WHAT'S BEING SAID ABOUT *THE POPULATION FIX:*

A book for every American environmentalist to read ... and ponder.
—Yeh Ling-Ling, Executive Director
Diversity Alliance for a Sustainable America

A fine book which should have a major impact on the population stabilization debate. —Virginia Abernethy, Ph.D., Chair
Carrying Capacity Network

Environmental health, public health, and population stabilization are all interdependent ... and this book makes that three-way connection come alive. —Bill Van Ry, Hospital CEO (Ret.)

A wealth of information and reference material for those concerned with a sustainable ... and a healthy America.
—Alan Kuper, Ph.D., President
Comprehensive U.S. Sustainable Population

A book clearly dedicated to preserving a certain quality of life for future generations of Americans.
—Anne Manetas, Director Environmental Projects
NumbersUSA

Public health is only one of many environmental and societal problems discussed in this book ... logically and unemotionally.
—William C. Ross, M.D., Board Certified
American Board of Family Medicine

An excellent book written so readers can understand the reasons for America's addiction to population growth ... a "must-read" for every thinking American. —Byron Slater
Population Stabilization Activist

Food for thought for every defender of America's soil, air, woods, water, and wildlife. —Jack E. Weir, Life Member
Izaak Walton League of America

A financial advisor performs due diligence on America's population growth rate ... and finds our societal and environmental books out of balance. —Thomas Spear, Ph.D., President
Wealth Management, Inc.

The Population Fix

The Population Fix

Breaking America's Addiction
To Population Growth

Edward C. Hartman

Think Population Press
Moraga, California

Cover design by Weston Thomson
Book design by Pete Masterson, Aeonix Publishing Group
Editing by Vicki Weiland
Back cover photograph by Diane Gysin

First Edition: 2006

ISBN: 0-9776125-0-3 paperback
ISBN: 0-9776125-1-1 case bound

LCCN: 2005911000

Published by
Think Population Press
P.O. Box 6366
Moraga, CA 94570-6366

Visit our website at: *www.ThinkPopulation.org*

Printed in Canada

CONTENTS

"(P)eople from other developed countries will say, 'America is a nice place to visit, but you wouldn't want to live there!'"

In The Beginning ... 39; How Large A World Problem? 40; How Large An Explosion? 41; What Causes World Population To Increase Or Decrease? 43; What Causes America's Population To Increase Or Decrease? 43; Births And Fertility Rates 44; Deaths And Life Spans 45; Net Migration Equals Immigration Minus Emigration 46; Population Growth Today 46; Affluence, Consumption, And Technology 47; Population Growth And America's Future 48; Addictions Can Be Broken! 48; For Reflection And Discussion: 48; Quick Fix #2 49

"Population growth in America may not be a physiological addiction, but it is has become an economic, political, and psychological addiction, negatively affecting virtually every American!"

Why "Addiction?" 51; We Just Keep Growing! 52; "Can We Talk?" 53; How Large An American Problem? 54; Wake Up! Wake Up! 55; What Has Caused America's Population Growth? 56; Holding Hands With 3.3 Million People! 56; Lessons From China And India 58; The "Sergé Survey" 59; Do You Still Love L.A.? 60; You're The Doctor 61; Looking Back ... And Ahead 61; For Reflection And Discussion: 62; Quick Fix #3 62

"(T)hey have entered what psychologists would call a state of tolerance. That is, they have reached a state where increasingly larger doses (of population growth) are necessary to produce desired effects."

Builders And Developers 63; Farmers 64; Food Processors 66; Hospitality Industry Employers 67; Information Technology (IT) Employers 68; Media Owners And Executives 69; Middle-Class Americans 70; Good And Bad Addicts 71; Looking Back ... And Ahead 72; For Reflection And Discussion: 72; Quick Fix #4 73

"Producers will only stop producing when population growth addicts have been cured and stop buying what the producers are selling."

"America's population growth pushers have a variety of motives. However, many—probably most—have one trait in common: They have never asked themselves the question, 'How many Americans are enough?'"

"Enablers' tacit acceptance and implied blessing of population growth provides population growth addicts with some semblance of justification for not seeking a cure."

"Some enablers of America's destructive population growth may not be able to grasp the connection between population growth and its deleterious effects. Others may be able to grasp the connection—but may not want to see it."

"If you do no more than read this book and continue to think carefully about what you have read, you will have taken a first step toward breaking America's addiction to population growth."

DEDICATION

"In this world,
who can do a thing, will not;
and who would do it, cannot …
and thus we half-men struggle."
From Andrea del Sarto by Robert Browning

This book is respectfully dedicated to
those half-men and half-women
who continue to struggle.

FOREWORD

America's Great Debate

THIS BOOK REQUIRES THE RETICENT, the fearful, and the intimidated to think about a subject they have previously wiggled their way around—*too many people*. Overpopulation in the U.S., what causes it, and what must be done about it is a subject that Ed Hartman, author of *The Population Fix*, approaches head on.

If you are not already a believer in a smaller, more manageable, and environmentally healthy community, state, nation, and planet, *The Population Fix* will alert you that no other subject is more important to the quality of life. Overpopulation is certain to narrow your choices and diminish the well-being of those who come after you.

Unfortunately, limiting the size of our national family is not the path we are embarked on today. If immigration and births continue at their present rates, the United States is on course to a population that will come close to the *one billion* people mark at the end of the century. That's three times our current population, in only a few generations.

So before the forces of demography, politics, and economic policy etch that unfortunate outcome in stone, nothing is more urgent for everyone to grasp than the immediate need for a change in direction. The author makes that case exceptionally well, explaining what can and must be done.

Although altruistic Americans are deeply concerned about world population, they have been reticent—and yes, irresponsible—by failing to do something about the overpopulation crisis in their own country. It often seems that the further away the population problem is and the less control Americans actually have in achieving a solution, the easier it is to be an advocate for a smaller population.

While good American citizens agonize about the problems of environmental degradation, famine, and poverty overseas, opportunists in our own country push us in the same undesirable direction because we have refused to insist on appropriate action to limit our growth here at home.

When an American President says we should "match willing foreign workers with willing American employers"—and when agribusiness and multinational business leaders applaud—the result is that building contractors, farmers, food processors, hotel operators, and the foreign workers they hire determine America's ultimate population, not you and fellow citizens.

When Congress passes legislation offering amnesty to illegal aliens, and increasing the number of "anchor babies," "family reunifications," "temporary workers," and "refugees"—and when courts expand those rewards—the result is that "coyotes" and human smugglers, criminal groups, along with refugee contractors, midlevel State Department employees, and Non-Governmental Organizations determine America's ultimate population, not you and fellow voters.

When a major American-based, internationally distributed newspaper like the *Wall Street Journal* declares "We believe in open borders"— and when other multimedia conglomerates "give the nod" to that idea on their editorial pages—the result is the economic and political goals of foreign governments, multinational corporations, and ethnic advocacy groups determine America's ultimate population, not you and your neighbors.

When environmental organizations insist that "population growth is a global problem requiring global solutions"—and when wealthy donors and major foundations say "Amen"—what they are demanding is that cheap labor be "king" and that five billion people living outside America and surviving on a few dollars a day decide what America's ultimate population should be, not you and your family.

For too many years America has let its ultimate population be determined by all the groups mentioned above—most with a clear financial or political interest in continuing our accelerating population growth for their benefit, not ours.

Until recently, this debate was being won by those who believe that *Americans do not have the right to determine America's ultimate population.* But the results of such policies, as Ed Hartman makes clear, have been bankrupt hospitals, crowded classrooms, declining water supplies, endangered wildlife, failing highways and bridges, growing land fills, overpriced and poorly constructed housing, polluted air, uncertain energy supplies, resurgent diseases, shrinking farmland, spreading urban sprawl, vanishing forests and wilderness, and ... and .... And I apologize if I left out your own favorite affliction brought about by these producers, pushers, enablers, and addicts of America's population growth.

Too often lost in the rancor and minutia of arguments over biometric identification and tamperproof Social Security cards, over special visas for "temporary" farm, hospitality, and information technology workers, over driver's licenses, tuition subsidies, and health care for illegal aliens, over border control, interior enforcement, and homeland security, over language and culture and assimilation, and over the dozens of other issues making their way to the front pages of newspapers and news-magazines and news broadcasts on TV and radio is the fact that the heart of that raging debate remains:

"Do Americans have the right—and the responsibility—to determine America's ultimate population?"

If you are still sitting on the fence, *The Population Fix* will help you find your way through difficult intellectual territory. But the author wants your participation in finding needed solutions. He is passionately committed to exposing the central role of population growth in the big scheme of America's societal and environmental problems and is determined to enlist you in helping with this mission.

The Population Fix is divided into digestible segments and the ingredients are infused with a deep understanding. At regular intervals, the author acknowledges and anticipates readers' questions and poses important queries of his own. As a result, *The Population Fix* takes you on an important intellectual safari and the author warns you about the tigers out there ready to eat you alive if you interfere with their real or perceived need for perpetual growth.

As a hopeful sign Ed Hartman points out many political leaders are reconsidering which side of this debate they want to espouse. Will they support individuals and institutions with vested—and often criminal—interests in rampant growth, or will they support the men and women who put them into office—and who can remove them from office?

After reading *The Population Fix*, I believe you will want to add your voice to this discussion. And once you have made up your mind, resolve to take action, firmly and quickly, knowing that your participation will make all the difference in the world!

Diana Hull, Ph.D., President,
Californians for Population Stabilization
Santa Barbara, California
www.capsweb.org

ACKNOWLEDGMENTS

"Abuse is often of service. There is nothing so dangerous to an author as silence." —Samuel Johnson

IF YOU HAVE READ THE acknowledgments of more than one book, undoubtedly you have inferred that writing and publishing a book is a collaborative endeavor. Only if you have written and published at least one book yourself do you fully appreciate just how true that is.

The Population Fix (TPF) would never have been started nor would it have been completed were it not for the enthusiastic encouragement, support, and, yes, criticism, of two close friends: Jack Weir and B. A. "Jug" Javorski. Like me, they share a deep concern for the America we will leave for our descendants, unless Americans awaken to their responsibilities to future generations.

While *TPF* was only an idea in the back of my head, a friend from Army CIC Inchon days, Brian L. Griffin, meticulously answered all of my questions about what to expect from an expedition into the publishing world. As author and illustrator of *Humblebee Bumblebee—The Life Story of the Friendly Bumblebees and Their Use by the Backyard Gardener* (available through *www.knoxcellars.com*), Brian's answers were prophetic as well as useful. Also, Luis Carrillo, author of *A Child Of No Importance*, and Betty Iverson, author of *A Time To Flee* and *Tabea's Story,* each provided me with the benefit of their experiences writing and publishing books.

Long before there was an outline—only thoughts on napkins—Peter Goodman, of Stone Bridge Press, publisher of quality books and software about Japan (*www.stonebridge.com*), gave me encouragement along with sound advice. His advice included, "Join Bay Area Independent Publishers Association (BAIPA)." That gem alone made all the difference! Throughout this project I received valuable counsel from many BAIPA members such as Sumant Pendharkar, author of *Raising Yourself,* a book for young people, and Pete Masterson, *TPF*'s book designer and owner of Æonix Publishing Group in El Sobrante, California. (Learn more about BAIPA at *www.baipa.net*.)

Through BAIPA I met Vicki Weiland, without whose conscientious, constructive, and professional editing, *TPF* might never have become a readable book. A thank you also to Ricky Weisbroth for her thorough proofreading, and to Desta Garrett for bibliographical assistance. Vicki and I both want to thank Chuck Stinson, Duane Stinson, Tom Stinson, and Mary Ann Bostwick at Sinbad's Restaurant in San Francisco, CA who provided us use of one of their booths as our home office away from home office while serving us fine food. Similarly, Steve and Elizabeth McIntyre, owners of Kaffee Barbara in Lafayette, CA and their exceptional staff kept appetites sated and coffee cups filled during countless hours of discussions with friendly, but candid reviewers.

Several friends—and some friends of friends—who so generously contributed their time to reading and commenting upon *TPF* are listed here with deep appreciation for their willingness to share their perspectives with me: Bob Crouch, Barbara George, Susanne Guyer, Joyce Hartman, Bob Hinshaw, Phyllis Hinshaw, Bert Hughes, Brian Jones, Matt Larson, David Lucas, Linda Reidt, Bill Ross, Pat Ross, Susan Sharpe, Byron Slater, Craig Smith, Joyce Smith, Rich Snyder, Bill Van Ry, Mauna Wagner, and Lois Webb.

To a considerable extent, *TPF* is a collection of ideas and information gathered from a variety of experts from a variety of fields. While I have hopefully accredited them properly within the text, I would herewith like to name and thank those who also read and commented upon the final draft: Virginia Abernethy, author of *Population Politics*, Chair, Carrying Capacity Network, and Board Member, Population-Environment Balance, Jim Baird of Izaak Walton League of America—Sustainability Education Program, Lindsey Grant author of *The Collapsing Bubble: Growth and Fossil Energy*, Alan Kuper of Comprehensive U.S. Sustainable Population, Caron Whitaker of National Wildlife Federation—Population and Environment Program, and Yeh Ling-Ling of Diversity Alliance for a Sustainable America.

Three gentlemen, whose names and comments appear on the back cover of this book, deserve special mention: Joseph L. Daleiden, author of *The American Dream: Can It Survive The 21st Century?* has not only written about dangers thrust upon our nation, states, cities, and towns by rampant population growth, but has rolled up his sleeves and worked as a grassroots proponent of population stabilization within his own community. Mark Kirkorian, Executive Director of Center for Immigration Studies, has helped create America's premier migration information think tank, recognized throughout the nation for its talent, knowledge, and fair-mindedness. Richard D. Lamm, former Governor of Colorado and Co-Director of The Center for Public Policy & Contemporary Issues at the University of Denver, has devoted much of his life to public service and continues to manifest his dedication to solving environmental and societal problems through his writings and his speeches.

I want to extend a special and heartfelt "Thank you" to Diana Hull, Jo Wideman, Shawn Flynn, and Gretchen Pfaff of Californians for Population Stabilization (CAPS) who so generously shared with me their time, energy, experience, and enthusiasm. Each and all are deeply appreciated!

I wish also to thank our daughters: Leanne Hartman who shared with me her knowledge of and experience in marketing and PR and who, working with talented artist, Weston Thomson, *(entoptic@hotmail. com)*, designed and coordinated *TPF*'s cover; Paula Hartman who brought her keen eye and legal experience to bear on the finer points of the final draft forcing me to close the circle on matters of logic and persuasion and who introduced me to the incredibly patient, persistent, and professional photographer, Diane Gysin *(www.portraitsbydiane. com)*. Thank you, also, to Ken Steele for introducing me to Weston.

And, like many authors before me, I am most thankful to have a spouse whose cheerful comfort and support continued throughout this project, even in the company of a sometimes reclusive and somewhat distracted husband. Thank you, Marolyn.

In the acknowledgments to *Schott's Original Miscellany*, Ben Schott thanked approximately three dozen people for their advice, encourage-ment, expert opinions, suggestions, and so forth, concluding: "If glaring errors exist … it's probably their fault." Not having the surfeit of forgiv-ing friends Mr. Schott apparently had, I must say, if glaring errors exist in *The Population Fix*, they are undoubtedly my fault!

And if you care to be acknowledged in the next edition of *TPF*, please visit *www.ThinkPopulation.org* and let me know what glaring errors—or slightly squinting errors—you have found.

PROLOGUE

A BABY ... AND A BOOK ARE BORN

Waiting outside a birthing room, I wrote the following "Letter" published a few days later in my local newspaper:

"On August 6, at 12:51 P.M., our younger daughter gave birth to a boy. Like her parents and her sister, she and her husband will plan to limit their family to two children. Yet, while our families plan sustainable, replacement-size families, our federal government, by failing to plan, makes it likely this boy, if he lives to my present age, will see America's population grow from approximately 300 million to 600 million and California's population grow from 36 million to 70 million.

"Year after year, Congress after Congress, administration after administration have chosen to ignore recommendations from their own agencies, commissions, committees, and constituents to consider population growth and its long-term threat to the United States and the world. Instead each administration proposes policies and each Congress enacts legislation designed to encourage more births and more immigrants—*in other words, more people!*

"While a few independent thinkers in Congress express concern about our *de facto population growth policy,* the majority in Congress, including our county's representatives, continue to vote in favor of polluted air and water, overcrowded schools and highways, depleted wilderness, wildlife, and fisheries, and failing infrastructure, all caused or exacerbated by unsustainable population growth. Such a sad legacy to leave our new grandson."

... Two months later, I began *The Population Fix.*

INTRODUCTION

"Ignorance and incuriosity are two very soft pillows."

—French proverb

WHO I AM

I AM A BUSINESSMAN, AN American citizen with a wife, two daughters, two sons-in-law, and four grandchildren. I am a person who is concerned about the legacy of agricultural debilitation, educational deterioration, *environmental* degradation, infrastructure disintegration, and other societal problems we are leaving to future generations of Americans. I believe most of these problems are exacerbated by population growth in the world, in America, and in the state, county, and town where I reside.

I am not a professional writer. Who was the literary critic who wrote of one author, "His work will be remembered long after Shakespeare's has been forgotten ... and not before?" Sounds like my work. I'm a businessman who thinks and probably writes in a businesslike way. In *The Population Fix,* I believe you will find mine a simple, straightforward style with an occasional dash of humor.

I am not a numbers man. Well, actually, I am. I like numbers and statistics and tables and such. But you may not guess that from reading this book. The concept of "Too many people" doesn't require a multi-colored graph. All it requires is a glance out of an auto's window while traveling on a crowded highway!

Taking it a step further, an understanding of how many current problems could be mitigated by population reduction won't require much more than a thoughtful mind while reading newspapers and newsmagazines, or while watching or listening to newscasts. Broad numbers and simple statistics should work just fine for our purposes, shouldn't they?

Because I plan to keep numbers broad and statistics simple, if the U.S. Census Bureau says America's population is 294,567,890, I'll probably say it's 300 million. That isn't exaggeration; that's just keeping it simple.

While some friends may disagree, I do not think of myself as a "population expert." My father used to say, "An 'expert' is anyone over 500 miles from his home office." Since I'm writing this in my home office, his definition alone would disqualify me.

From me you'll get bits and pieces borrowed from true experts who have helped me understand how America and the world got itself into its current fix and how we can get America, if not the world, out of it. You will learn how you can understand just as much as I do and become just as much of an "expert" as some people suggest I am about population growth simply by keeping your mind alert to connections between (a) societal and environmental problems and (b) population growth.

For this book, I am not "politically correct." If facts and logic lead me to a conclusion which is currently not favored by those who set today's standards for what one should not think, say, or write, please forgive me, because I'm liable to write it anyway. And if someone thinks they can read my words and thus read my mind and motives, great! Please contact me and we'll talk about forming a mind reading act.

I am neither a Republican nor a Democrat. I am neither pro-choice nor anti-choice. I am neither pro-immigration nor anti-immigration. I am neither a nativist xenophobe nor an open-borders one-worlder. I am not concerned about population growth in America *only*, but I am concerned about population growth in America *especially!*

I believe rampant population growth in America is neither inevitable nor desirable. A primary purpose of this book is *to demonstrate* rampant population growth in America is neither inevitable nor desirable and to offer you the means to help America recover from its population growth addiction.

WHY THIS BOOK

In 1997, my wife and I concluded the money we, our families, and our friends had been contributing to various *environmental* organizations was going to be wasted unless something was done to address human population growth and the damage it was doing to the *environment* worldwide and in America. We wrote to the *environmental* organizations we were supporting at that time and requested information about each organization's policies and activities regarding population growth.

Most, but not all, responded to our request and, based upon our assessment of the material received, we created a population-*environment* connection matrix and allocated our contributions for the year according to how much or how little connection each organization appeared to make between population growth and *environmental* degradation.

In 2000, after using our population-*environment* connection matrix for our own personal purposes, I mentioned it in a conversation with Sharon Stein, who at that time was Executive Director of Negative Population Growth (NPG). Sharon expressed interest, and over the next year or so I worked with Christopher Conner of NPG's staff to make the matrix more inclusive and professional.

Later, after Christopher moved on to work for an Eastern *environmental* organization, I asked NumbersUSA (NUSA) if it would be interested in helping me finish what Christopher and I had begun. Anne Manetas, NUSA's Director-*Environmental* Projects, and her boss, Roy Beck, a former *environmental* journalist, helped me further refine our personal matrix into the "Population-*Environment* Connection Scorecard" which went online on the Internet in 2001.

In 2002, during a "What next?" meeting with Jack Weir, a longtime friend, colleague, outdoorsman, and *environmentalist*, we concluded there was room for a comprehensive website devoted (a) to educating website visitors about the causes and effects of rampant human population growth and (b) to encouraging website visitors to support organizations actively addressing visitors' concerns regarding causes or effects of population growth.

With encouragement from Jack and a critical editing eye from B. A. "Jug" Javorski, a friend and mentor, I drafted website pages which eventually went on the Internet in August 2003 as *www. ThinkPopulation.org (TP.org)*. The "Population-*Environment* Connection Scorecard," which scores twelve *environmental* organizations, became a page within *TP.org*, reached via our "Think *Environment*" button.

EVERY PROBLEM A NAIL?

Have you heard the expression, "For the man whose only tool is a hammer, every problem seems a nail?" As a personal financial advisor, I can assure you that not every major event or problem my clients encounter can be solved with money. However, I can also assure you that virtually every major event or problem my clients encounter affects and is affected by money.

Similarly, as you read this book you may begin to wonder, "Does Ed think every problem can be solved by population stabilization or population reduction?" The answer is: No! America and the world have many problems which population stabilization or population reduction *alone* will not solve. But, just like money in the personal finance arena, most of America's and the world's problems will be *more difficult to solve,* if we fail to address population growth.

IF I SEEM CRITICAL …

As you read *The Population Fix* you will see I am critical of individuals and of industries, of positions of power and of positions of neglect, of organizations and of operations, and … well, critical of many things. For example, in a number of places I will refer to articles or letters published in my local newspaper. Some of my references to my local newspaper may seem uncomplimentary. However, I want to say at the outset, it is a good newspaper managed by and produced by good people. On the other hand, newspapers and I have totally different perspectives on America's addiction to population growth. That, as you will read later, is because media conglomerates in general and newspapers in particular desire population growth; it is the lifeblood of circulation growth and of advertising revenue growth.

It is not my intent to be a scold nor to denigrate the motives of the many on the receiving end of my criticism. All of us—you, me, all of us—are collectively responsible for America's addiction to population growth. If we are old enough to vote, we are old enough to have recognized something was wrong and old enough to have recognized contributions we may have made to an unsustainable situation. During my lifetime, America's population has more than doubled and during their lifetimes, our daughters and their children will likely see America's population double again and again. Yet I have waited until my "silver" years to try to do something about those disastrous projections.

So, yes, there is plenty of blame to go around and some of my criticism can and should be directed at me for failing to write more, to speak out more, and to seek more action from our elected representatives on a problem I could see with my own eyes.

What is that expression, *"If not now, when? If not me, who?"*

Well, now is the time, in my opinion, for each of us and for all of us to face the reality of America's rampant population growth.

Now is the time for us to accept our share of criticism and to accept our share of responsibility.

Now is the time for us, regardless of our past roles or our current roles—whether as addicts, as producers, as pushers, or as enablers—now is the time for us to become reformers.

Now is the time for each of us to help America end its dependence on the population fix and to contribute to breaking America's addiction to population growth.

Chapter 1

THE POPULATIONISTS

"Every journey has a secret destination of which the traveler is unaware."
—Martin Buber

altruist *n.* One with unselfish concern for the welfare of others; selfless.

ARE YOU AN ALTRUIST?

LET'S ASSUME YOU ARE DRIVING down an empty highway (yes, a *few* still exist in America) and you have just finished drinking a can of soda. You are far from home and this is not a route you expect to travel again. Nobody can see what you do. Do you toss the empty can out of the window? No? Why not?

"Well, Ed," you say—at least I hope you say—"if everybody did that, what a mess America would be. Maybe I won't have to look at this particular road again, but I don't want to create a mess for those who *will* have to look at it later."

Good for you! You may be an altruist.

The reason that is important is because this book is written for altruists—readers with an unselfish concern for the welfare of others. This book is for readers who can borrow the American Indian philosophy of the seventh-generation: *The present generation, which is making decisions for the tribe, needs to think of their impacts seven generations down the line.*

So, I may as well tell you up front ... this book may do *you* little good. If you absorb every thought contained herein and if you do everything recommended herein, *you* personally may gain little, except possibly the good feeling that can come from doing something good for future generations.

You see, it has taken many years for America to develop its addiction to population growth and it will take many years for America to deal with the producers, pushers, and enablers, and to help America's population growth addicts through withdrawal and recovery. By the time that happens, *you* may not be around to see many of the benefits of the recovery. If that proves true, you may have to obtain *your* satisfaction in knowing you have unselfishly—altruistically—done your best for the welfare of future generations.

ARE YOU—OR COULD YOU BECOME—A POPULATIONIST?

- Are you one who relates population growth to international, national, and local problems which cross your personal radar screen?
- When you read about a water shortage do you ask yourself, "Could it possibly be a 'people overage?'"
- When you hear about a bond issue to build another highway bridge or to bore another highway tunnel or to add highway lanes do you think to yourself, "Fewer people would mean fewer drivers and that would mean less need to raise taxes to pay for highway bond issues?"
- When a neighbor says, "Our schools are simply getting too crowded—we need to build more schools" do you reply, "If our population wasn't growing so rapidly would we need so many more schools?"

If you don't react to those and similar situations in similar ways today, do you think you could learn to do so tomorrow?

That is one of the purposes of *The Population Fix*—to help you learn *to think like a populationist* and to immediately react to every major societal and environmental problem with the question: *"Will population growth help or hinder the mitigation of this problem?"*

WHY "POPULATIONIST?"

"So, Ed," you might ask, "exactly what is a populationist?"

Good question!

Because there are so many different views about what should be done relative to population growth it seems to me an umbrella term is called for. Let me show you what I mean by listing just a few varying views regarding population goals:

- Stabilize world population below 6 billion or
- Stabilize world population at 6 billion or
- Stabilize world population above 6 billion.
- Stabilize America's population below 300 million or
- Stabilize America's population at 300 million or
- Stabilize America's population above 300 million.

Now, let's list some of the varying views regarding methods of achieving population goals:

- Address world population only or
- Address world and America's population or
- Address America's population only.

There are additional views I could have listed such as:

- Concentrate on improving education and/or governance in developing countries.
- Concentrate on increasing family planning funding domestically and/or internationally.
- Concentrate on reforming immigration policies.

Each of these views represents a concern about population growth, but no two concerns are quite alike. Therefore, I combine all people with views and concerns about population growth under one term, *"populationists."*

HOW MANY ARE ENOUGH?

Financial advisor James Schwartz once wrote a paper titled, "How Much Is Enough?" to remind his wealthy clients that there should be more to life than simply making more money.

Similarly, it may be time to remind America's leaders that there is more to American life than simply making more Americans.

My *primary* question to you as you begin this book is: *"How many are enough?"*

There are approximately *300 million* people living in America, approximately *10 million* of whom are living here illegally. Ultimately, how many people would you like to have living in America? One-quarter billion? One-half billion? Three-quarter billion? One billion? More?

I don't expect you to be able to answer that question now—that's why I'll ask it again at the end of this book. There is no *right* answer, so you needn't turn to the back of the book now to find the answer. All I ask is that you *think* about that question as you read this book and gradually formulate your own answer.

While reading this book, if you discover you are an addict, a producer, a pusher, an enabler, or a victim of America's addiction to population growth or have multiple roles, your answer may reflect your role. That's fine.

Regardless of your role, you may find your *personal answer*—and possibly your role—evolving and changing between now and when you encounter that question again.

PROFESSOR BARTLETT'S CHALLENGE!

Dr. Albert Bartlett, Professor of Physics at Colorado University, has issued a challenge. As you begin thinking about America's addiction to population growth, why not accept Professor Bartlett's challenge:

"Can you think of any problem on any scale, from microscopic to global, whose long-term solution is in any way aided, assisted, or advanced by having larger populations at the local level, state level, nationally, or globally? Can you think of anything that will get better, if we crowd more people into our towns, cities, states, nations, or world?"

Please pause here … Take a moment to think about Professor Bartlett's challenge: *"Can you think of anything that will get better, if we crowd more people into our towns, cities, states, nations, or world?"*

I can't. Can you? Whether used as a verb or as a noun, "crowd" is a word which suggests problems, not solutions. Professor Bartlett challenges you to *think like a populationist*. As you read this book, I encourage you to accept his challenge.

"POPULATIONIST" DOES NOT MEAN PREJUDICED

You will figure that out on your own, but I think it is worth stating. My reason?

I recently read a paper by Dale Allen Pfeiffer published by Carrying Capacity Network and titled, "Eating Fossil Fuels." It is filled with all kinds of statistics such as, "1.4 liters diesel equivalent per kilogram of nitrogen equates to energy content of 15.3 billion liters of diesel or 96.2 million barrels," and is replete with words such as photosynthesis, thermodynamics, endosomatic, and exosomatic.

Yet the paper's last paragraph contained the phrase, "Though this article may provoke a flood of hate mail ..."

Hate mail? How can such an esoteric discussion of the relationship between consumption of food and consumption of energy *possibly* provoke hate mail?

Here is how. Any time a person thinks about and writes about consumption—food consumption, energy consumption, any kind of consumption—that person will automatically begin to think about and write about population and what size population is sustainable with what level of consumption. Pretty soon that person is thinking about and writing about population stabilization and/or population reduction. And that is—apparently—all it takes to provoke hate mail!

No doubt many things in this book will be controversial to some— more overtly controversial than *anything* in Pfeiffer's paper. If you begin to *think like a populationist,* perhaps *you* will also have thoughts and express views which some people will consider controversial. The fact that you or I express controversial ideas does not mean that you or I are prejudiced against someone or something or that you or I are biased in favor of someone or something.

Incidentally, did you notice when you read the Introduction, words such as *environment* and *environmental* were italicized? I did that to illustrate the point that, of the people I have met who are constantly thinking about the effect of population growth upon America's problems—people I call populationists—perhaps 90% of them became involved with population issues because of their concern for the environment. Only later, after studying issues further, have they also become concerned about crime or culture or economics or education or one or more of the many other problems exacerbated by rampant population growth. Thus, when I read or hear a populationist described as a racist or a xenophobe or a nativist, I tend to be skeptical. Such has not been my experience.

DEFINITIONS

This might be a good place to indicate what I mean when I write "alien" and when I write "immigrant." According to *The American Heritage Dictionary of the English Language, Fourth Edition,* "alien" means: "An unnaturalized foreign resident of a country. Also called *noncitizen.*" So, any resident of any country who is not a citizen of that country is an alien.

Under "immigrant," the same dictionary says: "A person who leaves one country to settle permanently in another." Therefore, a citizen of one country who is in another country is an alien. Whether or not that person is also an immigrant depends on whether or not that person intends "to settle permanently" in that other country. This is how I will be using these two words throughout *The Population Fix*.

I assume you know what "illegal" means, so I need not define "illegal alien." Some people prefer to use the term "undocumented workers" to describe illegal aliens. There are two problems with that term: First, many illegal aliens are not "workers." Some are parents or spouses or companions of workers while others are children of workers and may be students in American schools.

Second, many illegal aliens are not "undocumented." Some, perhaps a majority, have many documents. The problem is that most of the documents held by illegal aliens are illegal documents. They may be documents created by criminal networks in the business of creating illegal documents for illegal aliens. Those aliens involved in the September 11, 2001 attack on the World Trade Center were hardly "undocumented." They had an abundance of documents! I don't believe I would describe them as "undocumented workers."

AMERICA AND AMERICANS

America 1. The United States. 2. also the Americas. The landmasses and islands of North America, Central America, and South America.

American *adj.* 1. Of or relating to the United States of America or its people, language, or culture.

I decided early in the writing of *The Population Fix* that I would use the primary definitions from *The American Heritage Dictionary of The English Language, Fourth Edition,* for America and Americans. Writing "America" uses less time, paper, and ink than writing "United States of America." Likewise, "Americans" is more efficient than "citizens and other legal residents of the United States." No inference should be drawn from this choice other than that I prefer to keep things simple.

CALIFORNIA! CALIFORNIA! CALIFORNIA!

As you read *The Population Fix* you will find many of my examples of problems created by or exacerbated by rampant population growth are "California problems." Why is that?

First, I was born, raised, and live in California and am more familiar with its problems than those of any other state.

Second, to say I live in California is certainly not a boast—so do more than 36 million others! But does it surprise you to realize that *one out of every eight people living in America lives in California?* Consequently, California's problems represent a large chunk of America's problems.

Third, what first happens in California—good or bad—often ends up moving on to the rest of America. Yesterday's population growth problems in California are today's population growth problems in much of America and will probably be tomorrow's population growth problems throughout America.

Finally, if ever there was a living, breathing counterargument to the "population growth is good" proposition, California is it. Or consider a letter to the editor from my friend, Jack Weir, published in my local newspaper:

"I must conserve power. I'm working by the light of my trusty Coleman.™ I'm appalled by the decline of our state. I feel like I'm back in Korea. Coming home in 1962, I drove on the nation's best highways and sent my kids to the nation's finest public schools.

"Now we start the millennium in a Third World context. The population has exploded, but highway capacity has not increased. Roads and bridges are in terrible repair. Our kids can't read, spell, make change from a purchase, or name our state's capital. Our energy infrastructure is in collapse. People's lives and livelihoods are in jeopardy."

If population growth is so good, where did California go wrong?

MIGRATION! MIGRATION! MIGRATION!

This book is about America's addiction to population growth. As you read on you will learn that in some decades America's population growth was the result of increased births and that in other decades population growth was the result of increased immigration. My primary concern is not with the cause of America's increasing population—though it may be necessary to understand causes to find cures. My primary concern is with the population increase itself and with its deleterious effects upon America. Whether population growth comes by trains or planes, boats or buses, shoe leather or stork-power—too many people are simply too many people!

You will find a significant portion of this book deals with migration. Why? Because *today the primary driver of America's addiction to population growth is net migration*—immigration, legal and illegal, into America minus emigration out of America. If net migration was zero and population was still increasing, I would be campaigning for Fish and Game Commissions across America to declare year-round, open season on storks! And the title of this section might be, "Storks! Storks! Storks!"

While it is also true that high fertility rates among some groups in America—including certain alien groups—are contributing to America's population growth addiction, the greater contributor today is the amount by which immigration exceeds emigration. That is why you will read so much about net migration in this book and why you will find American populationist organizations invariably spend much of their time thinking about, talking about, and writing about unsustainable net migration into America.

A REMINDER TO DISAGREE

Remember, I *expect* you to disagree with something you read somewhere in *The Population Fix.* That's great! It means you are thinking about what I have written. Mark the margins and when you have finished reading, go to *www.ThinkPopulation.org* and let me know what you disagree with and why you disagree. I assure you, I will welcome your views. They may give me fresh food for thought.

PLEASE FEEL FREE TO SKIP AROUND

The Table of Contents is relatively descriptive and sections within chapters are generally arranged alphabetically for easy thumbing. Please feel free to jump to chapters and to sections within chapters of particular interest or of particular concern to you. You can return later to chapters and sections you have skipped, if you choose to do so. However, before skipping around, may I suggest you read the next chapter, "An Overview," which will give you some background regarding the population growth problem worldwide as well as in America.

REFLECTION AND DISCUSSION QUESTIONS

You will find questions at the end of each chapter related to the chapter you have just read. You may find they help you pause a few minutes and reflect on what you have read. You may want to pose one or more of these questions to others to obtain perspectives different from either yours or mine. If you are part of a reading group or discussion group, perhaps you will find some of these questions encourage useful conversation and fresh thinking. As the expression goes, "Use them in good health!"

FOR REFLECTION AND DISCUSSION:

1. How well do you think the definition of altruist applies to you?
2. How easy or difficult do you think it would be for you to consider the "seventh generation" as you think about population growth in America?
3. How easy or difficult do you think it would be for you to *think like a populationist?*
4. What situations have previously caused you to think about the size of America's population?
5. How do the dictionary definitions of immigrant and of alien differ from your previous *personal* definitions?

QUICK FIX #1

Several readers of early drafts of *The Population Fix* became so concerned about America's population growth addiction that they wrote such comments as, "I feel as though I want to do something about it right now!" and "Isn't there something I can do today?" Consequently, I have added "Quick Fixes" at the end of each chapter. They will enable you to do something right now—today—and they have been designed to do quickly, in 20 minutes or less.

If you turn to Appendix C, "Quick Fix References," you will find a spot to enter name, address, and telephone number information. I suggest you use pencil as such things sometimes change. You may already know the information required or you may have to make a telephone call or scan pages in your favorite newspaper or newsmagazine. In any event, I believe you can gather the information called for in "Quick Fix" time.

Let's begin by collecting names, addresses, and telephone numbers of people who can influence America's addiction to population growth. For Quick Fix #1, enter information about the editor of your favorite newspaper or newsmagazine.

Chapter 2

AN OVERVIEW

fix *n.* *(slang)* An intravenous injection of a narcotic.

fix *n.* A difficult or embarrassing situation; a predicament.

fix *v.* To restore to proper condition or functioning; set right; repair.

IN THE BEGINNING ...

IT MAY BE USEFUL TO recognize the phenomenon of destructive, exploding growth of human population has no precedent in history. For most of its existence, mankind has struggled to reproduce and maintain itself in the face of infant mortality, early adult diseases, pestilence, natural catastrophes, tribal warfare, starvation, and fluctuating extremes of climatic change. Only when populations became of a sufficient size to support hunting and gathering and to produce surplus food was civilization able to establish footholds.

As civilizations flourished, the need for more people to provide inexpensive or free labor—think slaves—grew unabated. From time to time there were setbacks—epidemics were common. The "Black Death" reduced Europe's population by one-third and it took several generations to replace those who had died. In America, from the 16th century through the 19th century, there was a constant need for additional population—additional workers—to work in the mills and mines, the factories and farms. It was not until the 1950s that some scientists and political leaders became aware of the changing tempo of the world's—and of America's—population growth.

For the first time in the long history of our world, it became possible to say: *"We may have too many people; our population may be growing too rapidly."*

"Sex for Pleasure" was the title of a short item in the April 2004 issue of *Scientific American*. Leave it to those scientists to know how to get our attention! After that title, *SA* printed a paragraph from their *April 1954* issue which began: "Social, political, and public health leaders ..." from many countries are "seriously concerned" about population growth and are taking steps to distribute family planning information in order to create "... a better balance between resources and populations."

Just imagine ... leaders were "seriously concerned" in 1954, when world population was less than three billion—*less than half of today's population.* How concerned should they be now? Yet, how much evidence of concern do you see today among America's and the world's political leaders?

How many world problems are exacerbated by the world's accelerating population growth? Think about famine and food shortages, depletion of ocean fisheries, destructive logging of rain forests, threatened extinction of endangered wildlife, international conflicts over water or land usage, and so on.

Ask yourself, "Would these problems be more easily addressed if there were fewer people to feed, clothe, house, and employ?"

The answer is obvious—having fewer people would not solve all problems, but it would mitigate and make more solvable almost all problems.

HOW LARGE A WORLD PROBLEM?

Let's begin by discussing population growth not only in America but around the world:

- In 1800, world population was approximately one billion.
- In 1960—160 years later—it was approximately three billion.
- In 2000—40 years later—it was approximately six billion.
- And it is projected to be approximately nine billion in 2050.

In other words, it took 160 years for world population to increase by two billion, but it took only 40 years for it to increase another three billion!

Now, official projections are world population will increase another three billion in 50 years. My unofficial prediction is, it will take less than 50 years.

You might look at those numbers and dates and say:

"Well, look, Ed, things are getting better. Growth from three billion to six billion is 100% growth while growth from six billion to nine billion is only 50% growth. Things *are* looking better ... aren't they?"

Unfortunately, population growth "things" are not looking better; in fact, they are looking grim. In the first place, projections are just that—predictions about the future. In general, demographic projections for world population have turned out to be on the low side. Even with famines and wars, world population has tended to grow more rapidly than generally predicted.

More important, measuring population growth as a percentage of some base is, in many cases, not useful; it is the *added number of people* which adds to our problems. Let's illustrate how a "percentage argument" can be—and often is—misused by enablers of our population growth addiction.

Imagine a container designed to hold ten gallons of gasoline. Your car is out of gasoline so you take the empty ten-gallon container from your trunk, go to a service station, and ask for five gallons of gasoline.

The attendant puts five gallons of gasoline in your container, then asks, "Wouldn't you like me to add two gallons more?"

You say, "I think five gallons will be sufficient."

With a smile the attendant says, "Well, two gallons more will only be 40% more."

Not wanting to argue, you say, "OK."

Then the attendant asks, "Why don't I go ahead and add two more gallons?"

You say, "Well, that will make the container heavier to carry."

He says, "Yes, but only 28.5714% heavier." (Just your luck—a math savant pumping gasoline.)

Finally, he says, "Let me add another two gallons—that will only be 22% more."

Unfortunately, he just tried to pour 11 gallons of gasoline into a 10-gallon container and we all know what that can lead to. Likewise, with world population, if we pour nine billion people into a—let's say—four or five billion people world, we should not be surprised when there is an explosion.

HOW LARGE AN EXPLOSION?

Some nations have already had their population "explosions." If you have a strong enough stomach for such things, you have probably seen pictures of tens of thousands of starving people in Africa, Asia, Latin America, and elsewhere in the world. Let's consider just one nation, China, the most populous nation in the world, with over one billion people.

China's economy grows, but it's food production fails to keep up with its population. Fortunately for China, because its economy provides sufficient resources for it to buy food on the world market, it does so. Unfortunately for poorer nations of the world, China's demand drives food prices higher, and sometimes makes it unaffordable to those in would-be developing nations.

So, let them eat fish!

OK, let's think about the world's oceans for a minute. As large as they are, it is easy to think they will never lose their ability to meet humans' need for food. However, in *Nature Conservancy* magazine, Winter 2003, in an article titled, "Just The Facts" and subtitled, "Isn't There Always Another Fish in the Sea?" here is what William Stolzenburg writes:

"Over the past 20 years, the widespread disappearance of ocean life has contradicted the cornucopians. Consider just the fish. After climbing steadily from 1950 (when the United Nations' Food and Agriculture Organization, or FAO, began collecting global statistics), the world's marine-fish catch topped out in the late 1980s, and has since been on an ominous decline. For example, one acclaimed study found that between 1988 and 1998 the world catch decreased by 360,000 tons per year.

"Sixty-five percent of commercial fish stocks are either being fished to their maximum sustainable limits or worse ... *[and]* about 30 percent are overfished, some to the point of being commercially dead..." Think about it for a minute and you will realize *fish are the only wildlife hunted for food on such a large scale worldwide.*

Not only are we taking wildlife out of the world's oceans as the world's population grows, we are replacing it with growing tons of trash. According to an article in *Natural History* written by sailor and ecologist Charles Moore, there is a "patch" of floating plastic debris in the North Pacific about the size of Texas.

Hideshige Takada, an environmental geochemist at Tokyo University, and his colleagues have discovered floating plastic fragments are sponges for DDT, PCBs, and other oily pollutants. Japanese investigators found that plastic resin pellets concentrate such poisons to levels as high as a million times their concentrations in the water as free-floating substances. These pellets degrade and break into fragments and disperse. The dispersed pieces are eaten by nature's "vacuum cleaners," the jellies and salps living in the ocean. Jellies and salps are eaten by fish, and the poisons pass into the food chain ... with humans at the top!

Reflecting on this chain reaction, Moore concludes: "Farmers can grow pesticide-free organic produce …" but, he wonders, can nature grow a pollutant-free organic fish? "After what I have seen firsthand in the Pacific, I have my doubts," he concludes.

As consumers—especially children and pregnant and nursing women—receive increasing numbers of warnings about eating seafood, we can all share his doubts.

WHAT CAUSES WORLD POPULATION TO INCREASE OR DECREASE?

There are countless cultural, economic, religious, and personal factors contributing to billions of people making trillions of decisions which ultimately lead to increasing or decreasing populations. However, from a purely mathematical perspective, population increase or decrease *worldwide* is a function of *two* factors:

- births *and*
- deaths.

If births exceed deaths, population increases. If deaths exceed births, population decreases.

You might ask, "Don't births always exceed deaths, Ed? And, therefore, isn't population growth inevitable?"

Well, yes and no. Yes, today, worldwide, births do exceed deaths and have done so for many years. However, in many countries today—say, Germany and Japan—births do not exceed deaths. If you think about it, if the world's "average woman" had two children (one to replace herself and one to replace one man) rather than three or more children, ultimately births would approximately equal deaths and world population would stabilize. (Note: Experts would say the "average woman" should have 2.1 children—a "total fertility rate" of 2.1 in order to account for early mortality—to stabilize population. But we're not experts so we'll just say 2.0 children, preferably a 1.0 girl and a 1.0 boy.)

WHAT CAUSES AMERICA'S POPULATION TO INCREASE OR DECREASE?

Population increase or decrease within a political unit such as a nation, a state, or a county is a function of *three* factors:

- births,
- deaths, *and*
- net migration, e.g., immigration minus emigration.

For example, if in Country X each birth is matched by a death (i.e., each woman has two children) and each immigrant (a person entering Country X) is matched by one emigrant (a person leaving Country X), the population of Country X will be stable!

However, if the population of Country Y is increasing, either births are exceeding deaths (i.e., women are having an average of more than two children each and/or life spans are extending) and/or immigrants are outnumbering emigrants.

Facts about population growth in the world are not difficult to understand: *If births exceed deaths, world population grows.*

Facts about population growth in America are not difficult to understand: *If births exceed deaths and/or if immigrants exceed emigrants, America's population grows.*

In the opinion of most who have studied the situation, population in the world is growing at an unsustainable rate. In my opinion, population in America is growing at an irrational rate.

BIRTHS AND FERTILITY RATES

To illustrate how births and fertility rates affect population, let's look at a purely hypothetical, and mathematically easy to understand, situation.

Imagine a remote—and unique—island populated by 2,000 children, half girls, half boys. As they grow older they pair and have children. By age 30 they have had 2,000 children—half girls, half boys—and have no more. The island's fertility rate is 2.0 (2,000 children divided by 1,000 women) and its population is now 4,000. Imagine the second generation of 2,000 children grow, pair, and have children. By age 30 they have had 2,000 children and have no more. The island's fertility rate remains 2.0 (4,000 children divided by 2,000 women) and its population is now 6,000.

Now, imagine the third generation pair and have children, *and* the first generation begins dying at the same rate as a fourth generation is born. *For each birth, there is a death. For each death, there is a birth.* As a result, the population of our imaginary island remains stable at 6,000. A fertility rate of 2.0 (or 2.1 if you're an expert) is one element of a stable population because it results eventually in one death for each birth.

Let's take our illustration to another level. What happens if on an imaginary island women have *more* than an average of 2.0 children each? Let's imagine a second island populated by 2,000 children. As they grow older they pair and have children. By age 30 they have had 4,000 children and have no more. The island's fertility rate is 4.0 (4,000 children divided by 1,000 women), double that of our first island, and its population is now 6,000 (2,000 plus 4,000). Imagine the second generation of 4,000 children pair and have children. By age 30 they have had 8,000 children (2,000 women times 4.0 children) and have no more. The island's fertility rate remains 4.0 (12,000 children divided by 3,000 women) and its population is now 14,000 (2,000 plus 4,000 plus 8,000).

Imagine as the third generation pair and have children, the first generation begins dying. When the first generation is gone, the population is reduced by 2,000, but with the fourth generation of children added, *the population is* 26,000 (4,000 plus 8,000 plus 16,000 minus 2,000).

The fertility rate is only *twice* that of our first island, but its population is more than four times as large—*and it continues to grow!*

Our world *is* an island—an island in the universe. If the women on our world island had an average of 2.0 children each, the population of the world would eventually stabilize. Since world population has grown from one billion in 1800 to three billion in 1960 to six billion in 2000 and continues growing toward nine billion, we know the average woman on our world island has had more than 2.0 children ... and continues to do so today and for the foreseeable future.

DEATHS AND LIFE SPANS

Remember our first remote—and unique—island. The island's fertility rate was 2.0. For each death, there was a birth and the population of our imaginary island remained stable at 6,000.

Now, imagine a third island similar to our first island, but on this island people live 30 years longer than they live on the first island. In other words, unlike the first island where the first generation is dying as the fourth generation is being born, on this third island, the first generation lives until a fifth generation is born. That means 2,000 more babies would be born before the first generation died. On such an island, population would stabilize at 8,000.

In other words, *as life spans increase, population stabilization occurs at a higher level.*

NET MIGRATION EQUALS IMMIGRATION MINUS EMIGRATION

Remember our first remote—and unique—island? The island's fertility rate was 2.0. For each death, there was a birth and the population of our imaginary island remained stable at 6,000.

Now, imagine each year, 30 children, half girls, half boys, *immigrate onto* this island from another part of the world and no residents *emigrate from* the island. Net migration of 30 immigrants represent only 0.5% of the island's otherwise stable population of 6,000. However, by the 90th year, when the first generation of "natives" have died, approximately 2,700 immigrants have come to the island (30 x 90) and produced 1,830 children and 930 grandchildren.

Together, they have nearly *doubled* the otherwise stable population of the island to 11,460 (6,000 + 2,700 + 1,830 + 930). Of course, if the fertility rate of these immigrants is, like the fertility rate of some of America's immigrants, greater than the replacement rate of 2.0, growth of the island's population will be even greater. Further, *if net inward migration continues endlessly, population growth will continue endlessly!*

Even with a seemingly low net migration rate of 0.5%—approximately the net migration rate of America—and even when immigrants have low fertility rates—often not true of America's immigrants—the result can be a *near doubling of population in three generations!*

We should and we do welcome legal immigrants to America. At the same time, we should consider the numbers. *If we do not want America's population to grow from 300 million to 600 million to 1.2 billion,* we may want to consider reducing net migration, possibly by balancing the level of immigration with the level of emigration. At present rates of emigration, that suggests perhaps 200,000 to 300,000 immigrants per year—*rather than over one million.*

POPULATION GROWTH TODAY

Today in America, increasing life spans and birth rates of native-born Americans is not a major factor in our increasing population. Today net migration, i.e., immigration (inward migration) exceeding emigration (outward migration), plays the major role. However, in some developing countries, improved sanitation, diets, and health care dramatically increase life spans which in turn leads, *for a time,* to increasing population.

We want people to live longer, healthier lives. At the same time, we should understand the role of life spans as we learn about population growth in developing countries. Further, if families in certain underdeveloped nations are accustomed to having extra large families to make up for high mortality rates, that custom may exacerbate the population growth problem. Remember, if modern medicine and hygiene reduce mortality rates without a corresponding reduction in fertility rates, population can soar!

AFFLUENCE, CONSUMPTION, AND TECHNOLOGY

Before closing this Overview, I want to say a few words about affluence, consumption, and technology. I believe it was 1974, when population and environmental scientists Paul Ehrlich and John Holdren presented the equation:

$$I = P \times A \times T$$

This equation is sometimes used by environmentalists to illustrate how negative environmental *Impact* (I), results from the interaction between *Population* (P), consumption and *Affluence* (A), and the polluting effects of *Technology* (T).

The Ehrlich/Holdren formula suggests population growth is one of three factors which negatively affect our environment. For example, if a population is stabilized, but consumption and affluence are increased and/or the polluting effects of technology are increased, the negative impact upon the environment will also increase.

Put differently, one million people in an affluent, technologically advanced country—think cars and factories—are likely to create a greater negative impact upon the environment than one million people living in an underdeveloped country—think bikes and basket weaving.

According to this formula, in order to minimize the deleterious impact upon our environment, we should not only minimize population growth, but also minimize consumption and affluence and polluting technology. However, as you know, people worldwide yearn for more consumption and affluence, not less and for the benefits of more technology, not less.

Therefore, I hereby take note there are other factors besides population growth which contribute to environmental degradation. But I also take note that *even if world population growth stopped,* population migration from less affluent nations and from less technologically advanced nations to America and to other developed nations *would tend to add to the world's environmental degradation problems.*

POPULATION GROWTH AND AMERICA'S FUTURE

"So, Ed, where do things stand now—what does the future hold for America?"

Projections of current trends tell us that children born in America today will likely live to see most American cities looking like Hong Kong, Kolkata (Calcutta), Mumbai (Bombay), Mexico City, Sao Paulo, Singapore, Tokyo, and (gasp) Los Angeles and New York City. And that's the *good news.* The bad news is: That projection is based upon the Census Bureau's "most likely" scenario of future births, deaths, and net migration.

Because the U.S. Census Bureau has used, in my opinion, some optimistic assumptions about reductions in America's fertility rates, most likely the actual scenario will be worse than their "most likely" scenario. In short, even in the most unlikely event of the "most likely" scenario, these newly born children will live long enough to live in an America about which *people from other developed countries will say, "America is a nice place to visit, but you wouldn't want to live there!"*

ADDICTIONS CAN BE BROKEN!

If you have had a personal experience with addiction or if you have known someone who has had experience with addiction or if you have followed news stories about people with addictions, you know addictions are *not* easy to break. However, it can be done and the starting point, as you may know, is for one to accept the fact that one is dealing with an *addiction!*

In Chapter 3, "The Addiction," you will learn why I describe America's rampant population growth as an addiction. In subsequent chapters, you will read about the addicts who are hooked on population growth, about some of the victims of that addiction, and about the producers, the pushers, and the enablers of America's addiction to population growth.

While I have tried to lighten the material with my irreverent sense of humor, it is not a "smiley-face read." However, as you read further, remind yourself: *Addictions can be broken! You* can join tens of thousands of others who are working to break America's addiction to population growth!

FOR REFLECTION AND DISCUSSION:

    1. What examples have you seen or heard of someone using irrelevant percentages to "measure" population growth?

2. What is your reaction to those who say or write that population growth is not a problem to America or the world?

3. In what ways does the difference between the factors affecting world population (births and deaths) and a nation's population (births, deaths, and net migration) affect the way you think about population growth in America?

4. How might you illustrate the effect upon America's population (a) of births and fertility rates, (b) of deaths and life spans, and (c) of net migration (immigrants minus emigrants) to a group of young people?

5. What thoughts come to mind as you consider the Ehrlich/Holdren equation ($I = P \times A \times T$) as it applies to environmental degradation in America and in the rest of the world?

QUICK FIX #2

Obtain information about your Representative in the U.S. House of Representatives to enter into Appendix C, "Quick Fix References." If you or a friend have access to the Internet, *www.Vote-Smart.org* provides all the information you need or call them at 1-888-868-3762. Also, many telephone directories provide some of this information and a telephone call to your Representative's office will provide the remainder. Or, a call to your local newspaper may provide the information you are looking for. Ignore spaces for *"NumbersUSA.com* scores" for now. We'll use those spaces later.

Chapter 3

THE ADDICTION

narcotic *n.* An addictive drug, such as opium, that reduces pain, alters mood and behavior, and usually induces sleep or stupor.

addiction *n.* Compulsive physiological need for a habit-forming substance."

"Every form of addiction is bad, no matter whether the narcotic be alcohol or morphine or idealism."
—Carl Jung

WHY "ADDICTION?"

A PARENT SMOKES TOBACCO AND says, "I know it's bad for my health. I know it makes my clothes smell bad. I know it sets a bad example for our children and may even be bad for their health. I know it's a sad waste of money. But I can't stop!"

We could substitute "alcohol" for "tobacco" or we could substitute more destructive drugs such as "heroin" or "morphine" or "methamphetamine" and the negatives would be similar, "I know it's bad," and the conclusion the same, "But I can't stop."

Addicts know what they are doing is bad for themselves and bad for others—but they can't stop! They may deny they are addicted—but they can't stop! Their worlds may be imploding around them and they see it happening—but they can't stop!

America's addiction to population growth is like that. We know—if we take a moment to think about it—*none* of the problems we face today as a nation or within our states and communities will be easier to solve if we continue to increase our population—but we can't stop!

Presidential and Congressional commissions, academic committees, and intelligence community reports have consistently warned of the dangers of perpetual population growth. Yet we can't seem to stop ourselves. We can't seem to stop our legislators. We can't seem to stop our officials from doing things which ensure our population will continue to grow, thereby making our societal and environmental problems that much more difficult to solve.

Population growth in America may not be a physiological addiction, but it has become an economic, political, and psychological addiction, negatively affecting virtually every American!

WE JUST KEEP GROWING!

When my father's father was born, America's population was approximately 45 million. When my father was born, America's population was approximately 87 million. When I was born, America's population was approximately 125 million. When our first child was born, America's population was approximately 185 million. When our first grandchild was born, America's population was approximately 265 million. At the current rate of growth, when our first child reaches my present age, America's population will be approximately 375 million. When our first grandchild reaches my present age, America's population will be approximately 485 million. When our first grandchild's grandchild reaches my present age, will America's population be 650 million or 750 million or 850 million? Nobody knows for sure. However, whether the correct answer is two-thirds, three-fourths, or four-fifths of one billion, I'm glad I won't be around to find out.

Since the census of July 1, 1900, America's population has grown every year except one! Between June 30, 1918 and July 1, 1919, America had one million troops in Europe and one-half million people in America died from an influenza epidemic. The U.S. Census Bureau showed a population *decline* of 60,000 for that year, a one-time aberration, as annual *growth* was 1.3 million both the year before and the year after.

As a professional financial advisor, how I'd love to recommend an investment to my clients that had *only one down year every 100 years!* Unfortunately, as you will read later on, perpetual population growth does not make America richer. As America paves over its farms and wetlands, as it pollutes its air and water, as it degrades the quality of its schools, as it increases the cost of housing, as it ... Well, you name it. Ultimately, America's population growth is a good investment for only a few. Meanwhile, it makes most Americans economically poorer.

"CAN WE TALK?"

Odds are you are too young to remember this old vaudeville gag. (Odds are you are too young to remember vaudeville!) Here is an updated version:

"According to the U.S. Census Bureau, every time I breathe a man dies."

"Perhaps you should use mouthwash."

According to *USA TODAY*, the U.S. Census Bureau reported that as of January 1, 2004, America was recording a birth every eight seconds and a death every thirteen seconds, while adding an immigrant every 25 seconds. The result: an increase in America's population of one person every twelve seconds. The result: since 1980, America's population has *grown* more than the *total population* of either France or Great Britain! Imagine adding the population of France or Great Britain to our population! During the period 1990 to 2003, while Japan's, Germany's, and France's populations grew approximately 3%, 4%, and 6%, respectively, *America's population grew 16%!* Using an old financial advisor's trick, divide 72 by 16 and you learn America's population would double in 4.5 decades, if it continued growing at the same rate.

Lindsey Grant, former Deputy Assistant Secretary of State for Population and Environment, is author of several books including *Too Many People: The Case for Reversing Growth, How Many Americans? Elephants in the Volkswagen,* and *Foresight and National Decisions: The Horseman and the Bureaucrat.* In an article for the organization Negative Population Growth, Mr. Grant tells of collecting, during a three year period, over 1,500 news stories about crowding in America. The range of issues he cited was enormous:

- Rising housing prices and the displacement of the less prosperous;
- Urban sprawl;
- Stalled traffic and the transportation crisis;
- Infrastructure costs and rising taxes;
- The deterioration of public and social services;
- The impact of massive housing developments;
- Rising school populations and inadequate schools;
- Worsening local air quality;
- The polarization of local politics and the deadlock of government;

- Rising unemployment in some areas and the dislocations caused by new industry in others;
- The spread of paving and the attendant problems of runoff and flooding;
- The failure of water supplies;
- The destruction of woodlands, farmland, and natural landscapes;
- The sense of lost quality of life and the feeling that growth has somehow gone bad.

The news stories he compiled also pointed out some of the reasons for the complaints—such as a new development or shopping center, rising school populations, the construction of superhighways (or lack of them), diminishing rivers and aquifers.

But as Mr. Grant wrote, "They are all silent about the underlying driving force!

"A conservation group announces that excessive consumption is draining rivers across the country—and it blames 'U.S. irrigation habits, urban sprawl, increased ground water pumping and loss of wetlands … more often than not government policies …' and excessive municipal consumption. Not a word about population growth!"

It is time to break that silence!

HOW LARGE AN AMERICAN PROBLEM?

Let's try this and see if it helps: In 1800, each square mile of American soil served 6.1 people. Since one square mile equals 640 acres, perhaps a better way to say this would be, each person in America was served by 105 acres (640 divided by 6.1).

Now, even people who have never set foot on a farm have some general idea of what an acre looks like. Perhaps their house sits on a quarter-acre lot or their apartment complex sits on a five-acre plot. So, hopefully we can say to ourselves, "Well, each person had the benefit of 105 acres on which their house might sit, on which the crops and livestock to feed them might be raised, on which roads and stores and town buildings might be set to serve each person's needs. Yes, 105 acres sounds like a pretty reasonable amount of acreage for each person."

By 1960, when world population had tripled, American population had increased 36 times and there were 50.6 people for each square mile of American land. How could America's population increase 36 times, but people per square mile increase only 8 times (50.6 divided by 6.1)?

Well, America's land mass had increased (think Louisiana, Florida, Texas, Oregon, Washington, Alaska, etc.) along with its population. So, by 1960, each person in America was served by 12.6 acres. Hmm ... from 105 acres to 12.6 acres. That's not exactly what one would call "generous," but doable. Yes, 12.6 acres per person—doable.

Now, by 2000 there were 79.6 people per square mile in America and that "doable" number of 12.6 acres per person had been reduced to 8.0 acres per person. Oh, my! When we fly from one coast to the other we can see millions of those acres were never "designed" to raise crops or livestock nor will they ever hold stores or public buildings.

Oh, my, indeed! It seems we are getting down to nitty gritty numbers where one might reasonably ask, "Have we just about reached America's carrying capacity when we expect 8.0 acres to be sufficient to serve all the food, water, recreation, civic, and social needs of each citizen?"

If we have reached that point, then 2050 will really get uncomfortable when America will have only *5.5 acres to serve each resident!* That is, if we're lucky ...

When it comes to America's addiction to population growth, the important numbers are usually not percentages but numbers of people occupying America's land. For example, according to a publication issued by the organization Population-Environment Balance, "The USDA, National Agricultural Statistics Service data show that the amount of harvested land of principal crops has declined from 1.5 acres per American in 1980 to just over 1 acre per American in 2002. Not only did the population increase by 60 million between 1980 and 2002, but the number of harvested acres also fell by over 50 million acres." And for the first time in half a century America becomes a net importer rather than net exporter of agricultural products.

Remember: *Forget percentages. Count people ... and mouths!*

WAKE UP! WAKE UP!

OK. I told you earlier I was going to resist my natural urge to present you with lots of mind-numbing numbers. I think I just failed in that objective and some of you may have dozed off. If so, let me summarize:

(1) Unlike the vaudeville joke—"Every time I breathe a man dies ...," more appropriate would be: Every other time you breathe, a person is added to America's population!

(2) Virtually every societal and environmental problem in America is exacerbated by America's population growth.

(3) Percentages related to population growth are often mean-ingless—it's the number of additional people that usually matters.

(4) Each additional person requires additional land, water, and natural resources for food, housing, and infrastruc-ture—additional land, water, and natural resources of which America no longer has a surplus.

WHAT HAS CAUSED AMERICA'S POPULATION GROWTH?

Perhaps you are wondering, "Ed, what has caused and what is causing *America's* population growth—a high fertility rate or high net migration?"

The answer is: Both! After World War II and through the mid-1960s, the American fertility rate was well above the 2.1 replacement level which resulted in what has been called "The Baby Boom." Starting in the mid-1960s and running through the 1970s, America's fertility rate was well below replacement level resulting in "The Baby Bust." From the early 1980s on, the fertility rate in America for native-born American women has been at approximately replacement level.

"But, Ed, if the fertility rate in America for native-born American women has been at approximately replacement level since the early 1980s, why has America's population continued to soar at an unprec-edented pace?"

Because America's population increase has been fed (a) by a high rate of net migration, i.e., by the number of immigrants exceeding the number of emigrants and (b) by high fertility rates among some groups.

Let's put it another way: If net migration after the 1970s had been zero, i.e., if the number of immigrants had equaled the number of emi-grants, America's population growth would have slowed dramatically and America's population would be stabilized at approximately 250 million. *Yes, it would be stabilized at one-quarter billion, rather than crashing ahead with approximately 3.3 million more people every year* (approximately 33.3 million between July 1, 1994 and July 1, 2004).

HOLDING HANDS WITH 3.3 MILLION PEOPLE!

"Ed, you say America is adding approximately 3.3 million people every year?"

That's right.

"I've seen other figures that say America adds only 2.5 million or maybe 3.0 million per year. How did you come up with 3.3 million?"

The U.S. Census Bureau estimated America's population was approximately 260.3 million on July 1, 1994, and approximately 293.6 million on July 1, 2004. Subtract 260.3 from 293.6, divide the result by ten years, and you get 3.33 million people added annually. (Confirming this calculation: (1) A March 28, 2004 article by Alan J. Heavens of *Knight Ridder Newspapers* referring to a calculation of 33 million in ten years by Professor James Johnson Jr. and (2) a Carrying Capacity Network *Action Alert* dated November 2004.)

But more important, what does 3.3 million more people actually mean? What do 3.3 million more people look like?

Remember that old line, "If you laid all the economists in the world end-to-end, they still wouldn't reach … a conclusion?" Well, we don't want to lay 3.3 million additional people end-to-end, so let's try this instead.

Imagine 3.3 million people standing side by side, five feet apart, arms outstretched, hands touching—like a gigantic protest or demonstration. That line of people would stretch along Interstate 80 from San Francisco, CA, east through Reno, NV, Salt Lake City, UT, Cheyenne, WY, Omaha, NE, Des Moines, IA, to the suburbs of Chicago, IL, to Cleveland, OH, across the length of Pennsylvania, to the outskirts of New York City, then southwest on Interstate 95 through Philadelphia, PA to Baltimore, MD. And that would be *just twelve months population growth in America!*

Can you visualize that line of 3.3 million people? Can you visualize the line of cars that line of 3.3 million people will drive on our already crowded and deteriorating highways? Can you visualize the houses and apartments that have to be built to house that line of 3.3 million people? Can you visualize the number of classrooms that will have to be constructed and the number of teachers that will have to be hired to educate the children—and some adults—in that line of 3.3 million people?

Can you visualize the number of hospital rooms and beds that will have to be made available—the number of doctors, nurses, and other health care professionals that will have to be made available—to provide health services for that line of 3.3 million people? Can you visualize the amount of food and water and energy that will be required to feed and serve that line of 3.3 million people?

Probably not. I know I can't. I can get a pretty good visualization of 3.3 million people lined up clear across America—we've seen enough handholding demonstrations over the years to get some sense of what 30 or 300 or even 3,000 people lined up hand in hand might look like. Then, I can more or less imagine that line extending along the shoulders of various highways we have driven. So, yes, I *can* visualize that line of 3.3 million people across America.

But when I try to visualize all the cars they will drive, all the houses they will live in, all the schools they will attend, all the health care services they will require, and all the food, water, and energy they will use … No, that is more than I can visualize.

As it happens, that is also more than America has been able to keep up with for the past three decades. That is one reason why America's highways and other infrastructure have been deteriorating. That is one reason why so many people can't find "affordable housing." That is one reason why the health care industry is in crisis. That is one reason why the quantity of American-grown food goes down while food imports and America's population goes up. That is one reason why Western states try to equitably divide more of various rivers' water than normally flows in those rivers. That is one reason why small power problems have become multi-state, multi-day blackouts. *Yet, 3.3 million additional people is just one year's population growth in America!*

LESSONS FROM CHINA AND INDIA

What can Americans learn from China's population growth? While census numbers from China are always a bit suspect, China's population was approximately *600 million* in 1970, when the Chinese government decided *something had to be done* about its rapidly growing population. China contains approximately the same land area as America, so the numbers are particularly relevant.

China's leaders used their Communist Party control over housing, employment, and salaries to institute three reproductive norms: (1) late marriage, (2) longer spacing between births, and (3) fewer children, i.e., two children for urban families and three children for rural families. In 1979, rules were changed to promote only one child per family.

How successful has China's drive to reduce its population been? The good news is, China's population is now projected to decline. The bad news is … not until 2050, when it is projected (with fingers crossed) to *decline to 1.4 billion.* When will China's population return to the 600 million which troubled its leaders so long ago? Not during my lifetime and, if you are old enough to read this book, not during your lifetime either.

What can we learn from India's population growth? To begin with, India has about one-third the land area of America. Yet, it has a population of more than 1 billion. Does India have a problem and does India know it has a problem? You bet! But India has a democracy and their politicians—like our politicians—have never really put their arms around their problem. The result: in 2050 when China's population is projected to be in decline, India's population is projected to be *over 1.5 billion ... and growing!*

What lessons can America learn from China and India? First, America will eventually break its addiction to rampant population growth ... it is simply a matter of time. Eventually, population growth becomes so disastrous that a nation's leaders, whether autocratic or democratic, must acknowledge the problem and make some gesture toward addressing it.

Second, in a democracy, it is likely to take longer to effectively address a population growth problem than in a dictatorship. India learned that giving away free portable radios for having vasectomies wasn't enough ...

Finally, even when population reduction measures are imposed autocratically upon a nation, it takes many generations before positive results are seen ... several generations during which quality of life declines and human life may be devalued.

THE "SERGÉ SURVEY"

Randy Newman and his chorus sing about how much they love L.A. For years I thought he was being sarcastic, but after seeing him drive Wilshire Boulevard in his high-powered convertible in a television special, I concluded, he really *does* love L.A.

Mr. Newman, I suspect, does not share a three-bedroom house with four other families. Perhaps it is the people who do—among others—who made up the 70% who answered the most recent poll I have seen with, "We'd rather live somewhere other than Los Angeles."

Of course, I don't know the operative question. If it was, "If you were given $1 million to move elsewhere, would you rather live somewhere else?" then that survey doesn't tell us much. But for me, the acid test of the population growth addiction's destructive effect upon Los Angeles was not that opinion survey ... it was the "Sergé Survey!" Let me explain.

A friend asked, "Have you heard from Sergé recently?"

I replied, "No, I haven't ... have you?"

"Yes and, believe it or not, he has moved to Mesquite, Nevada!!!"

I was struck dumb. Now, to appreciate our mutual shock you need to understand that Sergé was an "Angeleno's Angeleno." Not only was Sergé born, raised, educated, employed, married, divorced, married, divorced, married, divorced … well, you get the idea … in Los Angeles, but his father also was born, raised, educated, employed, married … etc. in Los Angeles. In the early days of "motoring," at a time when the Southern California Auto Club was young and was responsible for stop signs and mileage signs along Southern California highways, Sergé's father's membership number was something like #000006!

In short, Sergé, and his father before him, "loved L.A." They could have been part of Randy Newman's chorus … at one time. When they heard other Californians derisively say such-and-such city, "Is becoming more and more like L.A. all the time," they thought that was a compliment for such-and-such city! They lived their lives in Los Angeles and had no desire to live anywhere else. That is, until Sergé moved to Mesquite, Nevada.

So, I called him at his new address and asked, "What happened?" I assumed he would say he had moved for health reasons, perhaps to address chronic asthma or rheumatism or something or other. But that's not what he said.

What he said was, "Ed, I got sick and tired of too many people!"

That is the "Sergé Survey," and Los Angeles polled poorly. And—here is where this affects you: Unless something is done—*and you are the one to do it*—the rest of America is headed for where Los Angeles is today.

DO YOU STILL LOVE L.A.?

Now I suppose I shouldn't pick on Los Angeles, should I? After all, Los Angeles is really Southern California these days—from the border with Mexico to the borders with Kern County (Bakersfield) and Santa Barbara County. In the San Francisco-Oakland Bay Area where people have long said, "It's looking more like L.A. all the time," it now looks, feels, and smells like L.A. much of the time.

Or take "laid-back, surf's up" Santa Cruz, CA. Out of 114 medium-size cities, it was recently ranked the nation's 13th most stressful. How can that possibly be? Traffic congestion! As Bert Sperling whose firm produces *Best Places* guides explains, the most frequent reason people give for moving from one city to another is traffic. "I can't put up with the traffic anymore!" Sounds like the "Sergé Survey" result, doesn't it?

Even in the once-bucolic county where I live, Contra Costa County, the good life is no longer considered so good. My local newspaper printed responses to their "Question of the Week: Do you perceive your quality of life in California improving or worsening?"

Every letter published was of the "worsening" variety! Since our newspaper is generally good about printing letters on both sides of issues, I'm guessing they didn't receive any of the "improving" variety.

Of course, when California sneezes, the rest of America catches the flu. For example, I recently asked a friend about his commute in metropolitan Washington, DC.

"Twenty to thirty-five minutes, depending on when I leave," he responded.

"Well, that's pretty reasonable. How far are you from your office?"

"Six miles."

YOU'RE THE DOCTOR

Like self-diagnosing the flu, *you* have to be your own diagnostician regarding America's addiction to population growth. Just like Sergé, *you* have to decide when *you* "are sick and tired of too many people."

You can decide when *you* think enough is enough and when *you* think too many are too many.

You can look at *your* driving times between various points and decide whether or not *you* think they are reasonable.

You can look at *your* tax bills and decide how much *you* want to pay to support people who moved to America supposedly sponsored by friends and relatives, who vouched for the newcomers' ability to support themselves.

Understand, not everyone will agree with you, if *you* decide America is overpopulated.

Remember, *some* people *still love L.A.*

LOOKING BACK ... AND AHEAD

In this chapter, we have considered reasons why I call America's rampant population growth an addiction—we know it is bad for us, but we continue it anyway. We tried to get our mental arms around this growth by discussing the dwindling number of acres in America available to support each resident. We created an imaginary line of 3.3 million people—the number of people added to America's population annually. And we saw one example that *the population growth addiction which has destroyed much of California is moving to the other 49 states ... and the District of Columbia!*

In the next chapter, we will take a look at some of the population growth addicts to understand not only who they are, but how and why they became addicts. Perhaps you will run across someone you know.

As you read further, remind yourself: *Addictions can be broken! You* can join tens of thousands of others who are working to break America's addiction to population growth!

FOR REFLECTION AND DISCUSSION:

1. How helpful or unhelpful do you find the analogy between America's addiction to rampant population growth and a physiological addiction?

2. If America's population can grow from 125 million to 485 million in three generations, what do you think the population will be for our *"seventh-generation"* unless we break the population growth addiction?

3. Why do you think America's news media extensively document problems which are obviously exacerbated by rampant population growth, but seldom suggest America address that underlying and exacerbating factor?

4. How comfortable are you with the concept that the number of acres of American land supporting each American has dwindled from 105 acres in 1800, to 13 acres in 1960, to 8 acres in 2000, will be approximately 5.5 acres in 2050, and will continue to dwindle as our population continues to grow?

5. How easy is it for you to visualize 3.3 million people holding hands across America and how easy is it for you to visualize all the cars they will drive, all the houses they will live in, all the schools they will attend, all the health care services they will require, and all the food, water, and energy they will consume?

QUICK FIX #3

Obtain information about one of your two U.S. Senators to enter into Appendix C, "Quick Fix References." If you or a friend have access to the Internet, *www.Vote-Smart.org* provides all the information you need or call them at 1-888-868-3762. Also, many telephone directories provide some of this information and a telephone call to this Senator's office will provide the remainder. Or, a call to your local newspaper may provide the information you are looking for. Ignore spaces for "*NumbersUSA. com* scores" for now. We'll use those spaces later.

Chapter 4

THE ADDICTS

addict v. To cause to become compulsively and physiologically dependent on a habit-forming substance.

addict n. One who is addicted, as to narcotics.

"The chains of habit are too weak to be felt until they are too strong to be broken." —Samuel Johnson

THERE ARE MANY POPULATION GROWTH addicts, some hardly aware they have become addicted. Others are so badly addicted *they have entered what psychologists would call a state of tolerance. That is, they have reached a state where increasingly larger doses (of population growth) are necessary to produce desired effects.*

Let's consider some of America's population growth addicts and the state of their addictions.

BUILDERS AND DEVELOPERS

Samuel Gompers, one of the early founders of the labor union movement, once was asked, "What does labor want?" His reply, "More!" That is exactly what today's builders and developers want—"More!" They want more population so they can build more houses, build more apartment buildings, build more "affordable housing," build more office complexes, build more shopping centers, and build more and more and more!

Increasingly, they also want more cheap labor. And they know the more people they have vying for jobs, the easier it is to keep labor cheap—especially if some of those people broke laws to enter the U.S. and join the labor force, and are not hesitant to break more laws by working off the books and by accepting cash instead of payroll checks.

Many builders and developers also like the idea of being able to keep such workers submissive by threatening to reveal their illegal status to law enforcement authorities. In other words, many builders and developers have become addicted to population growth.

If you doubt that, talk with any builder or developer and ask, "What would happen to your business, if population in your area stopped growing?"

You'd better be sure your builder or developer is sitting down when you ask. Otherwise, you may see a grown person melting like "the Wicked Witch of the West" on the floor before your very eyes! Visions of withdrawal pains rush to the head and weeping begins.

"Impossible!"

"We will always have population growth!"

"This nation depends on population growth!"

"My industry depends on population growth!"

"Our entire economy would collapse without population growth!"

"Motherhood and apple pie would mean nothing without population growth."

OK, perhaps not the last, but the perception is clear: Many builders and developers simply cannot conceive of life being worth living without more and more people—even if that means eventually leveling and building over every square mile of buildable land in the country. And of course, logically—mathematically—that is *exactly* what it does mean, if there is *infinite* population growth.

Does this suggest that many builders and developers care more about building and developing and making money than they care about the quality of life in America—the quality of life for humans as well as for wildlife? You betcha! That's exactly what it suggests.

And if that suggestion is wrong—if you run across a builder or developer who answers your question about, "What would happen to your business, if ...?" with, "Oh, we'd have plenty of work refurbishing all of the old and outdated residences and industrial buildings that were built over the past fifty years," please visit *www.ThinkPopulation.org* and let us have that *hero's* name and telephone number!

FARMERS

Believe it or not, American farmers once planted, tended, and harvested their own crops without help from cheap, foreign, and often illegal labor. If you are too young to remember such a time, then, as it is said, you're much younger than I. Believe it or not, in some parts of America, farmers still plant, tend, and harvest their own crops without help from cheap, foreign, and often illegal labor.

How is that possible? Well, fifty years ago, many schools in agricultural communities adjusted their school schedules to accommodate young people helping with the planting or harvesting of crops. That is still done in some communities. Also, fifty years ago, there were many American-born workers who traveled agricultural circuits following, in particular, the harvesting of crops.

Too many farmers today have become addicted to using cheap, illegal aliens to plant, tend, and harvest their crops. Ask many farmers what would happen if all illegal aliens were returned to their various homelands. They will tell you:

"Why, we couldn't farm without illegal aliens. We'd go out of business because Americans won't do this kind of work."

But, of course, Americans did "do this kind of work" for decades. You may have known some of those workers. You may very well be a descendent of some of them. What too many farmers today are *really* saying is, "Americans won't do this kind of work for the paltry wages I'm currently paying and for the poor working conditions I'm currently providing."

But, suppose, magically, all illegal aliens were returned to their various homelands. What would happen? Wages paid for planting, tending, and harvesting crops would go up. Working conditions associated with planting, tending, and harvesting crops would improve.

"But, Ed, wouldn't the price to consumers of food also go up?"

Undoubtedly, this would be the case, though not nearly as much as some farmers want us to believe, since the farmers' portion of the cost of most food sold in stores is a minor portion. And while consumers' cost of food would go up, taxpayers' (often the same people) cost of welfare would go down as they no longer would have to pay taxes to subsidize farmers for having paid puny wages and for providing poor working conditions.

You might say, "Well, OK, Ed, I understand some farmers are getting a free ride on the backs of illegal aliens and taxpayers, but what does that have to do with population growth?"

Well, every illegal alien is another person added to our population. Today, America's population is approximately ten million larger than it would be without illegal aliens. In many American communities they make up a significant portion of the population. In a few American communities they make up a majority of the population.

"But aren't most illegal alien farm workers temporary workers?

Don't they return to their home countries seasonally when they are not working in the fields, and don't they return to their home countries permanently when they have earned a sufficient grubstake?"

As someone once said and as Mark Krikorian, Executive Director of Center for Immigration Studies (CIS), repeated in his February 2004 report, "Flawed Assumptions Underlying Guest Worker Programs": "There is nothing more permanent than a temporary worker." For most, living on the wrong side of the tracks in America is preferable to living where there are no tracks—or trains or freeways or televisions or hospitals or schools or clean water or … Well, you name it.

Most illegal alien temporary farm workers remain in America, raise families in America—often large families of newly minted American citizens—live and die in America. And, as they age and must retire from farm work, they are replaced by additional younger, illegal aliens who come to America to earn their grubstakes and also, in theory, to return to their home countries healthy, wealthy, and wise. Thus the cycle repeats and repeats and America's population grows and grows—just as some farmers' addiction to population growth grows and grows.

FOOD PROCESSORS

When I was in college, I worked one summer for a tuna cannery in San Diego, California. Most of the workers in the cannery were immigrants or children of immigrants. Virtually all were legal immigrants or citizens born in the U.S. to legal immigrants. Had I worked for any of the many fish canneries on the West Coast between the Canadian and Mexican borders, I believe I would have reported the same thing—many immigrant workers, but few illegal alien workers.

I don't know what I would have reported had I spent that summer working for a fruit or vegetable packing facility in the Central Valley of California. But I am pretty sure that three decades earlier my relatives would have reported the majority of immigrants working in those plants were from other states, not from other countries, and those who were from other countries had entered America legally.

Today, not only fruit and fish processors have become addicted to a growing population of illegal aliens, but so have beef, pork, and poultry processors. People smugglers smuggle people across borders specifically to serve food processing plants. People die in vans and trains and trailers used to smuggle people across borders and to transport them on to food processing plants.

People are fined and threatened with jail time for soliciting people smugglers to smuggle people to their food processing plants. But the smuggling goes on, the population of illegal aliens goes up, and the number of U.S. born Americans out of work because they were displaced by illegal aliens willing to work for paltry wages and benefits grows. Not surprisingly, so does the bitterness of unemployed American citizens and legal immigrants.

HOSPITALITY INDUSTRY EMPLOYERS

It's rather difficult for the hotel, motel, and food service industries to say, "Americans won't do this kind of work," because tens of millions of Americans do wash and change linens, vacuum rooms, clean bathrooms, serve meals, and wash dishes. They perform these tasks in their own homes, of course. But if you travel around America, you will still find many places where Americans do any and all tasks required to maintain hotels and motels and to provide service at restaurants.

How in the world did so many in the hospitality industry become so addicted to cheap, illegal alien labor when there are obviously Americans willing to do such work for reasonable wages and benefits? Like other illegal substances, one taste may be enough.

"If I can get my dishes washed for $5 per hour less and if I pay cash and don't have to pay workmen's compensation and Social Security taxes, I can keep $10 (or more) per hour for myself."

Making more money is addictive—just look at the multimillionaires who go to jail because they had to make "just a few million more."

John Burnett of National Public Radio (NPR) reported on the hospitality industry in Vail, Colorado. He interviewed several illegal alien workers. Here are two examples as provided by a translator:

"Because an American won't do *(that work)*—not for what they pay us. Our boss contracted three Brazilians on temporary visas, but she wouldn't pay them what she promised. Even they quit after three days. And how long have we tolerated these conditions? Six months now?

"We're not taking work from anybody. We're not doing anything bad. We don't look for trouble. Actually, we're very submissive people. For instance, I never complain, because if I don't do something, they can always throw me onto the street."

Burnett concluded, "American employers are hooked *[his word]* on cheap immigrant labor, both legal and illegal.

"But a longtime housekeeping supervisor in Vail offers a cautionary word to the backers of a new guest worker program. She says back in 1986, when immigration reform granted amnesty to more than two million undocumented immigrants, guess what was the first thing her Mexican hotel maids did when they got their papers? Many quit their jobs and looked for better ones. And what did the employer do? Rather than raise salaries, she replaced them with new immigrants who were, as she said, 'hungrier for the work.'"

INFORMATION TECHNOLOGY (IT) EMPLOYERS

During IT booms, IT employers find it convenient to import "temporary" foreign workers to meet their perceived need for a quick fix of manpower. Later, they find it economically beneficial as well, since many of these "temporary" employees are willing to work for considerably less than American IT employees.

Saving housing costs by sleeping four to a room hardly seems a deprivation to many of these foreign workers and it brings them one step closer to their ultimate goal—permanent residence in America. Meanwhile, IT employers pay lower wages and avoid the cost of training older American technicians and engineers.

Everybody wins … everybody, that is, except American IT workers who want reasonable wages, benefits, working conditions, and quality of life. Yes, and also you and I, who want our American IT workers to have those things.

"Ed, why do you say you and I want American IT workers to have reasonable wages, benefits, working conditions, and quality of life? Should I really care what IT workers earn and how they live?"

You should if you want America's IT colleges and universities to continue to attract some of the brighter young Americans to prepare for work in the IT industry and if you want those bright young Americans to have good, dependable jobs when they graduate, and if you want America's IT industry to continue to be the center of innovation and advancement. Yes, you and I *should* care.

Previously, reference was made to the "perceived need" of IT employers for "temporary" workers during IT booms. Funny thing, how their "temporary need" tends to become permanent, just as their "temporary" workers tend to become permanent. How do we know this? Well, when IT busts come along, IT employers continue hiring "temporary" foreign IT employees.

If you want to test the accuracy of that statement yourself, here are clues you can watch for: *H-1B* and *L-1*. Memorize those codes; they are your clues. You will read articles and hear reports about *H-1B* or *L-1* visas for foreign professionals. Read and listen carefully. Determine for yourself whether or not America's IT employers' addiction to population growth is in tune with America's economic cycles. Or, do IT executives simply want more and more low-cost employees, whether IT times are boom or bust?

MEDIA OWNERS AND EXECUTIVES

How do media owners and executives measure success? Readers. Viewers. Listeners. The more newspaper and magazine readers, the more television viewers, the more radio listeners, and the more ad revenue, the more successful media owners and executives feel. Even when a media outlet is losing money with every issue or with every broadcast, they still crave more readers, viewers, and listeners.

And what makes more readers, viewers, and listeners? *More people! A larger population!*

If you find a newspaper, newsmagazine, radio or television newscast which has staff journalists who are allowed to present anything but the "growth is good" party line, count yourself as lucky. A few such organizations exist, but not many. In my experience, most adhere to a more typical pattern: They are quite generous in the space they provide to letter writers who express concern about population growth in their areas. At the same time, they expect their columnists and journalists, as well as their editorial page writers, to present only one view: *"Growth, good or not, is inevitable."* And when they write "growth," that is a code word for population growth.

Even in its generosity to letter writers, a newspaper's quest for political correctness can lead to some amusing results. I wrote a response to a fairly negative article written by a local columnist, Jack Chang, about a well-known Bay Area populationist, Yeh Ling-Ling, Executive Director of Diversity Alliance for a Stabilized America (DASA). It had an amusing result:

"Dear Editor: Jack Chang has never met an immigrant he didn't like … until he met Yeh Ling-Ling. What's Jack's problem with Yeh? 'Can't be sure, but I suspect it's the fact that she can count. Yes, Yeh counts noses: black noses, white noses, brown noses, Christian noses, Hindu noses, Muslim noses, young noses, old noses.

"In other words, she counts all noses and she says—not in a 'panicked, quickened trill'—we have too many noses in this country, in this state, and in Contra Costa County. She 'put two and two together and saw the root cause of all these problems, from crowded schools to heavy traffic, which is we have too many people,' i.e., too many noses.

"If Jack Chang were the 20th passenger on an elevator with a sign reading, 'Maximum capacity 20 riders,' and a 350-pound Sumo wrestler asked if he could be the 21st rider, Mr. Chang might say, 'You look like an immigrant—get on board.' Now, lean over the elevator shaft and listen carefully. Echoing up from the basement you can hear Mr. Chang saying, 'Always room for one more.'"

The amusing part of that exercise was, when they published the letter, they changed "350-pound Sumo wrestler" to "250-pound wrestler." I've never learned whether they were concerned about offending people who weigh 350 pounds or concerned about offending Sumo wrestlers!

More to the point, I suspect there was little likelihood Jack Chang could offend his newspaper's editors and owners by writing an article criticizing Yeh Ling-Ling, an outspoken critic of rampant population growth in America.

Of course, to criticize American media executives—in press, radio, or television—for wanting more Americans is like criticizing bird hawks for wanting more song birds in their territories. That's how each survives!

Show me a media executive who is willing to go to his or her Board of Directors and say, "I've decided America is crowded enough. From now on, we're going to let our readers/listeners/viewers know that rampant population growth is not good for America and it is not inevitable!"

Show me a media executive who is willing to say something like that and I'll show you a media executive whose employment contract has a *fabulous* severance clause!

MIDDLE-CLASS AMERICANS

"Ed, who would wash our cars and mow our lawns, if all the illegal aliens returned to their home countries?" my friend asked.

"Well, who mowed the lawns when you were a girl?"

"… My brother."

Exactly! Her brother mowed lawns. I mowed lawns. Widows could hear my steel-wheeled lawn mower, with its rattling grass catcher and banging lawn edger, half-a-block away and would be out on their porches waiting to flag me down. Across America, millions of American boys mowed millions of American lawns.

Later, my girlfriend, along with her friends and millions of other American girls, baby-sat millions of American babies for millions of

American parents, and ushered millions of patrons to their seats in thousands of American movie houses.

And all over America, millions of young men and young women flipped tens of millions of hamburgers, shook tens of millions of milk shakes, and washed tens of millions of dishes as they served tens of millions of Americans at diners, drive-ins, and family restaurants.

Wealthy Americans have always been able to hire others to do the jobs they did not care to do nor—too often in my opinion—care to have their children do. Today, too many middle-class Americans have decided they not only don't want to mow their own lawns, they don't want their sons to mow their own or others' lawns, nor do they want their daughters to baby-sit for others.

Not only are children of middle-class parents not learning the rewards of honest labor nor learning the true value of their tennis lessons and soccer uniforms, they are often taught it is OK to break the law when it benefits them—for example, by paying low wages in cash to illegal aliens to mow lawns and care for children.

This is, in my opinion, an unfortunate form of parenting, the ultimate cost of which may not be known for several decades.

GOOD AND BAD ADDICTS

A friend told me about being in a restaurant studying a wine list when he noticed two waiters were hovering nearby. One was smiling while the other was scowling. My friend looked up and said, "Now, don't try to pull the old 'good wine steward, bad wine steward' trick on me."

I don't want to pull the old "good addict, bad addict" trick on you ... but not all of America's population growth addicts are bad people. Many—perhaps most—are simply people who haven't thought about what their addiction is doing to America's future—in many cases, the futures of their own children, grandchildren, and further descendants. Many, perhaps most, are a little lazy—or very busy—and don't care to spend the time, energy, money and/or thought necessary to address their personal or political "needs" without requiring America to add to its already burgeoning population.

Most middle-class population growth addicts are good people, i.e., "good addicts." Perhaps thoughts cross their minds occasionally about wages and working conditions, about the underground economy, about subsidized health care permitting them to pay lower wage rates, and about deteriorating schools whose problems are multiplied by multitudes of students who speak little English. But they probably do not think about the total range of problems created by increasing population.

Nor is it likely they think of their lack of thought as adding to America's population growth. They may be good people—they may be "good addicts." But they are addicts all the same and they will have to come to grips with this, if America is to recover from its addiction to population growth.

But there are some truly bad population growth addicts. Ranking high on my "low life" list are: Employers who work with people smugglers who recruit bus loads and truck loads of illegal aliens as workers. And employers in whatever industry who fire American citizens and legal immigrants and knowingly hire illegal aliens in their places. I will shed no tears for any of these who are heavily fined … or sent to prison!

LOOKING BACK … AND AHEAD

In this chapter, we have discussed some of the industries—and individuals—who have become population growth addicts. Perhaps you know a few personally. We have considered economic reasons why some addicts find it easier to remain addicted than to seek recovery.

In the next two chapters, we will take a look at some of the many victims of America's addiction to population growth. The next chapter discusses living-and-breathing victims; the following chapter discusses some of the American concepts and institutions which are also victims of America's addiction to population growth. Perhaps you will run across someone you know or something you are already concerned about.

As you read further, remind yourself: *Addictions can be broken! You* can join tens of thousands of others who are working to break America's addiction to population growth!

FOR REFLECTION AND DISCUSSION:

1. Who have you known personally—yourself included—whom you might describe as "a population growth addict?"
2. What experience have you had with farmers and/or food processors which would permit you to comment on their addiction to population growth?

3. What experience have you had as a customer of America's hospitality industry that would lead you to believe not all of their managers are addicted to population growth?

4. What experience have you had as a consumer of the American media industry that would lead you to confirm or refute their being described as population growth addicts?

5. Of the population growth addicts you have known, would you describe any as "bad addicts?"

QUICK FIX #4

Obtain information about your other U.S. Senator to enter into Appendix C, "Quick Fix References." If you or a friend have access to the Internet, *www.Vote-Smart.org* provides all the information you need or call them at 1-888-868-3762. Also, many telephone directories provide some of this information and a telephone call to your Senator's office will provide the remainder. Or, a call to your local newspaper may provide the information you are looking for. Ignore spaces for "*NumbersUSA.com* scores" for now. We'll use those spaces later.

Chapter 5

THE VICTIMS

Living, Breathing

victim *n.* 1. One who is harmed by or made to suffer from an act, circumstance, agency, or condition. 2. A person who is tricked, swindled, or taken advantage of.

"It is not until the well runs dry, we know the worth of water."
—Benjamin Franklin

VICTIMS OF AMERICA'S ADDICTION TO population growth are generally, but not always, innocents. For example, it is difficult to think of victims more innocent of blame than wildlife destroyed by encroaching land development. On the other hand, taxpayers, who certainly are victims of the cost of additional schools and infrastructure to support rampant population growth, include some who welcome population growth when it mows their lawns and tends their children or when it reduces their labor costs and increases their profits.

Like some drug addicts, some population growth addicts are also victims.

AMERICAN INDIANS

It is obvious that America's population growth in the 18th and 19th centuries had a disastrous effect upon Indian tribes and Indian populations. The "New Americans" brought ways and means which not only destroyed Indians ways and means, but Indians themselves. Those who survived—a fraction of the original Indian population—were often force-marched to "foreign" lands within America's vast territories. As Mary Austin wrote in *Land of Little Rain*:

"Oppapago looks on Waban, and Waban on Coso and the Bitter Lake, and the campoodie looks on these three; and more, it sees the beginning of winds along the foot of Coso, the gathering of clouds behind the high ridges, the spring flush, the soft spread of wild almond bloom on the mesa. These first, you understand, are the Paiute's walls, the other his furnishings.

"Not the wattled hut is his home, but the land, the wind, the hill front, the stream. These he cannot duplicate at any furbisher's shop as you who live within doors, who, if your purse allows, may have the same home at Sitka and Samarcand. So you see how it is that the homesickness of an Indian is often unto death, since he gets no relief from it; neither wind nor weed nor skyline, nor any aspect of the hills of a strange land sufficiently like his own."

Yes, we can see how it is, when today we continue to chip away at what is left of Indians' lands—often sacred lands—to build power plants, coal mines to feed power plants, and highways taking people to and from power plants and to and from growing cities requiring power plants. Four-lane freeways replace two-lane highways across Indian lands, rearranging "… the land, the wind, the hill front, the stream" as casually as you or I might rearrange the furniture in our houses.

DRIVERS

By virtually any standard, we have more cars and trucks on our highways than our highways were designed to carry. And the number of drivers increases annually. How many alien drivers do you think we have on American highways who never drove a car until they came to America, e.g., alien women drivers who came from countries where women are not allowed to drive cars? How many aliens do you suppose we have on American highways who come from countries where "driver education" in schools is nonexistent, where traffic laws are observed only when they are impossible to ignore, and where horns are used more frequently than brakes?

Our roads and highways are overcrowded and deteriorating. There are too many rude and crude drivers for whom overcrowded and under-maintained conditions bring out their worst driving behavior. How many ill-prepared and inexperienced drivers have we added to that volatile mix? How many road rage explosions has that mix created?

EMPLOYEES

Syndicated columnist Ruben Navarrette, Jr., author of *A Darker Shade Of Crimson—Odyssey of a Harvard Chicano,* believes it is too late for America's workers to value hard work. He wrote that it is time to dispel the notion that illegal aliens are taking jobs from Americans. There are no waiting lists, he wrote, for native-born workers who want to pick lettuce or to pack meat or to pound nails, in "… harsh, unsanitary and sometimes even dangerous conditions," often for minimum wages.

Now, you may not personally know someone who has picked lettuce or butchered and packed meat, but surely you know someone who has pounded nails. In other words, have you known someone who is or has been a carpenter? As for packing meat: For decades native-born Americans and legal immigrants earned good wages and benefits packing meat, if not in great working conditions. Then, greedy employers found they could hire illegal aliens to do the work for less … much less. Much less, because taxpayers picked up the cost of supplemental food, health care, education, and even, in some instances, housing.

Or, think of this: According to the 2000 census, over 80% of taxicab drivers in New York City (NYC) were foreign-born. Yet in Cincinnati and Detroit less than 10% were foreign-born. Assume all the foreign-born cab drivers had never migrated to NYC. Do you think there would be no cabs in NYC, or do you think cab owners would pay sufficient wages and benefits to attract American-born drivers—as they do in Cincinnati and Detroit?

Mr. Navarrette reported America has created at least one and probably two generations of workers who are "soft-around-the-middle" *[his words]* and who were raised to think of many dirty and low-paying jobs as "immigrant work." In a letter I asked him if his position was that America should continue the process and "create third, fourth, fifth, and sixth generations of soft-around-the-middle workers by bringing in immigrants to do 'immigrant work.'" No reply.

My concern is that "soft-around-the-middle" workers may become America's downfall. My suggestion: Let economics—American economics—compensate American employees for doing the work that needs to be done and encourage American employers to provide the wages, benefits, and working conditions appropriate for the work that needs to be done.

Simultaneously, American voters should instruct their federal, state, and local elected representatives to enforce all relevant laws—from labor laws to loitering laws, from immigration laws to identity theft laws. Such enforcement would encourage employers to meet their responsibilities to their employees and to their communities.

In the first paragraph of this section about employees, Mr. Navarrette is quoted as suggesting American workers do not want to work in "sometimes even dangerous conditions." Let's examine his supposition further.

Les Cristie, *CNN/Money* Contributing Writer, listed "America's Most Dangerous Jobs" based upon Bureau of Labor Statistics data as follows: (1) lumberjacks, (2) fishermen, (3) commercial pilots, especially general aviation pilots (e.g., bush pilots, air-taxi pilots, crop dusters), (4) steel workers, (e.g., building skyscrapers and bridges), (5) driver-sales workers (e.g., pizza deliverers and vending machine fillers), (6) roofers, (7) electrical power installers, (8) farm workers, (9) construction laborers, and (10) truck drivers. How many native-born American workers do you know who perform some of these jobs? Of these ten dangerous jobs, how many do you think are largely performed by illegal aliens? Perhaps roofers and construction laborers. Other than perhaps those two—and there are certainly many native-born roofers and construction laborers—contrary to Mr. Navarrette's supposition, most of these dangerous jobs are performed by native-born Americans and legal immigrants.

Not surprisingly, there is a positive correlation between amount of danger and amount of pay. However, that correlation is becoming diluted as illegal aliens move into certain job markets and drive down wages. Eventually, Americans may refuse to do dangerous work for wages that fail to reflect the danger involved. Look again at Mr. Cristie's list of the ten most dangerous jobs and you can see for yourself that American workers will do all kinds of jobs—dangerous or not—if they are fairly and adequately compensated.

ENERGY USERS

As population grows, energy demand grows, i.e., the more Americans, the more energy America uses. While it is important for Americans to conserve energy, if each American uses 5% less energy, but the number of Americans increases by 10%, we still end up using more energy, despite our conservation efforts.

For example, America's *energy use per capita, i.e., per person,* was relatively unchanged between 1970 and 1990, *but total energy use in America increased 24%.* Why? According to Professor John Holdren (of

I = P x A x T fame—see Chapter 2, "An Overview"), 93% of that increase was due to population increase. In other words, per capita energy conservation was overwhelmed by an increasing number of people.

Another example: According to the California Energy Commission, *per capita* consumption of electricity in California dropped 5% between 1979 and 1999. However, during that same 20 years the state's population grew 43% largely as a result of immigration. Naturally, *total energy consumption grew.*

Viewed globally, international migration for economic purposes, e.g., better jobs, better living conditions, etc., tends to flow *from* nations with lower per capita energy consumption *to* nations with higher per capita energy consumption, i.e., to nations with more trains, planes, and autos, and more air-conditioned buildings. Not surprisingly, most aliens coming to America consume more energy *living here* than they did living in their home countries.

As long as population continues to increase in America, you may assume demand for energy will also increase, along with an accompanying increase in costs and in deleterious effects upon the environment.

HOMEBUYERS AND RENTERS

Read newspapers from cities across America and you'll read about local politicians who (a) brag about the rising "value" of residences and (b) complain about the shortage of "affordable housing."

The National Association of Home Builders and the National Association of Realtors asked recent homebuyers about the factors which influenced their home buying decisions. Here are the percentages of people responding "important" or "very important:"

- Houses spread out: 62%
- Bigger house: 47%
- Bigger lot: 45%
- Less developed area: 40%
- Away from the city: 39%.

"Bigger houses spread out on bigger lots in less developed areas away from cities!" Hold on—doesn't anybody want "smart growth?"

Oh, sure: Smaller houses (10%) on smaller lots (9%) closer to public transit (13%).

Costly Housing

"Well, Ed," you might ask, "What do these results mean for me or for someone I know who might be in the market to buy a house?"

They mean the cost of housing can go only one direction over the long run … up. As the supply of suitable land for housing declines, the price of such land goes up. As the demand for housing increases because of increasing population, the price of housing goes up.

Yet, the same politicians who want to create "affordable housing" for everyone refuse to work toward the one thing which would stop increasing demand for land and increasing housing costs—a stable American population.

Shoddy Workmanship

Obviously, increasing population means increasing demand for housing which in turn means increasing prices for land (since supply is limited) and, ultimately, increasing prices for houses and, indirectly, for residence rental units.

But there is another "cost" which new homebuyers in particular are suffering—shoddy workmanship. *Consumer Reports* interviewed Alan Mooney, president of Criterium Engineers, a Portland, Maine consulting-engineering firm with offices in 35 states. Mooney estimated 15% of all new-home construction is seriously defective. That represents 150,000 new homes a year. "That's a huge number," Mooney said, questioning whether "many of these houses will last 50 years." From what I have heard from friends and friends of friends about traumatized new homeowners, there is some question as to how long some of these new homeowners will last!

What is causing shoddy workmanship? According to *Consumer Reports,* "Shortages of skilled tradespeople sometimes contribute to …" shoddy construction. In fast-growing areas, such as parts of California, Florida, Nevada, and Texas, "… a lack of framers, plumbers, roofers, and electricians" often leads to use of less-skilled or unskilled laborers. "Lack of training and *language barriers*" *[my emphasis]* between bosses and their workers also contribute to "… poor workmanship."

America's addiction to population growth is creating an ongoing situation where we need more houses built than we have qualified workers available to build them. So we hire unskilled workers—often workers not able to read or speak English—to do work which should be done by skilled tradesmen. Or as a Duluth Trading Company catalog of tools and clothes for tradesmen states in its description of the book *Spanish On The Job—How To Get The Work Done,* "Trust me, yelling in English isn't going to help."

So, as unskilled workers move from unskilled work to work they may not be qualified to do, America's population growth-addicted builders import additional unskilled workers to replace them, thereby increasing demand for more houses—and schools—which are built by more and more unskilled workers.

ILLEGAL ALIENS

Illegal aliens are people who have not followed the rules of America's immigration laws—people who have not met screening requirements for matters such as good health, national security, no criminal record, adequate financial resources—but they are, nevertheless, in America. Then, how can they be *victims* of America's addiction to population growth? To obtain a full appreciation of the extent to which many illegal aliens and their families are victims, I urge you to read *Mexifornia,* a painfully personal and heartfelt book by Victor Davis Hanson.

Or, see a movie ...

An illegal alien employee has found something unimaginable while cleaning a hotel room. He shows it to his boss who casually responds that people come to hotels to do dirty things, and says that the employee's job is to make things look pretty again.

That is the scene from which the movie, *Dirty Pretty Things,* takes its title. (BBC Productions, with Celadon Productions, JonesCompany Productions; Stephen Frears, director; Steven Knight, writer; distributed by Miramax Films Corp., USA, 2003.) It is the way the hero's indifferent boss reacts when the hero shows him a human heart he has just removed from one of the guest rooms!

If you haven't seen it, let me assure you, this isn't a horror film—at least not in the way you may be thinking. This is a movie about the horrors of being an illegal alien in a relatively civilized nation and about the people who take outrageous advantage of illegal aliens' fear of deportation.

In a closing scene, in exchange for an illegal, but redeeming deed the hero has done, a big-league criminal hands him valuable, forged identity papers, then asks him why he's never seen him before.

The hero replies that they are the invisible people, the people who drive cabs, clean rooms, and ...

Well, I won't go further. Let me simply say, *Dirty Pretty Things* is a fine film. You will cheer the ending. And you will think long and hard about the damage done when people are encouraged to illegally enter reasonably civilized nations. You will definitely understand what I mean when I refer to illegal aliens as among the most injured victims of America's addiction to population growth.

Or, watch a PBS documentary, *Farmingville*, a 78-minute *POV* film (*www.pbs.org/pov* and *www.farmingvillethemovie.com*) about what happened when 1,500 Mexican day laborers moved into a New York town of 15,000 in the late 1990s. Early in the film, Paul Tonna, Suffolk County Legislator, says something about Farmingville having a prosperous economy in need of people willing to work. "We need day laborers." And throughout the film, one might surmise his loyalties were primarily with the day laborers—and their employers—rather than with his constituents.

However, near the end of the film he says, "There is a breaking of the faith when—and I go back to our federal and state levels where there are people who, I think, *[are in a]* very coordinated way say*[ing]*, 'This is good for our economy to have a *slave labor class* here and as long as we don't have any terrible open violence, we'll keep on doing a two-step. We don't care, if *[they have]* a problem in Farmingville and it ruins or hurts the residents there and creates tensions for those day laborers there—because the greater good—where our economy is good, *[is]* because we have this *slave labor.*'"

Just as white Southerners in the early 19th century convinced themselves they could not survive without Black slaves, many Americans have convinced themselves that they cannot survive without cheap illegal alien labor.

Or, read what Justin Pritchard of Associated Press reported in 2004 about deaths of Mexican aliens:

In several Western and Southern states work-related deaths of Mexican workers are four times the rates for American-born workers. Most often these deaths are preventable—and gruesome! Falls from roofs, impalings on farm and factory equipment, drowning in cattle feces are a few of the personal tragedies repeated over and over as newly hired, illiterate, and ill-trained illegal aliens replace those who have died or moved to safer jobs. Mexican aliens represent about 4% of America's workforce, but suffer about 7% of on-the-job deaths.

Dead and maimed illegal aliens—and their families—are indeed victims of America's addiction to cheap labor and population growth.

LEGAL IMMIGRANTS

Legal immigrants are people from other nations who have followed the steps required by America's immigration laws. They have met screening requirements for matters such as good health, no national security risk, no serious criminal record, and sufficient financial resources before migrating into America. Many of these immigrants came to America seeing it as a land of opportunity. Unfortunately, rampant population growth is making America, increasingly, the land of co-opted opportunity.

As population soars—especially as the population of uneducated and poorly paid illegal aliens soars—and as they take jobs which legal immigrants might have desired at reasonable wages, legal immigrants struggle to find the financial opportunities they were, figuratively and literally, banking on. Even the wages, benefits, and working conditions of jobs legal immigrants do find are often pegged at low levels, because of employers' ability to replace legal immigrants with illegal aliens.

There was a time when legal immigrants held many jobs in the construction, agricultural, food processing, hospitality, and service industries. Today, many of those jobs have been taken by illegal aliens who are willing to work for less than minimum wages, often without benefits, and with unsatisfactory working conditions. Meanwhile, legal immigrants, finding the jobs they used to have are gone, must turn to welfare to care for their families. Along with taxpayers, legal immigrants have become victims of America's addiction to population growth.

PAROLEES AND PROBATIONERS

"Parolees and probationers?" you may ask. "Who cares about parolees and probationers?"

Well, I do … and you should also, if you care about reducing—as much as practicable—recidivism, which is currently running at approximately 50%.

"OK, Ed, let's say I should care. Tell me, how are parolees and probationers victimized by America's addiction to population growth?"

Think about it. And *think like a populationist!*

We have a high percentage—too high a percentage—of felons being released from prison, and shortly later being arrested again and returned to prison for theft, burglary, and even worse crimes. We have too many criminals freed to their communities who fail to meet their probationary conditions. Why? For some, my personal suspicion is, it is because they are defective human beings and no amount of jail time or rehabilitation effort will ever cure their defects. However, for some percentage of parolees and probationers—I have no idea what percentage, but for some percentage—a decent job might be the difference between "going straight" and returning to a life of crime.

"A job? What kind of job?" you might ask.

Well, convicted felons probably have difficulty qualifying for executive positions with large corporations—unless, perhaps, they were executives who later ended up in jail! So, let's look at one potential source of employment: Restaurants. For run-of-the-mill parolees and probationers, perhaps jobs as dishwashers or as table busboys might lead to jobs as servers or even as cooks.

In an article titled "Second Chance Cafe" in *Gourmet* magazine Bernadette Verzosa tells the story of Jarvis Smith. Jarvis had been cooking since he was a little boy—three years old by his recollection—when he would hang out with his grandmother in the kitchen. But Jarvis got into trouble and went to prison. When he was released from prison, he was able to turn his cooking experience into a career. At the time the article was written, 19-year-old Smith was a fry cook at Cafe Reconcile, a "New Orleans restaurant founded by the late Father Harry Thompson..." Doing what he loves, staying out of trouble, Jarvis says, "I can hold my head a little higher." What is the connection between "Second Chance Cafe" and population growth?

Again, *think like a populationist.*

We have approximately 10 million illegal aliens in America with more arriving every year and adding to our population—adding to our illegally burgeoning population. What are most of these illegal aliens doing to earn money? Well, some turn to crime—drugs and robberies—ending up in the same jail Jarvis Smith left. However, many take jobs as janitors, hotel housekeepers, lawn mowers and ... right, as dishwashers, busboys, servers, and, some eventually as cooks.

So, for every illegal alien taking a job as a dishwasher or a busboy or server or cook, or a job as a janitor, a hotel housekeeper, or a landscape maintenance worker, there may be a parolee or probationer who might have turned away from crime and put his or her feet back on solid, honest ground, if he or she had been given an opportunity for one of those "starter" jobs.

Yeh Ling-Ling is also a naturalized citizen. She has given extensive thought to virtually all aspects of a sustainable society. *Thinking like a populationist,* she wrote:

"Incentives should be given to millions of low-skilled unemployed or underemployed legal residents, able-bodied welfare recipients, and nonviolent inmates to take the jobs now given to illegal aliens."

So, for all our sakes, I hope America's addiction to population growth isn't also contributing *unnecessarily* to Americans' addiction to illegal drugs and collateral crime.

STUDENTS

According to Valerie Strauss in "A Case For Smaller Schools," (*Washington Post,* August 8, 2000), education researchers believe ideal enrollments for elementary schools are no more than 300 students, for middle schools no more than 500 students, and for high schools 600 to 900 students. Yet high schools with enrollments of more than 1,000 account for 71% of American high school students.

High schools with 3,000 or more students are now common in large cities such as Los Angeles and New York. Some schools have as many as 5,000 students.

What has caused the growth in the school-age population? *Immigration has been responsible for almost 70% of population growth in the last decade.* And according to the National Projections Program, Population Division, U.S. Census Bureau, immigrants arriving since 1994 and their descendants will account for two-thirds of future population growth.

So America's rampant population growth not only forces school districts either (a) to build more schools than taxpayers can afford and/or are willing to pay for or (b) to cram more students into existing schools. The result, as expected: Diminution of the education process. Students are obvious victims of America's addiction to population growth.

TAXPAYERS

There are a number of ways in which taxpayers have become victims of America's addiction to population growth. Taxes are increased to pay for increased highway and roadway capacity. Taxes are increased to increase the number of schoolrooms and teachers. While taxpayers can, in theory, benefit from these and similar tax increases, it is difficult to see much direct benefit to taxpayers for the increases in taxes that are spent to pay for welfare for indigent aliens.

There are many different ways to define and to measure poverty. However, if we assume welfare use suggests a family's income provides an unsatisfactory standard of living, one might conclude America is importing poverty.

For example, among households in America in which the head of household is American-born, approximately 15% use one or more basic welfare programs, i.e., Temporary Assistance to Needy Families (TANF), food stamps, Supplemental Security Income (SSI), and/or Medicaid. But among households in America in which the head of household is not American-born, approximately 23% use one or more basic welfare programs. (Source: Center for Immigration Studies [CIS] analysis of March 2002 Current Population Survey data collected by the U.S. Census Bureau.)

Why should this be the case? As Dr. Steven A. Camarota of CIS wrote in a March 2003 report: "The high rate of welfare use associated with immigrants is not explained by unwillingness to work. In 2001, almost 80% of immigrant households using welfare had at least one person working.

"One of the main reasons for the heavy reliance of immigrants on welfare programs is that a very large share have little education. The American economy offers very limited opportunities to such workers, and as a result many immigrants who work are still eligible for welfare because of their low incomes." Thus, employers who hire alien workers at low wages let taxpayers pay for basic services that their low-wage workers can't afford.

As hard working as most immigrants and aliens are, not only limited education, but the large families of certain cultures, ensures that American taxpayers will be asked to pick up the tab for a variety of services.

An article in my local newspaper about Latino aliens leaving America's Southwest for other states traced the travels and travails of six Mexican families, each of whom came to America illegally. Living 43 to a three-bedroom house—which burned down because of an overheated electrical cord—they required years of subsidized housing and food. One family remained in government housing despite the fact that the father had a good job as a farm machinery mechanic. Why? Perhaps having eleven children had something to do with it!

As a taxpayer, how do you feel about supporting a family of illegal aliens with eleven children?

As a taxpayer, how do you feel about being a victim of America's addiction to population growth?

TRAVELERS

If you have been an American air traveler for more than one decade, you have observed deterioration in service over time. Neither airlines nor airports have been able to keep pace with the increase in air travelers. Even if America's population had stabilized, the number of American air travelers would have increased sufficiently to challenge the ability of the industry to serve travelers adequately. However, piling on the additional air travelers created by increasing population has simply overwhelmed air travel capacity.

Airports are seeking permission—and billions of taxpayer dollars—to build runway extensions and to increase airport and plane maintenance facilities. How many million acres of land will be permanently paved over to create runways where swamps, bays, estuaries, and other wildlife habitat exist today? How many Americans *want* to increase America's population at the cost of decreasing America's wild lands and wildlife?

WATER USERS

According to the report, "Population, Water & Wildlife: Finding a Balance," by Don Hinrichsen, Karin Krchnak, and Katie Mogelgaard, published by National Wildlife Federation: Humans worldwide currently consume approximately 54% of all the accessible freshwater contained in rivers, lakes, and underground aquifers. By 2025, population growth may push this figure to 70%.

And according to a report by the Federation for American Immigration Reform (FAIR): "Water shortages which used to be limited to the dry western states, are now a problem throughout the U.S. Even regions which once seemed to have limitless supplies of water are facing predictions of shortages within a few years and are imposing water restrictions on residents.

"As our water supply strains under the constantly increasing demands generated by population growth, ground water is being pumped faster than it is being replenished. Underground aquifers, the source of about 60 percent of the U.S.'s fresh water, are being depleted, and surface water in lakes and rivers is endangered by our increasing population demands. Many towns are halting development because of a lack of affordable fresh water."

In your lifetime, you have probably read or viewed news reports about deaths in other nations caused by droughts and resulting reductions in food supplies. Depending on your age, those cumulative deaths may number in millions or in tens of millions. Less well reported by American news sources are deaths caused by wars—sometimes civil wars—fought over access to water. In America, we fight our "civil water wars" civilly, in courts and legislatures. Nevertheless, we have been warned: America's supply of water is decreasing while America's population of water users continues to increase!

WILDLIFE

There are twelve different environmental organizations scored on *www. ThinkPopulation.org's* "Population-Environment Connection Scorecard." As you might imagine, I read *many* articles about threatened wildlife in these environmental organizations' publications.

Interestingly enough, publications of only four of those twelve organizations consistently make the relatively obvious connection between human population growth and wildlife decline: Izaak Walton League of America, The Nature Conservancy, and, to a lesser extent, National Wildlife Federation and Sierra Club. Yet, one doesn't require a Ph.D. in wildlife management to recognize that as the footprint of humanity expands over the earth, the land area available to wildlife contracts.

Occasionally, wildlife retreats only reluctantly to its restricted territory and we read of runners, bikers, hikers, and small children being mauled or killed by reluctantly retreating wildlife. More often, particular communities of wildlife simply decline until they disappear.

The Nature Conservancy, working with government and private entities, tries to purchase land to preserve some of these wildlife communities. However, they can only try to protect *confined and limited* wildlife preserves against the inexorable march of America's population growth.

Incidentally, in this book "flora and fauna" includes all living things—except humans, which though often exhibiting their own special versions of wildness, are not what I have in mind. Therefore, I am as concerned about the decline of life in our oceans and rivers as I am about the decline of life in our forests and on our plains.

Writing in *Population and Habitat in the New Millennium* published by National Audubon Society and the Global Stewardship Initiative, Ken Strom points out that it is often the consumptive demand of growing population which makes the use of commercial pesticides and of depleting fishing technologies economically viable. These products and practices in turn "take their toll on wildlife" causing species losses which are "visible and easily measurable."

In other words, practices destructive to wildlife are often driven by the need to satisfy the growing consumption of a growing human population.

Mr. Strom asks us to look near our homes for examples of wildlife losses or habitat damage which have resulted, either directly or indirectly, from population growth.

I echo his request suggesting that, if you *think like a populationist,* you will automatically address *every* story about wildlife loss with the question: "Will human population growth make it easier or more difficult to mitigate this problem?"

I believe we both know what the answer will be.

YOUNG PEOPLE

Forgive me for beginning this section titled, "Young People," with words guaranteed to put young people to sleep, "When I was a boy ..."

Yes, when I was a boy I, and most of my friends, had jobs in order to earn money. We delivered newspapers, mowed lawns, baby-sat, ushered patrons in movie theaters, worked in warehouses, pumped gasoline, prepared and served food, and did whatever else would bring us some spending money.

What did we spend our spending money on? Well, I bought a football—the neighborhood football. A friend down the street on our block bought a basketball—the neighborhood basketball. There were seven or eight or nine boys—and one girl—in our neighborhood. The operative count depended on how far "down" the age ladder we needed to go to fill team rosters.

It was not unusual for one of those boys to knock on a door and ask, "Mrs. Young, ..." or at our house, "Mrs. Hartman, may we use the football until Ed finishes eating dinner?" Notice it was not "Ed's" football nor was it "Bob's" basketball, it was always "*the*" football or "*the*" basketball ... *the neighborhood's* football and *the neighborhood's* basketball.

Today, life is much easier for young people living in middle-class families—at least where I live. Few have jobs. Few know what it feels like to earn spending money. Very few learn to weigh choices about how to spend limited amounts of spending money. Yet, they have an abundance of footballs and basketballs and soccer balls and ... Well, you name it and they have it. No more, "Bob, can we keep on playing basketball while you eat dinner? We'll take good care of the ball." Yes, today life is much easier for young people living in middle-class families—at least where I live.

However, I am inclined to think life is *not necessarily better* for these young people who seem destined to grow into adulthood without ever learning the value of work or the value of money. The tricycles and bicycles, the bats and balls, the gloves and gowns, the skates and rackets, the lessons and teams and trips and uniforms all arrive "free" … and easy.

Life will not be free … and it may not be so easy when they grow up. Perhaps their adult lives would ultimately be easier if, as young people, they were performing some of the work currently "delegated" to aliens.

If so, and if this is true for young people living in middle-class families, how important might it be for young people living in less affluent families? When you see young people lounging on street corners in less affluent areas, do you ever wonder, "Might they—and society—be better off, if they were doing some of the work middle-class America has delegated to illegal aliens?"

LOOKING BACK … AND AHEAD

In this chapter, we have discussed some of the living and breathing victims of America's addiction to population growth. Perhaps you know or have observed a few personally. We have considered the nature of their victimization and have implied ways in which lives—human and non-human—could be improved by discontinuing their victimization.

In the next chapter, we will take a look at some of the American concepts and institutions which are also victims of America's addiction to population growth. Perhaps you will read about concepts or institutions you are already concerned about. Perhaps the next chapter will increase your reasons for concern.

As you read further, remind yourself: *Addictions can be broken! You* can join tens of thousands of others who are working to break America's addiction to population growth!

FOR REFLECTION AND DISCUSSION:

1. What was your reaction when you saw illegal aliens listed as victims of America's addiction to population growth?

2. What was your reaction when you saw parolees and probationers listed as victims of America's addiction to population growth?

3. How do you resolve in your mind the inherent conflict of homeowners who like to watch increasing demand created by increasing population increase the value of their homes, yet want affordable housing for future generations?

4. How concerned are you about generations of American young people who are missing opportunities to work at the jobs frequently filled by illegal aliens?

5. Who have you known personally—yourself included—whom you might describe as a victim of America's rampant population growth?

QUICK FIX #5

Write a short letter to the Editor of your favorite newspaper or newsmagazine asking that reporters, editors, and columnists consider the population growth issue when writing their pieces. Please feel free to borrow from the sample in Appendix C, "Quick Fix References."

Chapter 6

THE VICTIMS

Not Living, But Vital

vital *adj.* 1. Necessary to the continuation of life; life-sustaining; 2. Necessary to continued existence or effectiveness; essential.

"After 12 years of therapy my psychiatrist said something that brought tears to my eyes. He said, 'No hablo ingles.'"   —Ronnie Shakes

PEOPLE AND WILDLIFE ARE NOT the only victims of America's rampant population growth. There are many American concepts and institutions which suffer from America's addiction to population growth. Let's consider some of these conceptual and institutional victims.

COMMON LANGUAGE

When a German automobile company purchased an American automobile company, it quickly announced communications between the two companies would be conducted in what language? No, not German.

When non-English movies present interaction between characters of widely divergent languages (see *Lovers of the Arctic Circle*), what language do they speak? No, not Spanish nor Finnish.

When international pilots communicate with landing towers at airports around the world—even in France—what language do they use? No, not French.

When representatives from the three NAFTA nations conduct business, what language do they use? No, not Spanish nor French.

When the Chilean government initiated a program to make its population fluent in a second language within one generation, what language did they choose? No, not Portuguese nor German.

When the King of Jordan announced a plan to educate all young people in his country in computer sciences and one foreign language, what was his language of choice? No, not French nor German.

What language is studied and spoken by more people around the world as a second language than any other? No, not Mandarin Chinese.

In what language do students around the world take the Graduate Management Admissions Test (GMAT) to enter graduate business schools around the world? The answer to this and the other questions is: English.

When we in America make special effort to make it easy for new residents to live in America without learning English, are we doing them a service or a disservice? Are we doing American culture a service or a disservice?

When a population of non-English speaking people reaches a number so that population loses its desire to learn English, who suffers more, that population or America? In my opinion, both suffer too much and too needlessly.

CULTURE

America's culture is fortunate to be an amalgam of assimilated behavior patterns, arts, beliefs, institutions, and other products of human work and thought from every part of the world. The key to that good fortune: Assimilation! However, not all introduced culture is necessarily beneficial to America's culture. For example:

A Chinese-speaking American tourist visiting China stops a local resident from crowding into the front of a queue with, "That's not polite!" The native replies, "We have too many people to be polite."

An American tourist in Japan remarks on the courtesy of the Japanese ... until she is pushed and prodded aboard a subway car by a human hired to pack more people into an already packed car.

When these characteristics of Asia's response to overpopulation migrate to America, are they changed by America's culture or do they change America's culture? When you drive on America's crowded streets and highways, which do you think is more likely to have happened?

Does increasing traffic congestion caused by increasing population density lead to increasing "road rage" and, if so, does that ultimately change America's culture? Does increasing population density decrease the value placed upon each individual? Does it increase the "watching out for number one—*me*" factor? Is thoughtfulness for others part of America's culture? If not, was it once and, if so, has increasing population density caused it to diminish?

Travel around America and you see a variety of cultures, most bonded by a common language and by a mutual concern for a common nationality. Those communities with the highest population density tend to have the highest concentration of museums and concert halls. But do those communities have the highest concentration of friendly, thoughtful people? Do those communities set the standard for the culture you wish for a future America?

DEMOCRACY

I asked a friend to describe a problem which concerned him which was *not* affected by population growth.

He thought one major problem—one which was a root contributor to many other problems—was failure of our elected representatives to speak honestly with constituents.

I asked him, "Do you think elected representatives are more likely to speak honestly with their constituents when they have more constituents to represent or when they have fewer constituents to represent?"

He smiled and answered immediately, "When they have fewer constituents to represent."

In other words, when an elected official has fewer constituents to represent, each constituent's opinion—as well as each constituent's vote—becomes more important to that official and that official may be more inclined to speak honestly to each constituent.

There are 435 Congressmen and Congresswomen in the U.S. House of Representatives. Whether the population of America is today's 300 million or tomorrow's one billion, we will still have 435 in the House of Representatives. This means as America's population grows, each Representative represents more and more people, perhaps four times more before the end of this century.

Can one person communicate with and well represent 690,000 (300 million divided by 435) men, women, and children? It isn't easy, but imagine how much more difficult it will be to communicate with and well represent 2.3 million men, women, and children. Can it be done well? Probably not. So what is the alternative?

There are two alternatives, given our present system:

(1) Stabilize America's population or

(2) Accept the fact that ordinary citizens cannot be well represented and only the wealthy and powerful will be able to communicate with their Representatives in Congress.

"Well, Ed," you might ask, "why not increase the number of Representatives in the House?"

If you understand how difficult it is to make sound legislation with 435 Representatives, try to imagine how a Congress of 1,740 members would operate!

Which would you rather have: (a) Poorer representation in Congress and poorer legislation or (b) an American population stabilized at a reasonable level?

EMIGRATION NATIONS

In an article in *a Common Place,* the magazine of the Mennonite Central Committee, Tanya Chute, a Mennonite volunteer in La Ceiba, El Salvador, writes: "One in six Salvadorans now lives outside the land of his or her birth."

How sad. If one in six Salvadorans lived outside the land of birth because they were so wealthy they could afford to live anywhere and everywhere, that would be different. But to be driven from one's homeland by war, poverty, and corruption … How sad! I have no idea what the relative proportion of Mexican citizens living outside of Mexico is, but I suspect if we took the measure of certain states in Mexico, we would find the situation as bad or worse than the situation Ms. Chute described for El Salvador.

Have you ever gone to, or taken a friend or family member to, a doctor who had come to America from another nation to practice medicine?

A conscientious doctor from India, practicing in a small town in Nevada, treated our elder daughter after an auto accident. A charming doctor from Taiwan is my wife's primary care physician. A thoughtful and caring doctor from China was my mother-in-law's physician until her death. How fortunate we have been—how fortunate America is—to have such competent and well-trained professionals working in its health care field.

And yet … I can't help wondering what is wrong with these emigration nations that prevents them from retaining the best and the brightest of their professionals—*their* doctors, *their* engineers, *their* scientists, and, yes, even *their* political scientists.

I sometimes wonder—but there is no way to know—how much longer Eastern Europe might have remained in Communism's grip if those nations had let those who ultimately became heroes of freedom simply leave for the West way back when? In other words, *how much do emigration nations lose* when they emigrate their dissidents and rabble rousers along with their professionals?

Ms. Chute's story begins with: *"Teach me English. There's no future for me here. I'm going north."* She then tells the story of Silvio Miguel Rodriguez Lopez and his neighbors in La Ceiba and how they risk their lives and the lives of those they love in order to migrate to America. Travelers going north face such risks as dehydration, extortion, starvation, and suffocation.

Ms. Chute's story concludes, "'Teach me English …' Silvio's voice returns to haunt me. As a catechist and community leader, he represents the hope of his people. If he leaves, who will carry that hope? How I long for the day Silvio might invest his energy and the passion of his dreams in a new El Salvador."

Once again, America's gain will be an emigration nation's loss.

ENVIRONMENTAL HEALTH AND PUBLIC HEALTH

Writing in *Population Press,* Bill Van Ry, retired President and CEO of St. Mary's Health Network of Reno, Nevada, discussed the connection between a healthy environment and a healthy population.

"With each passing year, surrounding toxicity rises—water becomes a scarcer commodity for a swelling country. There may be glimmers of hope as air and water quality improve on a spot basis, but additional growth coupled with more business and industry, simply blunt these gains in time.

"As the population grows the environment is further wasted in spite of our faith that science and technology can somehow mitigate the damages. *A sick environment eventually leads to a sick people.* No health care delivery system, no matter how comprehensive and well funded, will be able to cope with the human misery that ensues.

"If America wants a workable *[health care]* delivery system that meets expectations, we must get on with the business of stabilizing our numbers as other developed nations have done and then strive for a more optimum size. Not only will smaller numbers better enable us to provide better health care, but restoration of the environment will be enhanced as well. Until then, the health care system we so desperately want and believe to be our right will remain an elusive dream. "

When we consider the logical connection Mr. Van Ry makes between public health, environmental health, and population stabilization, it is—once again—difficult to take seriously politicians or environmental leaders who harangue about societal and environmental problems without discussing the underlying cause of so many of those problems—rampant human population growth.

FARMLAND AND OPEN SPACE

How many millions have heard Joni Mitchell sing about paving paradise and putting up parking lots ("Big Yellow Taxi") or have heard Brenn Hill sing about building highways along the flyways and through the wetlands, farmlands, and fields ("Legacy Highway")? How many of those millions have stopped to ask themselves, "What can I do to protect the remaining farmland and open space for future generations?"

It may be hard to imagine, but according to an article in the May 2003, *Washington Post,* in the 1940s, the county which led the nation in farm income was Los Angeles. Now it leads the nation in human population density. Elsewhere in California, about 50,000 acres of farmland vanish each year. In other states farmland suffers the same fate. Take Georgia, Ohio, and Texas, which in recent years have each lost more than 150,000 acres of agricultural land because of population growth and the desire many homeowners have for more space: Average lot sizes have doubled in the past two decades.

The future holds more of the same for farmland. According to a study by the American Farmland Trust released in 2002, "Housing developments are encroaching on the wide open spaces of the rural West and could replace more than 24 million acres of ranch land by 2020." More food to feed more people suggests a need for more farmland and ranch land. Instead, both are disappearing rapidly.

Quoting from *www.SprawlCity.org:* "Although there are many definitions of sprawl, a central component of most definitions and of most people's understanding of sprawl is this: Sprawl is the spreading out of a city and its suburbs over more and more rural land at the periphery of an urban area. This involves conversion of open space (rural land) into built-up, developed land.

"For those who are concerned about the effect of sprawl upon natural environment and agricultural resources, the more important overall measure of sprawl is the actual amount of land that has been urbanized. Knowing the actual square miles of urban expansion (sprawl) provides a key indicator of the threat to the natural environment, to the nation's agricultural productivity, and to the quality of life of people who live in cities and in the small towns and farms that are near cities.

"About half of all sprawl nationwide is related to America's population growth and the other half is related to land use choices, according to the results of scientific analysis of U.S. Bureau of the Census data on the 100 largest Urbanized Areas of the United States."

To repeat, *approximately one-half of America's urban sprawl is caused by America's addiction to population growth.* The other one-half is caused by other factors such as demand for larger houses and for larger lots. Population growth is destroying farmland and ranch land at the very time we need more food to feed the growing population. From whatever cookbook, this sounds like a recipe for disaster!

INFRASTRUCTURE

Have you lived in a big city long enough to remember when radio traffic reports were given only on the half-hour, only during commute hours ... generally with nothing to report? Now, they come every ten minutes, 24 hours a day ... and there is *always* something to report. Have you driven on Interstate highways long enough to note their deterioration?

When Steve Heminger was Deputy Director of California's Metropolitan Transportation Commission, he was reported to have said no state or county was trying to match population growth with highway capacity. "We couldn't afford it even if we wanted to."

"Ed, you're saying America can't afford its population growth?"
That's right.

- Can't afford it for highway and bridge construction and maintenance;
- Can't afford it for school construction and maintenance;
- Can't afford it for sewage and wastewater treatment plants;
- Can't afford it for energy production and distribution;
- Can't afford it for airport facilities;
- Can't afford it for hospital and clinic construction;
- Can't afford to maintain state and national parks to meet the needs of an increasing number of visitors;

- Can't afford non-polluting and open space-preserving waste disposal facilities;
- Can't afford it! Can't afford it! Can't afford it!

Dan Weikel wrote a major piece for the *Los Angeles Times* about Interstate Highway 5, the 1,381-mile main artery from the Mexican border to the Canadian border, running the length of California and through Oregon and Washington. The article's assessment of I-5 can be summarized in three words: *It's falling apart!*

Ten mile per hour commutes in Washington, detours around metal fatigued bridges in Oregon, ten-lane sections widened to twenty-lane sections in California, and still traffic engineers can't find funds to keep up with increasing population and commerce. And legislators can't tap taxpayers for the estimated $50 billion required to catch up.

Everything that happens on the West Coast eventually reaches the rest of America. As Associated Press reported: "Arizona gained its 88th municipality ..." It was the state's first new city in almost ten years. A farm town about 25 miles south of Phoenix, Maricopa is expected to grow from 5,000 to approximately 200,000 in the next decade.

Cities, counties, states, and Congress can't afford to build needed new infrastructure or to properly maintain existing infrastructure. Yet Congress can't find the will to do what needs to be done to stabilize America's population so we have time to catch up with needed construction and maintenance of infrastructure.

Infrastructure: Another voiceless victim!

MUNICIPAL TRANSIT DISTRICTS

Should the "M" in transit district acronyms, e.g., "MTD," stand for monopoly, rather than municipal?

Show me a town whose population has grown into a city which "requires" a municipal transit district and I'll show you a city where a handful of union leaders and politicians probably hold taxpayers and *a small portion of commuters* hostage to wage and benefit and tax demands. That is one of many penalties of population growth—one of many penalties of towns growing into cities.

"Ed, how can you write, 'small portion of commuters?' We couldn't survive without our municipal transit district ... could we?"

Yes, actually we could. Actually, we do, whenever municipal transit districts are temporarily shut down. But set aside, for now, what I have written and read what an expert on the subject has to say.

Edwin Stennett has written a thoroughly researched book, *In Growth We Trust: Sprawl, Smart Growth, and Rapid Population Growth.* ('Sounds like a title I might have used, doesn't it?) Stennett's goal was "... to clearly and forcefully draw out the links between overpopulation and local, community-level problems" in the Washington, DC Metropolitan Area (WMA).

In a section titled, "What about Metrorail?" Stennett points out the system, *which is nearing capacity on some lines*, provides 650,000 trips per day while the number of non-Metrorail vehicle trips per day is 15,600,000. In other words, only one daily trip out of twenty-five is a Metrorail trip [15,600,000 + 650,000 =16,250,000 ÷ 650,000 = 25].

Further, daily vehicle trips in WMA are projected to increase by 5,500,000 over the next 20 years. Obviously, even if Metrorail doubled its trips per day—highly unlikely—it would have a negligible effect upon WMA traffic congestion. That is, even if Metrorail trips doubled, *non-Metrorail daily trips would increase from 15,600,000 to 20,450,000* [15,600,000 + 5,500,000 - 650,000 = 20,450,000].

The point is, municipal transit districts address only a fraction of cities' transportation needs and cannot save cities from traffic congestion problems.

As the populations of American towns grow, the probability also grows that a few local politicians will convince voters they need a municipal transit system—typically rail. Taxes will be increased to pay for such a system. Ultimately, local residents will find they are paying higher taxes to support a system they would never have needed in the first place, if population growth had been kept in check.

PRODUCTIVITY

"Ed, how is productivity affected by rampant population growth?"

Like a commodity, the price of labor goes down as supply goes up. When the price of labor is cheap, employers are less inclined to invest in labor-saving materials and equipment, without which, improved productivity is unlikely.

An example: I watched a group of laborers, being paid "off the books," manually lifting and dropping heavy steel pikes to break up a concrete slab. If the employer of those workers had to pay legal wages as well as payroll taxes and workmen's compensation, you can bet that employer would have had pneumatic tools to break up the concrete efficiently!

Another example: According to Mark Krikorian: "The production of raisins in California's Central Valley is one of the most labor-intensive activities in North America. Conventional methods require bunches of grapes to be cut by hand, manually placed in a tray for drying, manually turned, manually collected. Starting in the 1950s in Australia (where there was not a large supply of foreign farm labor), farmers were compelled by circumstances to develop a laborsaving method called 'dried-on-the-vine' (DOV) production.

"DOV involves growing the grapevines on trellises, then, when the grapes are ready, cutting the base of the vine instead of cutting each bunch of grapes individually. The new method radically reduces labor demand at harvest time and increases yield per acre by up to 200 percent. But this high-productivity, innovative method of production has spread very slowly in the United States because the mass availability of foreign workers has served as a disincentive to farmers to make the necessary capital investment."

Aside from the fact that "off the books" workers and their families often live in poverty and the fact that taxpayers are subsidizing "off the books" employers by paying for their workers' welfare benefits, it is unsound economics to allow "slave wages" to discourage mechanization and innovation.

Necessity, not slavery, is the mother of invention. Only when an American industry finds it is necessary to pay full and fair wages to its employees, will that industry advance into the 21st century!

PUBLIC HEALTH

Hospitals and medical facilities around America are in crisis mode. Like most infrastructure in America, construction, modernization, and repair of hospitals cannot keep pace with rising demand. Rising demand and falling revenue are functions of several causes, but high among them is increasing population and, in the case of legal and illegal aliens, approximately one-third of that population is without medical insurance or other means of paying for medical care as compared with only 13% of native-born.

For example, Los Angeles County produced a report estimating the cost of "… caring for uninsured illegal aliens alone …" was $350 million a year. For California as a whole, the corresponding estimate is $600 million a year.

Problems in America's health care system merited a special study and report by Federation for American Immigration Reform (FAIR). From that report titled, "The Sinking Lifeboat—Uncontrolled Immigration & the U.S. Health Care System," here are a few illustrative excerpts:

- "In some hospitals, as much as two-thirds of total operating costs are for uncompensated care for illegal aliens."
- "Aliens (legal and illegal) who arrived between 1994 and 1998 and their children accounted for 59% of the growth in the size of the uninsured population in the last ten years."
- "Lack of insurance leads many aliens to use hospital emergency departments—the most expensive source of health care—as their primary care provider."
- Los Angeles County Supervisor Michael Antonovich is quoted as saying, *"We're running an HMO for illegal aliens and if we keep it up, we're going to bankrupt the county."*

Bankrupt the county? Perhaps. Or perhaps simply give up the means to provide emergency medical treatment to anyone. Is the problem bigger than California? According to FAIR:

- "Arizona, facing a $1 billion state budget shortfall in FY2004 was forced to consider cutting 60,000 children from the State Children's Health Insurance Program. Yet in December 2001, the legislature had approved $3 million to cover kidney dialysis and chemotherapy for illegal aliens."
- "In El Paso, Texas, where nearly 40% of residents had no health insurance and the illegal alien problem was rampant, Thomason General Hospital was seeking a 12.5% property tax increase to offset its uncompensated care costs."
- "According to the Florida Hospital Association, non-citizens amass unpaid bills of more than $40 million a year at Florida hospitals."

"OK, Ed, but isn't the problem limited to border states …?"
Unfortunately, no. Here are some FAIR examples:

- "At Iowa's Buena Vista county hospital, which must now pay for translators on staff, uncompensated health care for aliens constitutes 25% of total services."
- "Hospitals throughout South Carolina say they have been left with at least $4 million in unpaid bills after delivering babies for illegal aliens who disappear before filing Medicaid paperwork."

- "In 2002, Pennsylvania and New Jersey hospitals gave almost $2 billion in free emergency and short-term care to uninsured patients, a large share of whom officials believe were illegal aliens."

And if you want more stories of how hospitals and taxpaying legal residents are being shortchanged on emergency care, there are stories from Illinois, Minnesota, New York, North Carolina, and more.

Disease Control

Another aspect of public health which concerns many in the medical profession is the introduction into America of new and exotic diseases and the resurgence of old and largely defeated diseases. One example is tuberculosis (TB). As reported by Melissa Healy in the *Los Angles Times,* World Health Organization and U.S. Centers for Disease Control tell us TB kills two million people each year. Most Americans had come to think of TB as a disease of the past. However, public health officials tell us approximately 33% of the world's population is infected with TB and approximately 10% of these will become sick.

Let's see: 10% of 33% of six billion people is … 200 million people sick with TB.

"But, Ed, that's not in America, is it?"

Well, yes and no. Most of these people will remain in other countries. However, illegal aliens do not take TB tests before they enter America and they may not be willing to obtain TB tests after they arrive for fear of deportation. Further, for those illegal aliens who do obtain TB tests and do learn they have treatable TB, they may not be willing or able to complete the demanding regimen of four drugs taken daily for six to eighteen months.

According to one study, "People with low literacy skills have four times greater health care costs than those with high skills." Why? Because they "… fail to take medications as directed." Why? Because they are illiterate in English and don't understand medical instructions. The result is, those TB patients who fail to follow medical instructions increase the chance of creating new strains of drug-resistant TB here in America.

PUBLIC SAFETY

A comedian tells us how much easier it is to solve crime in a small town than in a city:

"The small town sheriff asks a witness, 'Can you give me a description of the suspect?'

The witness says, 'Yes, I can, Sheriff ... Dwayne.'"

As small towns become cities, criminals become anonymous, crimes become more difficult to solve, and crime rates increase. One of the false solutions to rampant population growth is called "smart growth," an oxymoron, if ever there was one. Piling more and more people into less and less space does nothing to solve the need for more and more food, more and more water, more and more energy, and more and more infrastructure—with more and more damage done to the environment to meet those needs. Meanwhile the quality of life for the inhabitants of these man-made beehives goes down for everyone ... except for criminals.

What do you think: Would a criminal prefer to ply his trade walking down streets of family residences with windows on all sides—some with "Neighborhood Watch" stickers—available to provide observation of strangers on the street? Or would a criminal prefer to walk down dimly lit halls of "smart growth" multistory residence buildings where he passes only windowless walls? Doesn't it seem perfectly logical—from a criminal's perspective—that crime rates per capita should increase as population density increases?

RECYCLING

According to Californians Against Waste, "Recycling has come almost full-circle in the last 60 years." During World War II, Americans decreased wasteful consumption, recycled all kinds of items, and saved scrap for the war effort—metal for planes, rubber for military tires, and even leftover cooking fat for lubricants. Americans reduced, reused, and recycled it all!

Ten years after the war Americans re-learned how to waste. For several years we became the "Disposable Society." Then starting in the late 1970s and continuing right up to today, Americans realized they were choking on their own waste and depriving future generations of needed resources.

And yet ... according to an Associated Press article by Jim Wasserman, even as government, industry, and the public move toward a "Recycling Society," population growth is overwhelming that progress and overwhelming our capacity to handle our waste. For example, in 1991, California dumps accepted approximately 36,500 tons of trash.

Still, ten years later, despite the fact that recycling, diverting, and composting had increased significantly, trash delivered to dumps *increased*. Dramatic early drops in annual landfill tonnage were overtaken by waste from millions of new residents.

While there may always be more we can do to reduce per capita waste, so long as we have a rampant increase in the number of "capitas" (people) in California as well as the rest of America, waste will continue to increase and to become an increasing problem.

RULE OF LAW

We Americans tend to look down on nations ruled by power rather than by laws applied relatively equally to all citizens—nations where the wealthy or politically connected can obey or ignore laws as they choose. The American system of justice is devised and executed by humans and, like humans, is fallible. But it is something we can generally be proud of and something we should generally be willing to protect.

In America, is there anything which threatens the rule of law more than citizens deciding individually which laws they will obey and which they will ignore?

A friend told me about helping an illegal alien obtain an illegal loan in order to purchase a house. He hesitated before telling me, because he knew I would not approve—though I said nothing. He rationalized his action by telling me what a nice fellow this person was. I might have asked how satisfied my friend would have been with that explanation, if he had received it from his son explaining why he helped a nice friend of his cheat on an exam at school.

I might have asked him how he will teach his son the importance of working to change laws with which we disagree rather than simply ignoring them.

Had I read a column titled "Home loans for illegal aliens?" by Michelle Malkin, I also might have asked how he felt about requiring taxpayers to guarantee his friend's home loan. But I hadn't and I didn't. I didn't need to.

Like too many Americans, my friend knew what he had done was not only illegal, it was morally wrong—destructive of America's justly acclaimed rule of law.

No-Rules Residents

"You read about all these terrorists; most of them came here legally, but they hung around on those expired visas, some for as long as 10-15 years.

Now, compare that to Blockbuster; you are two days late with a video and those people are all over you. Let's put Blockbuster in charge of immigration." From Elko Shopper, Elko, NV

Advocates of open borders—which is another way of saying advocates of unlimited population growth—are fond of saying, "We are a nation of immigrants." It would be more accurate to say, we are a nation of *legal* immigrants. Even more than being a nation of legal immigrants, we endeavor to be a nation of law-abiding citizens and legal residents.

A sizable portion of public expenditure is devoted to enacting and enforcing laws and to detaining and punishing those who break laws. Illegal aliens enter America by breaking American laws. They extend their illegal activity by obtaining false identification documents and by participating in the underground economy.

"Oh, come on, Ed! Is public safety threatened by having a few million innocent dishwashers, hotel maids, fruit and vegetable pickers, and baby-sitters breaking a few obscure laws?"

Demand by these "innocent" lawbreakers for illegal transit and false identification papers creates a criminal supply which also becomes available to illegal aliens whose intentions may not be so "innocent." Literally tens of thousands of "OTMs" (Border Patrol-ese for Other-Than-Mexican) have entered America from Africa, Asia, the Middle East, South America, and elsewhere. The numbers are increasing as people smugglers and document forgers hone their skills.

While criminals have their way with America's borders, "homeland security" remains a political slogan rather than a functioning reality.

When citizens of countries lacking in respect for the rule of law move to America, do they bring those attitudes with them? Certainly, the answer in many cases is: "No, we came to America because we wanted to escape the injustices of our country."

However, there are undoubtedly others—particularly those who broke American laws to come here—who accepted their homelands' attitudes and mores and willingly brought them along. You will find their names on police blotters from California to Maine and from Texas to North Dakota.

SOLITUDE

Optimists like to believe science will find ways to solve all problems created by rampant human population growth. Food shortages? "Science will find ways to make food out of bacteria." Energy shortages? "Science will find ways to turn air into energy." Water shortages? "Science will find economical ways to make ocean water potable." There is one shortage caused by human population growth even optimists admit science will have a hard time replacing: Solitude!

Population Press quotes John Stuart Mill writing in 1848 when world population was just over 1 billion:

"There is room in the world, no doubt, for a great increase in population, supposing the arts of life to go on improving, and capital to increase. But even if innocuous, I confess I see little reason for desiring it.

"It is not good for man to be kept at all times in the presence of his species. A world from which solitude is extirpated, is a very poor ideal.

"Solitude, in the sense of being often alone, is essential to any depth of meditation or of character; and solitude in the presence of natural beauty and grandeur, is the cradle of thoughts and aspiration which society could do ill without."

Perhaps one day science will produce "Solitude Chambers" which people can enter to take walks in *virtual* woods, climb *virtual* mountains, survey *virtual* desert vistas, and study *virtual* creatures in *virtual* tide pools. Perhaps when America's population reaches one billion, people will have become so accustomed to *virtual* reality and so sickened by oppressive humanity, they will welcome the relief provided by a machine which can mimic the sights, sounds, smells, and feel of the great outdoors.

Perhaps.

For now, there are still many who would like their descendants to be able to take walks in real woods, climb real mountains, survey real desert vistas, and study real creatures in real tide pools—and to not have to make reservations a year in advance to do so.

TAX EQUITY

Should a couple with three, two, one, or no children pay more income tax than another family with identical Adjusted Gross Income, but with four or more children?

Granted, Congress changes tax law as frequently as some celebrities change spouses—well, perhaps not that frequently—but as of this writing, here is how federal tax law favors large families over small families:

For our example, take three families each consisting of a husband and a wife, each having annual Adjusted Gross Incomes of $44,000, and each taking the existing Standard Deduction. Couple A has no children, Couple B has two children, and Couple C has four children. The respective federal income tax (state income tax would be a separate issue) for these three couples would be: Couple A = $3,504, Couple B = $574, Couple C = [$2,356].

"Ed, why are there brackets around Couple C's tax amount?"

Good question! Well, Couple C would not only *not* pay any federal income tax, they would receive a $2,356 payment *from* the federal government—thanks to Couples A and B.

I realize fairness, like beauty, is in the eye of the beholder. Nevertheless, I have to ask: How fair do you think it is that a couple with no children, possibly not by choice, pays six times as much federal income tax as a couple with two children? Or how fair do you think it is that a couple with two children, possibly by choice, sends $574 to Uncle Sam, while Uncle Sam sends a check for $2,356 to a couple with four children—whether or not by choice? Do you think America might be better off if it *rewarded* couples for limiting the size of their families rather than *penalizing* them for doing so and then paying couples for *not* limiting the size of their families?

Since America has the *highest birth and fertility rates of any developed nation in the world* and since America's population is now the *third largest of all the nations in the world,* does it seem logical that Congress would want to encourage even faster population growth?

- Is Congress opposed to family planning and so taxes more those who practice it than those who do not?
- Does Congress favor religions which are opposed to family planning?
- *What is the logical basis for asking those who limit the size of their families to subsidize those who do not?*
- What is the Constitutional basis for such discrimination?
- Is it time for that basis to be challenged in court?

LOOKING BACK ... AND AHEAD

In this chapter, we have examined some of the institutions and concepts which have been and are being damaged by America's rampant population growth. *While some might argue these conceptual and institutional victims are not essential for America's continued existence, they may well be essential, if we want America to remain America.*

In the next chapter, we will consider how withdrawal from America's addiction to population growth can improve the lot of most of the victims discussed in this and the preceding chapter. Perhaps the next chapter will increase your desire to help rescue these victims.

As you read further, remind yourself: *Addictions can be broken! You can join tens of thousands of others who are working to break America's addiction to population growth!*

FOR REFLECTION AND DISCUSSION:

1. Why do you think so few American environmental organizations express concern about America's rampant population growth and those that do only address it as part of a worldwide problem?

2. How serious do you consider the effect of America's addiction to population growth upon public health and public safety?

3. How do you feel about families with three or fewer children paying significantly more income taxes than families with comparable earnings, but having four or more children?

4. Which of the conceptional and institutional victims discussed in this chapter most concern you?

5. What additional American concepts or institutions do you believe may be victims of America's population growth?

QUICK FIX #6

Write a short letter to your Representative in the U.S. House of Representatives asking him or her to consider the population growth issue when drafting legislation and when voting on legislation. Please feel free to borrow from the sample in Appendix C, "Quick Fix References."

Chapter 7

REHABILITATION

rehabilitate *v.* To restore to good health or useful life, as through therapy and education.

"When there is yet shame, there may in time be virtue."
—Samuel Johnson

"Rehabilitation? Wait a minute, Ed, don't addicts have to go through withdrawal—don't they have to kick the habit—before they can be rehabilitated?"

Absolutely right! There is no rehabilitation for addicts—or their victims—until addicts withdraw from their addiction. If you read to the end of this book you will see that is precisely what must happen.

However, if you have read the previous chapters, you have read an overview of the scope and the seriousness of America's population growth addiction. You have learned about some of its addicts and about many of its victims. Perhaps you have even recognized yourself or others you know among those addicts and victims. And, by this time, you may find your psychic wagon is dragg'n. So I think it is time to take a break from all the depressing and *distressing* information. Which reminds me of a story ...

An executive was hired to straighten out a failing company. During his first week on the job he was *distressed* by the number of subordinates coming into his office to tell him about this problem and that problem and so on.

At the end of the week he called all of his subordinates into his office and told them, "Beginning next week, I don't want any of you coming into my office with problems. We don't have problems! We have opportunities! Begin thinking of your problems as opportunities and let's see how that changes things around here!"

Sure enough, the following week was devoid of subordinates coming into the boss's office with problems. Whatever their problems were, they were learning to take care of them themselves. However, on Friday, one of the subordinates *did* come into his boss's office and, with a desperate look on his face announced, "Boss, ... we've got ... an *insurmountable opportunity!*"

Perhaps you are beginning to wonder if America's addiction to population growth is an "insurmountable opportunity?" The short answer is: No! Tens of thousands of Americans are, for a variety of reasons, taking a variety of steps to reduce the likelihood that future generations will suffer from the effects of that addiction. At the conclusion of this book, I will discuss some of those steps and explain how you can join them in their efforts to help America withdraw from its addiction.

First, though, I thought it might be helpful—as well as refreshing—to depart from the depression-inducing aspects of this addiction. Let's consider what would be some of the gains—along with a few of the pains—associated with rehabilitation after withdrawal from America's population growth addiction. Let's consider how the lives and well-being of many of its victims could be changed.

THE GAINS

While curing America of its addiction to population growth would involve some adjustments and, like all adjustments, some "pains," there would also be many "gains." Certainly, you could review the list of victims of America's addiction yourself (see Chapters 5 and 6, "The Victims") and understand in general how each might be better off with fewer people in America. However, let's consider together *a small sampling* of gains of withdrawal from America's addiction to population growth.

Common Language Expanded

How much money do you think American taxpayers would save if all taxpayer-funded publications, documents, forms, signs, and other media were in one language—English? Consider textbooks, voter instructions, street signage, and other official media now in multiple editions in multiple languages.

How much money do you think America's health care system would save if it was not required to serve multiple languages with interpreters and non-English forms?

How much money do you think America's criminal justice system would save if it was not required to provide interpreters to non-English literate accused and convicted criminals?

Money aside, how much richer culturally and socially do you think America would be if it did not have a large-and-growing population of *second-class residents identified primarily by their inability to read, write, or speak English?*

Democracy Strengthened

In Chapter 6, "The Victims," I wrote about problems created by a House of Representatives with an unchanging 435 members, regardless of how many people America has and regardless of how many people each member is supposed to represent. A few weeks after writing that, my wife gave me an Op-Ed piece by George Kenney, a U.S. diplomat serving in the senior President Bush's administration. His article explains the problem perhaps better than I did.

He writes that in 1913 the number of Representatives was increased from 391 to 435 and each Congressional District had a population of approximately *200,000*. Today that number has grown to approximately *690,000* meaning "… legislators tend to lose touch with voters." It is more expensive for campaigns to reach more people and "Dollars come first, constituents second." Increasingly, only the wealthy—or candidates who are supported by wealthy special interests—can afford to run for political office, which may explain why Congress sometimes passes laws with which a majority of Americans disagree. Kenney writes, "Americans face a crisis." His question is, will Congress "… represent people or lucre?"

Unfortunately, to address this problem, Kenney proposes increasing the size of the House of Representatives *five fold now and working toward a long-term goal of "districts of about 100,000 people."* [My emphasis.] Let's see, if we reach a population of 600 million people divided by 100,000 people would mean 6,000 Representatives. *Wow!* He admits his suggestion is "mind-boggling" and that it would "cause huge disruptions." But he writes "the alternatives are far worse" and finally, "Let's not quibble over practicalities."

No, let's not! Instead, let's ask ourselves—like true *populationists*—wouldn't it be better—as well as cheaper and more logical—to stabilize

America's population at a lower level rather than convert the Houston Astrodome to seat our House of Representatives?

As they say, *"To solve a problem, one must first define the problem accurately."* A populationist would define the problem not as too few Representatives, but as too many constituents. If we reduce and stabilize America's population, we reduce the problem of maintaining representative democracy!

Education Enhanced

The financial strain on schools and on taxpayers who support schools would obviously be reduced if population growth were reduced. But in addition, imagine how much money might be used to repair school buildings, to purchase textbooks and equipment, and to pay teachers, if only schools were not forced to educate the many children of aliens—often non-English speaking children—who came into America illegally.

Using Immigration and Naturalization Service data and average educational cost per pupil by state, Federation of Americans for Immigration Reform (FAIR) estimated the annual cost of educating *illegal alien students* in America as approximately $12 billion, and when the cost of educating *children born in America to illegal aliens* is added, total cost more than doubles to approximately $29 billion! Note: These estimates do not include the cost of special programs for non-English speaking students nor the cost of school meal programs for students from lower income families.

Let's take a look at the ten states with the largest expenditures to educate the children of illegal aliens:

- California = $7.7 billion
- Texas = $3.9 billion
- New York = 3.1 billion
- Illinois = $2.0 billion
- New Jersey = $1.5 billion
- Florida = $1.2 billion
- Georgia = $1.0 billion
- North Carolina = $.8 billion
- Arizona = $.7 billion
- Colorado = $.6 billion
- Total 10 states = $22.5 billion

Now, that could buy quite a few textbooks for children of legal residents, couldn't it?

Employee Wages And Working Conditions Improved

If America's addiction to population growth—especially America's addiction to illegal population growth—is broken, some of the biggest gains will fall to American employees whose wages will increase and whose unemployment rates will decrease. As the *supply* of cheap labor goes down, the *price* of labor will go up, especially at the low end of the wage scale which has been hit especially hard by illegal alien labor.

Similarly, legal American workers cannot be exploited by employers as illegal alien workers are exploited. Employers cannot threaten to report legal American workers to immigration officials. Consequently, legal American workers—and their union representatives—will insist on safety training and on safe working environments. Also, they will insist on being paid fully for time worked and will insist on being paid on the books so appropriate contributions will be made to their Social Security accounts.

Environmental Protection Increased

As I wrote in Chapter 1, "The Populationists," most populationists I know became concerned about America's addiction to population growth because of their concern for America's environment. Federal, state, and local governments, and organizations like The Nature Conservancy spend hundreds of millions of dollars trying to protect wilderness and wildlife from destruction by population driven development, i.e., houses, highways, malls, and more—everything required to support increasing population.

Yet the destruction is inexorable so long as population grows. There is not enough money in all the treasuries of all the world's nations to save all the lands and waters which should be saved for future generations, unless America's—and the world's—populations are stabilized.

Today, federal, state, and local governments, and organizations like The Nature Conservancy spend their hundreds of millions of dollars fighting a losing battle against developers' bulldozers. Just think how wonderful it would be if they could instead spend that money on maintaining and improving existing wilderness and wildlife populations. A stable American population would permit them to do so.

Highway Conditions Improved

Can you imagine the roads and highways you use today with 15% less traffic—15% fewer cars and trucks?

"Oh, Ed" you say, "I often imagine that and it's called fantasizing."

Well, it doesn't have to be a fantasy! Not only would traffic be less hectic, but if America's population stabilized at a logical level, governments could spend less on building new bridges, tunnels, and highways and spend more on retrofitting and refurbishing the bridges, tunnels, and highways we have now—the bridges, tunnels, and highways which civil engineers and inspectors tell us are threatening to fall apart.

Population stabilization is not a panacea! If America's population stopped growing tomorrow—an impossibility—it would still take decades to repair America's existing highways and related structures. But without an eventual respite from population growth, our states and our highway engineers will be like the fellow who said, "The faster I run, the behinder I get."

Homeland Security Increased

The 9/11 Commission Report—Final Report of the National Commission on Terrorist Attacks Upon the United States makes it clear that America ignores immigration laws at its peril. Under a section titled, "Permeable Borders and Immigration Controls," the Commission wrote: "There were opportunities for intelligence and law enforcement to exploit al Qaeda's travel vulnerabilities. Considered collectively, the 9/11 hijackers:

- included known al Qaeda operatives who could have been watch listed;
- presented passports manipulated in a fraudulent manner;
- presented passports with suspicious indicators of extremism;
- made detectable false statements on visa applications;
- made false statements to border officials to gain entry into the United States; and
- violated immigration laws while in the United States.

"Neither the State Department's consular officers nor the Immigration and Naturalization Service's inspectors and agents were ever considered full partners in a national counterterrorism effort. Protecting borders was not a national security issue before 9/11."

Among the Commission's recommendations and listed under

"Protect Against and Prepare for Terrorist Attacks" are the following:

"Target terrorist travel, an intelligence and security strategy that the 9/11 story showed could be at least as powerful as the effort devoted to terrorist finance.

"Address problems of screening people with biometric identifiers across agencies and governments, including our border and transportation systems, by designing a comprehensive screening system that addresses common problems and sets common standards.

"Quickly complete a biometric entry-exit screening system, one that also speeds qualified travelers.

"Set standards for the issuance of birth certificates and sources of identification, such as driver's licenses."

In other words, The 9/11 Commission recommends America devote more time, energy, research, and money to enforcing its immigration laws ... *quite the opposite of the recommendations of the addicts, the pushers, and the enablers of America's addiction to population growth!*

Migrant Deaths Reduced

As victimized as illegal aliens *living in America* might be by "coyotes" and other people smugglers, employers, and extortionists, perhaps the ultimate victims of America's addiction to population growth are the illegal aliens *who die on their way to America*. Who is responsible for those deaths? Specifically we may blame cruel deserts or cruel human smugglers, but ultimately it is our Congresses and our Administrations who bear responsibility for encouraging people from other nations to break our laws and take life-threatening risks.

Each time our politicians reward illegal aliens living in America, they send a message to tens of millions of citizens of other nations: "If you can manage to illegally enter America and, with the complicity of employers seeking cheap labor, avoid apprehension until our next amnesty declaration—of course by a different name—you will be rewarded with most of the benefits of American citizenship, including the right to bring spouses, children, parents, and siblings to America so they can obtain their citizenship and invite still others, *ad infinitum.*"

What a great day it will be when there are:

- No more "coyotes" and other people smugglers;
- No more manufacturers of false identification which can be used by terrorists as easily as by illegal alien farm workers and hospitality industry employees;

- No more employers making "campaign contributions" to government officials in order to have taxpayer subsidized cheap labor;
- No more pandering politicians buying ethnic votes at tax-payer expense.

Having encouraged millions of people of other nations to risk their lives as they break American immigration laws, do you sometimes wonder whether our politicians ever feel pangs of guilt when they read about the hundreds of illegal aliens who die on rafts at sea, who suffocate to death in ships' holds and in shipping containers, or who dehydrate and starve to death in American deserts? What do you think? Once we stop the pandering and the promising, we can stop unnecessary deaths of illegal migrants.

Recidivism Reduced

If there are some inmates and probationers who truly want to turn their lives around—and I believe there are—I would like to see our federal and state governments help those people find decent jobs with decent wages, decent working conditions, and decent benefits when they are turned back into our communities. Wouldn't you prefer your governments do that rather than encouraging illegal aliens to take those jobs for indecent wages, with indecent working conditions, and indecent benefits?

Tax Equity Advanced

We all know what virtually all politicians consider to be their most important responsibility: To get reelected. How, one wonders, did politicians come to the conclusion that providing tax subsidies for people with large families would win them more votes than they would lose from overtaxing families with smaller or no families? How, one wonders, have families with smaller or no families allowed politicians to impose this surtax on them without retaliating at the ballot boxes?

Not that one expects logic from Congress or from tax laws, but how illogical—as well as how contrary to America's best interest—it is to penalize those who plan and reward those who do not plan!

When America recognizes it has a population growth addiction and decides to break that addiction, taxpayers with smaller families will rise up against politicians who penalize them for having smaller families. When that happens, that part of the addiction will be broken in one night—election night.

Water Supplies Protected

A number of years ago, my wife and I were driving through parts of the South when I remarked on a crop I was not familiar with. I said it looked something like corn, but since it was only 12" to 18" high, it couldn't be corn. On the other hand, since miles and miles of this crop had been planted, it obviously was a valuable crop and I was surprised that I had no idea what it was.

It was a hot day so we stopped at a country store for soft drinks. I said to one of the fellows resting in the shade in front of the store, "I'm not familiar with the crop we have been seeing along the road. What is it?" He replied, "It's supposed to be corn—but without water, that's what it looks like."

Without water, that's what we all look like—stunted and wilted. Scientists have succeeded in inventing many things, but so far, their efforts to "invent" rain have been pretty futile. Yet, in America we continue to add water users as if our supply of rain and water is unlimited. Unfortunately, water is not unlimited. The only logical response to America's limited supply of water is to limit the supply of water users. In other words, limit America's population. Stabilize America's population and we automatically stabilize America's water quantity problems and can then apply more scientific and political effort to America's water quality problems.

Young People Employed

Nothing gives young people a more immediate appreciation for money and what money buys than working to earn money. If 10 million illegal aliens magically and suddenly returned to their home countries, what would happen? Well, America's population would decline by 10 million residents—not a bad start toward a stabilized American population.

However, in my opinion, an even bigger benefit to America would accrue from the millions of young people who would replace some of those illegal aliens at their jobs and thereby get some early, real world experience with performing work and earning money. Who knows what the effect of paying taxes at an early age might have on their voting habits when they reach voting age? Politicians beware!

THE PAINS

There will be some pains associated with breaking America's addiction to population growth. After all, we have become addicted to adding millions to our population annually. To gradually reverse that habit will require adjustments, some of which may bring some pain—to some degree

—to some Americans. Let's examine some of those potential pains.

Expensive Strawberries

Farm workers are in a field harvesting a crop. One, holding a newspaper says, "Look, $200 million in farm subsidies just signed into law." One of the other workers asks, "Do you think that means we'll get a raise?"

Let's say there are approximately 10 million illegal aliens in America. I have seen published estimates ranging from 8.3 million to 20 million illegal aliens. But let's use 10 million for our purposes.

We know a significant percentage of these people are working in the agricultural industry. We know they are working for minimum wages and benefits—wages and benefits not acceptable to Americans capable of doing the same work.

If these poorly paid workers were to leave America and return to their home countries, either:

(1) The crops they have been planting, tending, and harvesting would no longer be planted, tended, and harvested, or

(2) Those workers would be replaced by American workers who *would demand* better wages, benefits, and working conditions, or

(3) Those agricultural jobs would be mechanized so fewer workers would be required, or

(4) A combination of the above would occur.

In any event, it is not unreasonable to assume that the retail prices to consumers of strawberries and other labor-intensive crops currently planted, tended, and harvested by illegal aliens would rise. How much would prices rise? It would vary by the crop, of course, and according to which of the four approaches discussed in the previous paragraph were chosen.

But, in general, we know that planting, tending, and harvesting food crops usually represents the smallest portion of prices to consumers. Processing, packaging, transporting, and distributing frequently encompass up to 90% of a food product's price to consumers—think frozen strawberries.

Philip L. Martin, professor of Agricultural and Resource Economics at the University of California, Davis, wrote a book titled, *Promise*

Unfulfilled: Unions, Immigrants, and Farm Workers (Cornell University Press). In an article published by Center for Immigration Studies and adapted from his book he wrote:

"Fresh strawberries are picked directly into the plastic containers in which they are sold; most are picked in a 12-pint tray for piece rates of about $1.50 per tray, or $0.125 per pint. Farmers receive an average $0.40 to $0.50 a pint; pints of strawberries retail for an average $1.50 to $2 a pint."

So, according to Professor Martin, *strawberry pickers are paid approximately $0.125 for a pint of strawberries which sell for $1.50 to $2 a pint.* In other words, farm workers' wages for picking strawberries—which, of course, does not include planting and tending strawberries—appear to account for less than 10% of the retail price of fresh strawberries.

For purposes of this discussion, let's assume the very (unlikely) worst case: Let's assume the price of strawberries doubles! Would you be willing to pay twice as much as you currently pay for strawberries, if you knew you were (a) helping to break America's addiction to population growth and (b) helping to provide better wages, benefits, and working conditions to American farm workers?

Perhaps you would eat fewer strawberries. Perhaps you would save strawberries for special occasions. Perhaps you would eat more frozen strawberries. Perhaps you would grow your own strawberries. But in any event, it would not mark the end of life on earth as we have known it. In fact, it is a safe bet that there have been occasions in the past when you *have* seen the price of strawberries on the market take 50% – 100% seasonal swings, up and down. No, it would not mark the end of life.

Feelings Of Guilt

Since its inception, America has been viewed as—and Americans have viewed themselves as—a nation of immigrants. How can we—you and I—want to prevent others from having what we have?

We don't! Few Americans want to prevent others from *having* what we have. However, most Americans want to prevent others from *destroying* what we have!

Most important: I believe most Americans want others to have what Americans have—democracy, freedom, justice—*in those countries and on those continents where those others live today.*

Let me illustrate this point: David Brooks, columnist for *The New York Times*, wrote a column advocating poignantly that an *illegal alien worker* should be provided with all the benefits rightly provided to American citizens and legal immigrants. In response, Alan Kuper of Comprehensive U.S. Sustainable Population (CUSP) wrote:

"Sharing the society you enjoy: the schools, institutions, infrastructure, and the services of government is commendable. The only question in a democracy: Does a majority agree to it? Further, would a majority continue to agree in the future when natural limits such as water shortages prove that the U.S. is full? I'll gladly match Brooks' generosity, but only after we determine optimum U.S. population for living sustainably far into the future for the benefit of all life on Earth. And after we agree democratically to make that population number our goal."

While Americans are a generous people, common sense and experience tell us generosity alone cannot solve all the problems of the world's poor and mistreated. According to Population Connection, *the number of people living on less than $2 per day is "just over 2.7 billion."* Nor can all the world's poor and mistreated move to America without destroying much of what America has created over more than two centuries.

Consequently, most Americans feel sadness when they read about or hear about a community or a tribe or a family or an individual who would like to move to or remain in America, but cannot, because of some law or regulation or technicality. We would be less human, if we did not feel sadness in such situations.

But should we feel *guilt?* No ... not if we support policies and institutions which are working to bring improved political and social conditions worldwide so these people will be able to reside in safety and comfort in their own nations.

Sadness? Yes. Guilt? No.

Saving Social Security?

"OK, Ed, I'm willing to accept the pain of more expensive strawberries and even live with some occasional twinges of guilt knowing not all the poor people in the world can move to America. But don't some economists and politicians say we need to import more young workers from other countries in order to save our Social Security System?"

Good question, but let me ask you: Doesn't it make you smile when con artists, arrested for promoting pyramid schemes, say, "If only the authorities had let us operate a little longer, *everybody* would have gotten their money back?"

Yes, a few economists and some politicians sound analogous when they say, "If only we had 20 million more young workers, *everybody* would get their Social Security retirement benefits." Meanwhile, we have moved from 40 workers supporting each recipient of retirement benefits to 20 to one to 10 to one to 6 to one to … Will it end when each retiree has a personally assigned worker supporting that retiree's retirement benefits?

Like a rose by any other name, a pyramid scheme by any other name is still a pyramid scheme. So long as retirement benefits for retirees rely on current contributions from current workers, Social Security can only be "saved" by one or the other or both of the following: (1) Increasing revenue, e.g., increasing payroll taxes, increasing the earnings of trust fund investments or (2) reducing retirement benefits, e.g., increasing "normal retirement age," reducing cost-of-living adjustments. Adding more young workers today simply means adding more retirees tomorrow.

While a *few* economists and *some* politicians argue the solution to this pyramid scheme is to increase immigration of young workers to pay into the Social Security System, they do not explain where these imported young workers are going to find work … unless they take jobs from existing American workers. Nor do they explain how millions of low-paid young dishwashers, lawn mowers, baby-sitters, and hotel service workers are going to save Social Security, especially when many of them are part of America's growing underground economy, paying little or nothing in Social Security taxes.

There may be some "pains" associated with breaking America's addiction to population growth, but failing to save Social Security will not be among them.

Other Pains Of A Shrinking Population?

"But, Ed, aren't there some other pains associated with population reduction?"

I think we can safely say, there is almost always some pain associated with almost any major change—and going from population growth to population reduction would be a major change. On the other hand, barring some catastrophic event, because of population momentum *there is every likelihood America's population will continue to grow throughout this century!* This makes clear why we need to look seven generations ahead and take action now.

But, let's assume we do look ahead and we do take action now and America's population does begin to decline early in the next century—

what then? Well, in the first place, we will have had 100 years to prepare for the change. In the second place, we will have been able to look to the experience of several other nations—such as Japan and certain European countries—whose population declines should occur before ours. From their experiences, we can pick and choose the more successful strategies and tactics for dealing with population decline. Finally, whatever the problems created by a declining population, it seems to me they are certain to be less costly and less destructive than the problems currently created by our addiction to population growth!

LOOKING BACK … AND AHEAD

In this chapter, we have examined how some of the victims of America's addiction to population growth—individuals as well as institutions and concepts—would benefit if that addiction was broken.

In the next chapter, we will consider who is producing the population growth to which America has become addicted. While our influence on the producers is limited, it can be valuable, as you will learn, to understand who the producers are.

As you read further, remind yourself: *Addictions can be broken! You* can join tens of thousands of others who are working to break America's addiction to population growth!

FOR REFLECTION AND DISCUSSION:

1. Referring back to Chapters 5 and 6, "The Victims," what additional victims do you think might "gain" from rehabilitation?
2. What additional "pains" can you think of that Americans might endure if the population growth addiction is broken?
3. How do you feel about the possibility you might experience some withdrawal pain such as higher prices for some goods and services?
4. What thoughts come to your mind which tend to offset feelings of guilt brought on by withdrawal from the population growth addiction?
5. What ideas come to your mind as first steps which might be taken toward initiating a withdrawal process?

QUICK FIX #7

Write a short letter to one of your U.S. Senators asking him or her to consider the population growth issue when drafting legislation and when voting on legislation. Please feel free to borrow from the example in Appendix C, "Quick Fix References."

Chapter 8

THE PRODUCERS

producer *n.* One that produces, especially a person or an organization that produces goods or services for sale.

factory *n.* *(slang)* A place where drugs are packaged or manufactured.

"It is no use trying to tug the glacier backwards." —Tibetan proverb

DRUG ADDICTS CAN BE CURED. Drug pushers can change careers. Enablers of drug addicts can be taught not to make bad situations worse. Victims can eventually recover from their victimization. On the other hand, persuading producers of narcotics to cease and desist is an almost impossible task. By and large, producers only stop when addicts stop purchasing their products or when they die.

By the same token, it is unrealistic to think we can rehabilitate producers of America's addiction to population growth. *Producers will only stop producing when population growth addicts have been cured and stop buying what the producers are selling.* Still, I believe it serves a purpose to identify some of the population growth producers.

AMERICAN TRADE NEGOTIATORS

America's Office of the U.S. Trade Representative (USTR) is our cheerleader for encouraging "free trade" between nations. Economic theory hypothesizes that maximum economic efficiency will occur globally if all nations permit free movement of capital, labor, and products between nations. This is good economic theory for Economics 101. Unfortunately, too many trade negotiators perform as if they never completed Economics 202. Further, USTR negotiates with other nations and groups of nations without being restrained by America's immigration laws or concerns for America's population growth. As Jessica Vaughan, Senior Policy Analyst at the Center for Immigration Studies and a former U.S. Foreign Service officer wrote:

"The United States has signed on to an international framework for free trade in services that binds us to dysfunctional immigration policies, notably the professional guest worker programs.

"Without adjustments to both our planned treaty commitments on visas and our existing guest worker policies, continued U.S. involvement in future trade agreements could put the country on a one-way street moving toward wide open access for foreign workers under terms dictated by an international organization rather than our own democratically evolving immigration laws, with potentially disastrous consequences in professions such as nursing, technology, and even teaching.

"Before ratifying any new trade agreements on services, Congress must reform the temporary business and professional visa programs to allow for the legitimate conduct of trade in services without unleashing a flood of permanent guest workers."

In other words, if we are not careful—if the people we elect to Congress are not careful—America will be in a situation where a few—a very few—non-elected trade negotiators will be establishing America's *de facto* immigration policy while ignoring legitimate concerns about rampant population growth and deteriorating quality of life. If you want an easily understood, but thorough, explanation of how well-meaning diplomats can become producers of America's drug of choice, population growth, log on to *www.CIS.org* and request a copy of *Be Our Guest—Trade Agreements and Visas*.

Remember, American workers—and the citizens of most other developed nations—*do not want free movement of labor.* In other words, many, probably most, American workers *do not want to move* to other nations to work, even though for particular work, *economic theory* argues it might be more economically efficient for them to do so. It is difficult enough to encourage American workers to move from one part of America to another in order to find work. The number of Americans willing to move to other nations—especially permanently—is relatively small. Not surprisingly, the same is true for citizens of other developed nations.

Who does that leave to validate the free movement of the labor portion of the Economics 101 equation? *Workers in less developed nations* who are more than happy to move to developed nations to work ... or, in some cases, others who move to "work" host nations' welfare systems.

Unfortunately, our USTR either doesn't understand that or refuses to acknowledge it. Instead, it goes blithely on its way negotiating trade agreements which will permit other nations to emigrate millions of their citizens to America with little or no regard for the objectives of America's immigration laws, for America's taxpayers, or for America's quality of life.

LESS DEVELOPED NATIONS

Have you heard about the snake charmer who was so poor his snake didn't have a pot to hiss in?

Many countries are like that snake charmer—most of their citizens are so poor they can can barely dream of a marginally better life for themselves and their descendants. One manifestation of their dreams is the number who enter the annual "Diversity Visas" lottery. Fifty thousand lottery winners receive green cards which are granted to people from "underrepresented" countries, i.e., those countries which send relatively few emigrants to America.

When you realize five to ten million people enter the lottery annually to win 50,000 visas, you can see how strong their dreams must be. You also realize *how many people* dream of emigrating to America ... and can only imagine *how many more* would share that dream and enter the lottery, if America reduced the odds against winning by increasing the number of winners to 100,000 or 250,000.

In 1990, America had approximately 20 million foreign-born residents. Ten years later, America had approximately 31 million foreign-born residents. Think about what that means for just a moment. In one decade—the time it takes for a newborn to reach the fifth grade in school—America's population of foreign-born residents grew by 11 million people ... grew by nearly 60%! By the time our illustrative newborn graduates from college, will America's foreign-born population have increased another 11 million people? Twenty-two million additional foreign-born residents in America! That is greater than the population of any American state except California—approximately the population of Texas!

That, in my opinion, is no small matter, not something to be taken lightly nor accepted without careful consideration. So, let's consider some of these nations:

Central And South America

A large portion of the 11 million increase in foreign-born residents in America between 1990 and 2000 came from Mexico, Central, and South America. This should come as no surprise to anyone who reads newspapers or newsmagazines. However, the full extent to which Mexico, Central, and South America contributed to this increase may surprise you: Of the 11 million increase, nearly 7 million, or over 60%, came from Mexico, Central, and South America!

The second thing which may surprise you is the extent to which foreign-borns from Mexico, Central, and South America have dispersed throughout America. In 1990, Mexican, Central, and South American foreign-borns were the predominant category of foreign-borns in 11 American states. You can probably guess some of them, e.g., California, Arizona, New Mexico, Texas, Louisiana, and Florida. The other five you might not have guessed: Kansas, Wyoming, Idaho, Nevada, and Illinois.

However, in 2000, it would have been easier to guess the states in which Mexican, Central, and South American foreign-borns were *not* the predominant category. In 2000, they were the predominant category *in 32 of the 50 states.*

If you know someone who thinks America's addiction to population growth only affects coastal and border states, you might want to give them that statistic.

Primarily this book is about America's addiction to population growth. Only secondarily is it about the sources of that addiction and growth. If America imports over 11 million new residents each decade, that, in my opinion, is a population growth problem. However, it is a problem we—and our Congress—easily can do something about.

If America adds 7 million Mexicans, Central, and South Americans each decade, that, in my opinion, is also a cultural problem we must do something about, unless we are willing to incur the cost of a dual-language nation with all that means to our educational, health care, social services, law enforcement, and judicial structures.

While Mexico and Central and South American countries are producing the bulk of what has become the cross-border flow of America's population growth fix, I do not believe these nations are, with one exception, intentionally producing our population drug of choice—too many people. That exception is Mexico, which I will discuss in a separate section. I believe the Central and South American countries are trying, with varying degrees of success and with some cycles of failure, to provide for their citizens in their own lands. That their cycles of failure result in increasing emigration to America does not, to me at least, suggest that was an intended purpose of failure.

East Asia

Nearly 6 million of the 31 million foreign-born residents of America in 2000 were from East Asia. Somewhat surprising, their number increased by 2 million in the 1990-2000 decade. I believe this is indicative of what America's family-friendly, chain-reaction immigration policy has wrought.

What is your reaction when you hear on television or read in a newspaper an immigrant—in our state, often an illegal alien—quoted as saying, "I am so lonely without my … (you fill in the blank with husband, wife, son, daughter, mother, father, sister, brother) who is thousands of miles away." Hmm? Could that be because you traveled thousands of miles to come to America and left … (fill in another blank) behind?

Admit one million workers, who bring one million spouses, who bring two million children, some of whom bring one million spouses, who bring one million siblings, who bring … Well, you get the idea. Pretty soon you have enough for a fairly large family reunion picnic … or another state.

Mexico

Why separate Mexico from the Central and South American countries? Let me answer that question by quoting from an academic article by Yeh Ling-Ling. The article is titled, "Mexican Immigration and the Political Future of the United States."

"The Mexican government does not seem to be a passive observer in the massive Mexican emigration to the United States. Its political elite has made public statements, adopted policies, and systematically engaged in lobbying activities in the United States at the federal, state, and local levels. As a result, American domestic and foreign policies have been heavily influenced. The goal appears to be to, in effect, eventually erase the border between Mexico and the United States. Such an effort is unprecedented in U.S. history. Continued mass Mexican migration is seen as the key factor in achieving this objective."

There is a Mexican/American border, but it is much easier to cross that border than it is to cross the Atlantic or the Pacific. It is even easier to cross than it is to cross the Isthmus of Panama and, therefore, it is easier for millions of Mexicans to come to America, legally and illegally, temporarily or permanently, than it is for citizens of almost any other country in the world except Canada. The result is that we have more foreign-born residents in America from Mexico than from any other part of the world.

In 2000, Mexican-born residents in America equaled the foreign-born American residents from the next ten emigrating countries—China, Vietnam, Taiwan, Philippines, India, Cuba, former USSR, Korea, Canada, and El Salvador—combined! Of the approximately 35 million foreign-born in America in 2004, *Mexico accounted for nearly one-third!*

Perhaps more important is *the accelerating rate of migration from Mexico.* The increase of approximately 5 million Mexican-born American residents between 1990 and 2000 more than doubled the number of such residents in one decade. Further, Immigration and Naturalization Service estimates indicate that in 2000, *approximately 50% of Mexican-born residents in America were illegal aliens!*

Tapan Munroe, a Northern California economist, writes a column for my local newspaper. In an article titled, "NAFTA is still a work in progress," Munroe wrote of his concern that NAFTA had "not reduced the income gap" between Mexicans and Americans. Instead, the income gap had increased "more than 10% in the past decade." We shouldn't be surprised, he wrote, because Mexico's economic problems can't be solved by "greater Mexican exports via NAFTA alone."

Munroe listed education, health care, infrastructure, and research and development as areas where "Mexico has not invested enough." He also commented on Mexico's failure to create "a better business climate," which I believe must include reforming Mexico's judicial and criminal justice system. "According to a recent World Bank report," Munroe wrote, the way for Mexico to become "a globally competitive economy" is to make these recommended investments and reforms. Only then will it be able to "take full advantage of the benefits of NAFTA."

In other words, the Mexican government's failure to do its part to take full advantage of NAFTA and to improve the lot of its citizens means that *Mexico will continue to produce* emigrants to tempt America's population growth addicts.

A major Mexican failure which pours north across our mutual border is its inability to repair its broken criminal justice system. Every week we read articles about exceptionally brutal crimes committed in Mexico and about the members of the criminal justice system arrested *for protecting* the criminals responsible ... or about members of the criminal justice system being fired or murdered *for taking effective action* against criminals.

When Mexicans cross the border illegally they not only show little regard for American law, but their experience with and appreciation for criminal justice in general is likely to be quite different from our own. Kevin Sullivan, writing with Mary Jordan for the *Washington Post*, provided an example of the difference between America's and Mexico's criminal justice systems:

The bodies of 12 people were found buried in a Ciudad Juarez house reportedly used by drug dealers. Mexican federal officials were questioning 13 state police, including a state police commander, who were suspected of working with drug traffickers. The top federal organized-crime prosecutor suggested there was a "breakdown of law enforcement in Chihuahua state."

Lorenza Benavides is Co-Director of the Association of Relatives and Friends of Disappeared People. This is a Juarez group representing families of approximately 200 men who have disappeared since 1993. Benavides said she was not at all surprised by the corruption allegation against the police. She said most of the 200 missing men had last been seen in custody of police who, she suspects, kidnapped and, perhaps, killed them.

Apparently, offers of money from drug traffickers overwhelms the desire of police officers to serve the public. Even though approximately 300 officers had been fired, a police spokesman acknowledged they had not cleaned up the police force.

For several decades I have watched the Mexican political scene and Mexican politicians. Every six years I would say, "At last. They have elected a president who has the capacity to clean up the mess and to help Mexico reach its potential." And every six years plus three I would say, "Another loser. Another Mexican politician who has wasted three precious years that should have been devoted to educating the uneducated, breaking the back of the criminals in the criminal justice system, developing an efficacious tax system, and bringing justice to the Indians of Mexico."

Mexican history seems to be stuck in a vicious, vicious cycle.

"... A Change Of Heart"

Here is how another witness of the Mexican scene sees it. Ed Marston is Senior Journalist and former Publisher of *High Country News (www.*

hcn.org), a journal of and for Western America. Mr. Marston wrote a magnificent article titled, "The son of immigrants has a change of heart." I want to quote from it extensively. First, because it is so beautifully written, I want to retain as much of his eloquence as practicable. Second, because I want you to appreciate how his emotions as well as his logic led to his change of heart.

He begins his article with an anecdote about a traveling salesman who wrote to a hotel complaining he'd been bitten by bedbugs while staying at the hotel. He received a lengthy letter of apology back, saying that bedbugs had never been seen on the premises or even within blocks of the hotel. Inside the envelope, he also found a note: "Send the bedbug letter."

Marston wrote, "I believe the story because I once had a bedbug letter of my own. I sent it to people who wrote to tell me that *High Country News* was wasting its time reporting on mining, damming and overgrazing. The real problem? Overpopulation."

Marston always sympathized with such letter writers, because he also would have liked fewer people clogging up roads and trails. But he would tell them he "… didn't know how to fight population growth, except by writing about the effects of more people pressing on forests, rivers and open space. Reproduction, I said, was like the other primal emotions. We chose not to go head-to-head against overpopulation anymore than we went head-to-head against lust and greed or murderous hearts. That we left to the preachers.

"But life got more complex during the last decade. 'Overpopulation' now means immigration into the United States, mainly by Mexican nationals. It is no longer a matter of Americans' inability to control ourselves. It is now a matter of fellow human beings of other nationalities being unable to match their economies to their fecundity. It has also become a matter of obeying our laws and maintaining our borders."

However, as the title of his article states, Marston is a son of immigrants. He wondered how he could oppose others coming to America for work or to escape from squalor. Yet, as a professional journalist, he wanted to weigh the public-policy implications of immigration rationally, not simply emotionally. At the same time, he was, "overwhelmed by dispatches from the ground. Americans no longer care to mow their lawns or clean their toilets or slaughter the chickens we eat. Nor do we want to learn to do computer programming the way Asians do."

So what happened to break the stalemate between reason and

emotion? Marston spent time in Mexico and got to know a Mexican landscaper—the father of eleven children.

"He is proud of his life, and he should be. But he was also incredulous at our lives. He indicated that a father, mother, son and daughter wasn't a family at all. It was more an *hors d'oeuvre*, a *tapas*. I'd like to think he wasn't contemptuous of us personally. But he was dismissive of a culture where only two children might be the norm.

"This was the other, patriarchal face of immigration: one of the men who stands, invisible, behind the image of a young woman, babe in arms, wading the Rio Grande River at night. Should I be swayed by his attitude? Should I be swayed by knowing that some of his children will probably come to America, or may already be here? Should I be swayed by knowing that Mexico's second largest source of income after oil exports is expatriate workers sending money home? I think I should be.

"When it comes to important matters, we have no choice but to trust our emotions, tempered by our hearts and minds. Here's what they tell me: It would be good for Americans to clean our toilets, write our computer programs, slaughter our chickens and cattle, and pick our strawberries. And it would be good for Mexicans to cope with their population and economy without using the United States as an overflow tank, and without using the poor Mexican people as cash cows, to be exported as if they were crude oil or cattle."

Here is evidence Marston was right on target: Hernando de Soto is founder of the Institute for Liberty and Democracy in Peru and author of *The Other Path* and *The Mystery of Capital*. Working with the Mexican government, de Soto discovered some interesting things which he reported in a speech as he accepted Cato Institute's "Milton Friedman Prize for Advancing Liberty":

Approximately 80% of Mexicans work in the extralegal *[underground]* economy. They own approximately 6 million businesses, 134 million hectares of land, and 11 million buildings. All together, they are worth approximately $315 billion, i.e., approximately 7 times the value of Mexican oil reserves and approximately 29 times the value of all foreign direct investment since Spain granted Mexico independence.

This leads me to close this section on Mexico with a thought-provoking letter written by a local reader, published in my local newspaper:

"By continuing with such a liberal acceptance of illegal immigrants, we're really doing countries such as Mexico a disservice. Mexico is a large country with many resources: oil, forests, agriculture, minerals, ports, tourist hot spots, and a vast labor supply. By rights, it should be far more prosperous than it is. Yet 40 percent to 50 percent of the population lives in poverty. Why? There are only two possibilities—either Mexicans, as a people, have the ability to make their country prosperous, or they don't. I believe they do.

"I think the main reason for their failure is a lack of focus. From the top (the President) on down, the focus in Mexico is on moving as many people as possible to the United States. Instead, it should be on raising the standard of living in their own country. By continuing to allow the high levels of illegal immigration, we impede their progress. In other words, we need to encourage them to either sink or swim. They can swim, but they will need to be forced to do so. If Mexicans don't have the ability to improve their country, then why would we want them here at all?"

Other Nations

Since Mexico, Central America, South America, and East Asia were responsible for 80% of the 11 million increase in foreign-born residents in America between 1990 and 2000, do we need to be concerned about the other nations sending their citizens to America?

From a population growth addiction standpoint, not so much concerned, perhaps, as to be aware: If America wants to know when it has broken its population growth addiction and moved toward population stabilization, it will be when total immigration from *all* nations is about the same as it currently is from "Other Nations." In other words, it will be when total immigration and emigration are in balance at between 200,000 and 300,000 per year—not while immigration is approximately *1.5 million* per year as it is today.

"REFUGEE" CONTRACTORS

Who or what are "refugee" contractors? According to Don Barnett writing for Center for Immigration Studies (CIS) in October 2003, "Refugee" contractors are "charitable" (i.e., tax exempt) organizations. "Functioning as federal contractors and employing at least 5,000 in the U.S., most of their income is based on the number of 'refugees' they resettle to the U.S.—not to other countries."

In other words, these are organizations which can increase their income by increasing America's population with increasing numbers of "refugees." Why do I put "refugees" in quotation marks? Because, like so many federal programs initiated by Congress then allowed to run wild on its own, the "refugee" resettlement program has gone a little nuts and our definition of "refugee" has become even nuttier.

It is difficult for Americans not to feel sympathy for legitimate refugees. But today the "refugee" program has become so riddled with corruption and illegitimacy, it is difficult for Americans to know who is and who is not a legitimate refugee. According to Mr. Barnett, our government paid approximately $30 million to resettle approximately 100,000 "refugees" in 1995. But in 2002, we paid approximately $60 million to resettle fewer than 30,000 "refugees."

Again, according to Mr. Barnett, "The program began with the goal of encouraging direct private giving to refugees by providing a federal tax dollar ($1) for every dollar of value provided by the refugee contractor ... In 1996, the matching formula was rewritten to provide 1.4 federal tax dollars ($1.40) for every dollar of value provided by the refugee contractor. Then, in 1999, it started dispensing $2 for each dollar of value from the contractor."

And so on and so on. Once again, Congress fiddles while taxpayers burn—and "refugee" contractors produce more people to support America's population growth addicts.

How many million more would-be "refugees" are waiting to take advantage of Western benevolence? In the November/December 2003 issue of *Via,* the California State Automobile Association magazine, Pico Iyer wrote about Nigerians boarding Lufthansa planes bound for Frankfurt. During flights, they swallowed their passports. When they arrived, they were unable (because they had no papers) to enter Germany or return to Nigeria. They were given $6 a day to stay in so-called asylum hotels around the airport. They figured that was more than they could earn in Lagos.

When will this fraud on American and other Western taxpayers end? Based upon past experience it won't.

From Mr. Barnett's conclusion: "When the U.S. began taking Southeast Asian refugees in the late 1970s, refugee agencies hired *temporary workers,* thinking the program would only last a few months. Almost 30 years after the last American left Vietnam we are still taking 'refugees' from Southeast Asia. At least 1.5 million have come in as 'refugees' from this region."

Thus, it will not end until American taxpayers rise up and say to Congress, "We are tired of having our tax dollars spent to increase U.S. population and to exacerbate the very problems we elected you to mitigate!"

RELIGIOUS AND SECULAR LEADERS

Many years ago I saw a cartoon showing a patient lying on an operating table surrounded by doctors, one of whom is saying that the patient's problem has been narrowed down to one of seven possibilities. A quick count tells the reader the patient is surrounded by seven doctors.

As I investigated the relationships between various religions and fertility rates among various religions' adherents, I began to feel like that patient with seven opinions.

In some parts of the world—including parts of America—adherents of a particular religion might be discouraged from practicing family planning while adherents of that same religion in other parts of the world are encouraged to practice family planning.

From what I have read, my sense is that a little secular political and/or economic pressure applied at the right time in the right place sometimes results in a change from "discouraged" to "encouraged." For example, according to *Wall Street Journal* staff reporter Gautam Naik, Tunisia, a predominantly Muslim nation, reduced its fertility rate from 7.2 in the 1960s to 2.1 in 2004. The point is: Not all Muslims are automatically required to have large families. On the other hand, according to *www.IslamInAfrica.org,* the fertility rates of some generally Muslim nations was as follows: Bangladesh = 3.3; Kenya = 4.1; Jordan = 4.4; Tanzania = 5.7; Niger = 7.3.

For many people in the world—including many Americans—secular cultural influences such as *machismo* mix with religious influences to influence fertility rates. In some cultures, regardless of what religion is observed, there may be a tendency to revere large families. In such cultures, celebrities, the wealthy, and cultural icons may set examples—perhaps compete—by having large, larger, and largest families. Can you imagine how such examples play out in the daily lives of ordinary people?

TWO KINDS OF PRODUCERS

Among producers of America's addiction to population growth, there are producers and then there are producers. Yes, some producers, such as the Mexican government and "refugee" contractors, know they are adding to America's population growth addiction. Other producers, such as most other governments or sectarian and secular leaders, do not really think about—or probably care about—what their contribution is to America's addiction to population growth.

Which do you believe are the more destructive, those producers who take advantage of America's addiction for their own economic and political benefit, or those who are oblivious to the damage they cause?

PUTTING PRODUCERS IN THEIR PLACES

As you may remember from Chapter 1, "The Populationists," there are only two factors which cause world population to change: births and deaths. If births exceed deaths, world population increases. In America, as in any other nation, there are three factors which determine population change: births, deaths, and net migration (immigrants minus emigrants).

The producers of America's population growth addiction fall into two categories: (1) Those who promote increasing births and fertility rates such as certain religious and secular leaders, and (2) those who promote increasing net migration such as American trade negotiators and "refugee" contractors. No producer of addictive substances will willingly give up his trade, but, in my opinion, we have a better chance of stopping the latter than the former.

LOOKING BACK ... AND AHEAD

In this chapter, we have examined how some people and some institutions have been allowed to contribute to America's addiction to population growth. From this you can see it will not be easy to persuade many of them to change their ways. Our primary focus must be to make them irrelevant by curing the addicts and educating the pushers and enablers.

In the next chapter, we will consider the pushers of America's population growth addiction. We will discuss who they are and some of the reasons why they have become population growth pushers.

As you read further, remind yourself: *Addictions can be broken! You* can join tens of thousands of others who are working to break America's addiction to population growth!

FOR REFLECTION AND DISCUSSION:

1. How much latitude do you think American trade negotiators should have in making agreements with other nations which will produce additional population growth in America?

2. What do you think about the inference that most less-developed nations are not intentionally directing their citizens to emigrate to America?

3. What do you think about the inference that Mexico is intentionally directing its citizens to emigrate to America?

4. What was your reaction to the extracts from Ed Marston's article titled, "The son of immigrants has a change of heart?"

5. What did you read in the section about "Refugee" Contractors that you did not previously know?

QUICK FIX #8

Write a short letter to your other U.S. Senator asking him or her to consider the population growth issue when drafting legislation and when voting on legislation. Please feel free to borrow from the sample in Appendix C, "Quick Fix References."

Chapter 9

THE PUSHERS

pusher *n.* One who sells drugs illegally.

"If you board the wrong train, it is no use running along the corridor in the other direction." —Dietrich Bonhoeffer

AMERICA'S POPULATION GROWTH PUSHERS HAVE *a variety of motives. However, many—probably most—have one trait in common: They have never asked themselves the question, "How many Americans are enough?"* If they did, perhaps some of them would stop pushing to have an America of one billion or more residents.

ARMCHAIR ECONOMISTS

Whenever you hear somebody say, "Illegal aliens only do work American workers won't do," you know you are listening to someone who either knows little—or pretends to know little—about American workers ... *and who hopes listeners know even less about economics.*

American workers do plenty of mighty tough jobs. Think of high-rise steel workers or bridge and dam builders. But, also think of something as basic and as essential as a plumber. Follow a typical plumber around for a week and tell me you aren't tired *just from watching* the heavy duty and often dirty work he—or she—does. Or, think of soldiering. How is that for a job many Americans won't do—but many Americans *do* do?

Another example: One of my native-born friends cleans bathrooms, kitchens, and whatever else needs cleaning for a living on a daily basis and has done so for many years. Another native-born friend runs a small office-cleaning business. She lives in a lovely house in an upper middle-class neighborhood. Yet, when one of her workers is sick, she cleans offices, including bathrooms. My friend is an American citizen raised on hard work and motivated by dependability. When called for, she willingly does "the work Americans *[allegedly]* won't do."

Now, thinking about other work "American's won't do," I want you to try to imagine you are about to negotiate your price for a job I am going to describe. As to whether or not this is one of those jobs "Americans won't do," you be the judge.

Your imaginary job is seasonal ... you must earn enough money during the work-season to support yourself—and perhaps a family—for the full year, since you may not find another job during the off-season. During the work-season you may see your family only intermittently.

Imagine performing your job outdoors rain or shine, hot or cold. Much of the time you are bent at the waist to perform your work, but you can't put much of your weight on your hands, because you have to use them for the job you are doing. Obviously, your job is physically demanding—it took hard work for you to become fit enough simply to apply for the job.

Because of the physical demands of this job you know you probably will be considered too old to continue in this line of work by the time you reach age 40. Even now, young and healthy as you are, you recognize there are always other younger ones on the sidelines just waiting for a chance to take your place. In fact, each day when you perform your job you know someone is eager and willing to take advantage of every mistake you make. And at the end of every work-season you ask yourself, "Do I really want to continue taking such abuse to my mind and my body for another season?"

OK, how much do you want to earn to perform this job? Ten dollars an hour? Twenty dollars an hour? Fifty dollars an hour? Am I getting close to your price?

You say you're not sure you want the job at any price, but if you take it, you'll have to be paid enough to take care of your needs for the full year, not just for the season.

Fine. How about $1 million for the season?

You say you'd give that some thought?

Good. Now, let's go back to $10 per hour.

"No way," you say. "What do you think I am?"

Well, perhaps you've already guessed what you are—you're a National Football League center. We're now negotiating your price!

The point is, you and I may not want to get our bodies and brains bashed week after week by 250-300 pound titans. But there are plenty of Americans who are willing to perform that task—and other tasks considerably less glamorous—*for the right price.* That is how economics works!

That is how Americans work! *Americans will do the work that needs to be done … for the right price!*

Pseudo-Economists

Some media columnists fancy themselves to be economists—especially, if they write columns for *The Economist.* A fairly thorough "Survey of Migration" published in *The Economist* contained many suggestions that economics dictates that migration between countries is not only inevitable, but *automatically* beneficial both to sending and receiving countries. For example, "… migration of the unskilled delivers the largest global economic gains …" However, nowhere in their survey did the authors demonstrate—or even attempt to demonstrate—that this and similar statements were based upon some generally accepted or even occasionally accepted economic theory.

Personally, I find it difficult to understand how either America or the world make large economic gains when America admits one million aliens to wash dishes, one million to mow lawns, one million to make beds, and one million to care for children. When those four million invite three million parents and siblings, one million spouses, and have sixteen million children, and when a large portion of this added population requires taxpayer subsidized child-care, health care, education, food, etc., the global gains—and the gains for America—seem elusive at best.

The Economist's point may have some validity, but I find it easier to understand Professor Milton Friedman's point: *"You cannot simultaneously have open borders and a welfare state."* [My emphasis.]

FANS OF "FAIRNESS"

"Fair" and "diverse" are words columnists like to use to push their bosses' addictions. Certain secular and religious leaders and many open borders advocates also use the same words to push America's population growth via increasing immigration. Diversity doctrinaires are discussed in Chapter 11,"The Enablers," but let's address the fairness issue right now. "After all," fans of fairness will say, "we *are* a nation of immigrants. It wouldn't be *fair* to shut the door to those who simply want to have what we have." Let's talk common sense about fairness and about shutting the door.

In my town we have a spot where commuters on foot can line up and wait for other commuters in cars to come by and pick them up for rides to San Francisco. I work out of an office in our home, so I don't ordinarily go to San Francisco and, when I do, I often take municipal transit. However, one morning I had several errands to run in and around San Francisco and had to drive. Knowing I could use the express lane on the San Francisco-Oakland Bay Bridge if I had a few passengers in my car, I stopped at the commuter corner to pick up some would-be riders.

There appeared to be approximately 20 people in line and the first five opened the doors and got into my car, two in the front seat and three in the back seat. They were about to close the doors when the sixth person in line said,

"That isn't *fair*. I want to ride to San Francisco too."

I said, "Yes, but this car is only designed for a driver and five passengers."

"I don't care; that isn't *fair*. I can sit on somebody's lap." So, the sixth person in line got in the back and sat on somebody's lap and started to close the door. But before he could close the door, the seventh person in line said,

"That isn't *fair*. I want to ride to San Francisco too. I can sit on somebody's lap too." So, he did.

Then, the eighth person in line said, "That isn't *fair*. I want to ride to San Francisco too. I can sit on somebody's lap too." So, he did.

Then, the ninth and the tenth persons in line each said, "That isn't *fair*. I want to ride to San Francisco too. I can sit on somebody's lap too."

Well, it was crowded and not necessarily comfortable—and the vision to the rear was pretty much limited to what I could see in the two outside mirrors. But at least I had been "fair" to the first ten people in line.

Unfortunately, the eleventh person in line caught one of the doors before it could be shut and said, "That isn't *fair*. I want to ride to San Francisco too. I can lie on the floorboard in the back."

And the twelfth person in line said, "That isn't *fair*. I want to ride to San Francisco too. I can lie across the rear window panel."

And the thirteenth person in line said, "That isn't *fair*. I want to ride to San Francisco too. I can lie across the floorboard in the front."

And the fourteenth person in line said, "That isn't *fair*. I want to ride to San Francisco too. I can sit on the driver's lap."

And the fifteenth person in line said, "That isn't *fair*. I want to ride to San Francisco too. I can lie across the dashboard."

"Hey, wait a minute," I yelled. "I can't see where I'm going."

"That's OK," said Number 15, "I can tell you where to steer."

"Yeah, but I'm having trouble reaching the steering wheel."

"That's OK," said Number 14, "I can steer for you."

"But I can't feel the brake pedal or the gas pedal."

"That's OK," said Number 13, " I can push the pedals for you."

And with that, away we went heading for San Francisco.

Of course, we never made it. Before we had driven five miles, Numbers 13 and 14 misunderstood Number 15 and we ran off the road into an embankment at high speed and all of us were killed ... Now, talk about *ghostwriting* ...

The next time you hear a speech or sermon, or have a friendly conversation, or read a column in which "fairness" is used to push America's addiction to population growth, feel free to tell the pusher this story.

POLITICIANS

Politicians, both Democrats and Republicans, have been pushing America's addiction to population growth for many years. For example, according to a report by the Center for Immigration Studies (CIS):

"When the INS conducted raids during Georgia's Vidalia onion harvest in 1998, thousands of illegal aliens—knowingly hired by the farmers—abandoned the fields to avoid arrest. By the end of the week, both of the state's Senators and three Congressmen had sent an outraged letter to Washington complaining that the INS 'does not understand the needs of America's farmers,' and that was the end of that.

"So, the INS tried out a 'kinder, gentler' means of enforcing laws, which fared no better. Rather than conduct raids on individual employers, Operation Vanguard in 1998-99 sought to identify illegal workers at all meat packing plants in Nebraska through audits of personnel records. The INS then asked to interview those employees who appeared to be unauthorized—and the illegals ran off. The procedure was remarkably successful, and was meant to be repeated every two or three months until the plants were weaned from their dependence on illegal labor.

"Local law enforcement officials were very pleased with the results, but employers and politicians vociferously criticized the very idea of enforcing the immigration laws. Gov. Mike Johanns organized a task force to oppose the operation; the meat packers and the ranchers hired former Gov. Ben Nelson to lobby on their behalf; and, in Washington, Sen. Chuck Hagel (R-Neb.) made it his mission in life to pressure the Justice Department to stop. They succeeded, the operation was ended, and the senior INS official who had thought it up in the first place is now enjoying early retirement."

Can you imagine what such imperious action by politicians does to the morale and dedication of law enforcement officers who are actually trying to enforce immigration laws? They work long and inconvenient hours in uncomfortable surroundings—often putting their lives on the line—to enforce laws. Then, a few politicians and the companies and organizations making major contributions to those politicians, stand the laws on their heads and punish those trying to enforce laws.

Another way in which politicians push population growth is by encouraging "family reunification" in immigration laws. To hear most politicians talk you would think the validity of "family reunification" ranks right up there with motherhood and apple pie. Common sense tells us the reason an immigrant wants to bring a spouse, child, parent, or sibling to America is because that immigrant left a spouse, child, parent, or sibling at home to travel to America.

In other words, most immigrants were not kidnapped, separated from their relatives, and brought to America against their will. And for those very few who were kidnapped, free them, jail their kidnappers, and release the kidnapped back to their relatives in the countries from which they were taken. But politicians refuse to talk like that; they prefer fuzzy wuzzy terms such as "family reunification."

"If we bring temporary workers to America to do work for which there are insufficient American workers, shouldn't we let them bring their families with them?"

Accepting *for the purpose of this discussion only* the assumption of "insufficient American workers," the answer is, "No, not if you don't want those temporary workers to become permanent American residents."

"But, Ed," you might say, "that seems rather severe. After all, these are good, hardworking people."

Exactly. We should keep that in mind before we get carried away with programs to promote more "temporary" foreign workers. Or, as George Borjas, Harvard immigration economist, said quoting someone relating a similar German experience: "We wanted workers ... *but we got people.*"

RELIGIOUS LEADERS

Religious leaders are generally caring people. They care for the poor. They care for the needy. They care for the downtrodden. They preach to their congregations about caring for the poor, for the needy, and for the downtrodden. It is difficult to think of a group who, on the whole, are more poor, more needy, or more downtrodden than illegal aliens.

Some religious leaders are inclined to say, "They only come to America to work and to have a better life." Well, no. Actually, some come to America to steal and to cheat. Some come to smuggle drugs. Some come to smuggle people. Some come to fly airplanes into tall buildings. Some come to have babies who will become American citizens. Some come to obtain free medical care. Some come to escape from the criminal justice system in their own countries. There are *many* reasons people come to America ... and not all of the reasons are good reasons nor are all of the people good people.

Nevertheless, many congregations hear sermons about how it is their sacred responsibility to provide care for illegal aliens—even though such care may conflict with the objectives of America's immigration laws and, indeed, may simply push America's addiction to population growth.

"SHORTAGE SHOUTERS"

Californians for Population Stabilization (CAPS) refers to the employer organizations and spokespersons who maintain that America has a shortage of this or that kind of scientific or technical expertise as "shortage shouters." CAPS identifies three key "shortage shouters": Information Technology Association of America (ITAA), Indian-owned National Association of Software and Service Companies (NASSCOM), and American Immigration Lawyers Association (AILA).

It's easy to understand why AILA cries, "Shortage!" The more immigrants, the more work for immigration lawyers, and the more legal fees. NASSCOM? Well, if you follow financial news, you know that India is the nation to which so much American information technology work has been outsourced and that Indian is the nationality of so many of the workers coming here to replace American workers.

How about ITAA? Don't they know whether or not their member companies have shortages of technical workers? Yes and no. Yes, they know whether or not there are shortages and, generally speaking, ... no, there are not. What do I mean by "generally speaking?" Well, at any given instant for any given high-tech company, there may be a shortage of this or that given expertise or knowledge or experience within that company. Does that mean there is no person in America qualified to fill that position? Again, in general, the answer is: There is probably someone, somewhere in America who could fill that position. Whether that person wants to fill that position at the price the position-holding company is willing to pay is a separate issue.

"Well, Ed," you may ask, "aren't there occasions when so many companies want the same kind of expertise or knowledge or experience at the same time that America simply doesn't have enough high-tech talent available to meet all those demands regardless of the price companies are willing to pay?"

Yes, that does happen—occasionally. Those occasions are called "high-tech booms" during which high-tech workers command high prices for their labor. Such occasions are generally followed by "high-tech busts" during which the high-tech workers who commanded high prices begin looking for work at any price. During those occasional, temporary booms, there is some justification in allowing high-tech companies to bring high-tech employees to America to fill those occasional, temporary vacuums.

That is precisely what Congress did when it instituted the *H1-B* visa. This was supposed to be a temporary visa designed to meet temporary needs. Of course, employers who used such temporary workers soon found a permanent competitive advantage to using workers willing to work for from 25% less (according to an Immigration and Naturalization Services study) to 33% less (according to a University of California at Los Angeles study). So, the employers become addicted to low-paid high-tech workers and ITAA, NASSCOM, and AILA become "shortage shouters" and pushers of America's addiction to population growth.

"Wait, a minute, Ed! These are *temporary* workers!"

Please remember this, whether Mexican "temporary workers" in America or Turkish "temporary workers" in Germany: *There is nothing more permanent than "temporary workers."*

TAX-AND-SPENDERS

Tax-and-Spenders take two forms, rather like vampires and werewolves, I suppose. One is the Congressional form which concentrates its energy on "victimizing" its growing constituent populations by telling them how poor they are, how uneducated they are, how deprived of health care they are, and telling them how, if elected, their Representative will tax the rich and spend lots of money on constituent victims. The

Congressional form can only be killed by driving "polls" through their hearts … polls indicating enough American taxpayers have awakened to the daylight of what the addiction to population growth is costing them!

The other form of Tax-and-Spenders—the werewolf form—are nonprofit organizations which conspire with Congressional Tax-and-Spenders to spend all the money Congress appropriates on programs for "victims." Many of these "victims" are in America only because various Congresses and Administrations have refused to enforce America's immigration laws. Thus, they have encouraged poor, uneducated, and medically deprived illegal aliens to come to America in order to replenish the supply of "victims."

Of course, the more poor, uneducated, and medically deprived illegal alien "victims" Congress can induce into the country with lax immigration laws and lax law enforcement, the more money the werewolf organizations can claim they need to aid these "victims."

- Gap between rich and poor widening? Guess why.
- Classrooms too crowded? Guess why.
- Number of people without health insurance increasing? Guess why.

So, the cycle continues with some nonprofit organizations which are dedicated to easing the plight of "victims" lobbying Congress to increase America's population of "victims" so they can actually demand more financial aid from "Big Government" so Congress can justify taxing more and spending more! And this practice crosses party lines.

Perhaps you remember the story about the Congressional aide taking the Russian legislators on a tour of DC and explaining, "In this country we have two major political parties—the evil party and the stupid party. I am proud to say I am a member of the stupid party."

In my opinion the Democrats and the Republicans each have more than enough evil and stupidity to go around. Frankly, both parties are guilty of supporting policies and laws which have pushed America's addiction to population growth.

A Local Twist

Of course, Tax-and-Spenders are not limited to federal legislators and federal legislation. The Tax-and-Spend pigeons often come home to roost. My local newspaper's "Question of the Week" was: "What steps should be taken to relieve traffic congestion in the East Bay?" All ten of the published letters contained answers which involved either government spending additional money and/or directing life-style and economic changes. For example:

- Encouraging drivers to car pool or to drive more efficient cars.
- Taxing cars and car systems—and not letting them off cheaply.
- Charging for parking everywhere people work, shop, and live.
- Relocating businesses where people live.
- Upgrading existing conventional rail lines to modern passenger standards.
- Making all public transportation free of charge.
- Giving companies and individuals objecting to higher taxes the choice to move.
- Adopting smart growth strategies aimed for regional common good by advocating appropriate high density.
- Constructing six new under-the-bay tunnels.
- Persuading businesses to locate outside the mainstream business districts of the cities.

Frankly, I find it difficult to believe my local newspaper received no letters suggesting a solution to the overriding causative problem—rampant population growth in the county. Well, actually, I know they received at least *one* such letter ... mine. But since *they* didn't publish it ...

"How sad that we have politicians, both nationally and locally, so intent on *rewarding* aliens for breaking our immigration laws and, at the same time, so content with *penalizing* aliens who have respected our immigration laws and waited their turns.

"How typical that we have politicians so intent on *rewarding* employers unwilling to pay American market wages and so intent on *rewarding* immigration lawyers—both of whom contribute big bucks to election campaigns.

"How sad that we have politicians so intent on *rewarding* ethnic group 'leaders' for contributing big blocks of votes and at the same time so content with *penalizing* taxpayers and unemployed American workers.

"How sad ... How typical!"

UNITED NATIONS AND OTHER INTERNATIONAL ORGANIZATIONS

How many nations are there in the United Nations?—Over 190.

How many of those nations do you think are seriously concerned about America's quality of life? How many do you think are seriously concerned about our crowded schools? About our disappearing wild lands and wildlife? About our failing bridges and highways? About our … well, about anything that is adversely affected by population growth? Not many? I think you are correct.

Well, then, we shouldn't be surprised when the UN (United Nations) and WTO (World Trade Organization) and GATS (General Agreement on Trade in Services) and NAFTA (North Atlantic Free Trade Agreement) and CAFTA (Central American Free Trade Agreement) and SACU (South African Customs Union) and FTAA (Free Trade Areas of the Americas) and CSFTA (Chile and Singapore Free Trade Agreement) and the other alphabet soup of international trade negotiations and agreements sponsored by these organizations fail to be concerned about America's quality of life or its addiction to population growth.

WHAT PUSHES PUSHERS?

Does it make sense to you for some illegal aliens to obtain taxpayer-subsidized, in-state tuition at some state universities while some American citizens pay out-of-state tuition to those same universities? To me, our irrational immigration policies and our non-enforcement of immigration laws make no sense at all unless:

- One makes money by hiring illegal aliens at below-market wage rates;
- One increases political power by organizing and/or catering to selected categories of illegal aliens;
- One sells foreign language newspapers or owns foreign-language media outlets—which, for example, most of the large media chains do;
- One believes the larger the domestic market becomes, the better for everyone … without recognizing the downsides of growth.

For the rest of us who pay extra taxes to subsidize such irrationality, the only thing that makes less sense is the fact that we continue to elect politicians who subject us to such senseless subsidies!

LOOKING BACK ... AND AHEAD

In this chapter, we have examined some of the pushers of America's addiction to population growth—both individuals and organizations. We discussed some who are motivated by desire for power and influence, others who are motivated by greed, and still others who are motivated by compassionate feelings. Whatever their motivations, we need to push back at the pushers.

In the next two chapters, we will discuss who is enabling America's addiction to population growth. The first chapter discusses governmental enablers while the second discusses non-governmental enablers.

As you read further, remind yourself: *Addictions can be broken! You can join tens of thousands of others who are working to break America's addiction to population growth!*

FOR REFLECTION AND DISCUSSION:

1. What is your reaction when you read or hear, "They only do work Americans won't do?"
2. What do you think when you read or hear, "After all, America is a nation of immigrants?"
3. How do you react to the "It isn't fair" statement when you realize there are 300 million people in America and over 5 billion people in less developed countries?
4. How many broadcast anchors or newspaper and magazine columnists can you name who seem to have a concern about America's rampant population growth?
5. What experience have you had with your tax dollars being spent to mitigate the negative effects of population growth rather than addressing the causes of population growth?

QUICK FIX #9

Visit or ask a friend to visit *www.NumbersUSA.com* and click on "Report Cards" to look for your Representative's population growth "grade." Then record the date and the "grade" in Appendix C, "Quick Fix References."

Chapter 10

THE ENABLERS

Government

enabler *n.* A person or institution that makes addiction feasible or possible and gives legal power, capacity, or sanction to an addict.

"In politics, sincerity is everything. Once you can fake that, you've got it made." —Groucho Marx

AS AMERICAN AS MOTHERHOOD AND APPLEJACK

When I was young and my father's father was old, he used to keep a bottle of whiskey in my mother's kitchen cabinet. Once or twice a day he would "sneak" into the kitchen, find his bottle, pour a jigger of whiskey into a water glass, have his drink, rinse his glass, and replace his bottle.

Each time he went through this routine, my mother would wait until he had left the kitchen. Then, she would take his bottle from its cabinet, replace the jigger's worth of whiskey with tap water, then return the bottle to its cabinet. I suppose my mother was an "enabler," enabling my grandfather to enjoy his "whiskey" for more years than he might otherwise have done.

Like my mother, the enablers of our population growth addiction are not necessarily addicts themselves. However, to use the dictionary's language, enablers make it feasible or possible and give legal power, capacity, or sanction to America's addiction to population growth. *Enablers' tacit acceptance and implied blessing of population growth provides population growth addicts with some semblance of justification for not seeking a cure.*

Let's begin by examining the role federal, state, and local governments, including elected and appointed officials, have played—and continue to play—as enablers of America's population growth addiction.

AMERICAN PRESIDENTS

What follows is largely taken from three sources: (1) an article by Stephen Mumford published in Carrying Capacity Network's *Focus*, (2) a paper by Lindsey Grant published in Negative Population Growth's *NPG Forum*, and (3) a study by Roy Beck and Leon Kolankiewicz published in The Pennsylvania State University Press' *Journal of Policy History*. The data summarizes nearly 40 years of American presidential policy on population growth. I believe you will find it makes interesting reading:

1969 *(population approximately 203 million).* A 24-person "Commission on Population Growth and the American Future," chaired by John D. Rockefeller III, was established by President Nixon and Congress.

1970 *(population approximately 205 million).* Two months after the first "Earth Day," the First National Congress on Optimum Population and Environment convened in Chicago. Religious groups—especially the United Methodist Church and the Presbyterian Church—urged, for ethical and moral reasons, that the federal government adopt policies that would lead to a stabilized U.S. population. President Nixon addressed the nation about problems it would face if U.S. population growth continued unabated.

1972 *(population approximately 210 million).* The "Rockefeller Commission" issued its 186-page report concluding that further population growth would do more harm than good. It also offered suggestions for stopping that growth. Six months prior to seeking reelection, reportedly under immense pressure from religious leaders, President Nixon simultaneously received and renounced the report.

1974 *(population approximately 214 million).* President Nixon, recognizing the gravity of the overpopulation problem, directed in National Security Study Memorandum (NSSM) 200 a new study be undertaken to determine the "Implications of World Population Growth for U.S. Security and Overseas Interests." In August 1974, Gerald Ford succeeded to the presidency and work on the study continued.

1975 *(population approximately 216 million).* The 227-page report and its recommendations were endorsed by President Ford including one that America should try to reach population stability by 2000. This would have required a policy of encouraging one-child families!

Presumably, most Americans and religious groups were not ready for that.

1980 *(population approximately 227 million).* President Carter received a *Global 2000 Report* which (1) presented an integrated description of major world trends in resources and the environment and related them to population growth, and (2) evaluated the capability of the American government to conduct such integrated foresight on an ongoing basis. Its conclusion was that the federal government did not have facilities in place to relate declining resources to population growth in America or worldwide.

1981 *(population approximately 229 million).* At the very close of the Carter administration, the *Global 2000 Report,* which offered no recommendations, was followed by a booklet of action proposals from the U.S. Department of State and the Council on Environmental Quality. Included among eight recommendations were the following: "The United States should develop a national population policy which addresses the issues of population stabilization as well as just, consistent, and workable immigration laws." The recommendations were reasonable and measured and well-received by the general public. However, their impact on government policy and on the politicians who create policy was negligible.

1982 *(population approximately 232 million).* President Reagan established a "Global Issues Working Group" to "identify global environmental and resource issues of national concern ..." However, the "Group" went dormant about 1985 *(when America's population was approximately 238 million).*

1993 *(population approximately 258 million).* President Clinton created the "President's Council on Sustainable Development" and charged it with helping to "grow the economy and preserve the environment ..." objectives that might possibly be in conflict.

1996 *(population approximately 265 million).* The Council called for a "Move toward stabilization of U.S. population." The report and President Clinton's acceptance of it may constitute the first explicit acceptance by a President of the proposition that U.S. population should stop growing.

Unfortunately, America's population grew by approximately 62 million or 30% while five Presidents figured out America's rampant population growth was causing America major harm!

From the preceding historical review of presidential action and inaction we can draw our own "good news/bad news" conclusions:

- First, the good news is that intelligent politicians and intelligent members of their staffs know that rampant population growth in America and worldwide is a threat to America.
- The bad news is that they have been unable to fathom a politically adroit way to address America's addiction to population growth without—in their judgment—losing more votes than they gain.

By understanding our politicians' calculations we may eventually be able to show them they can win more votes by having the courage to help population growth addicts break their addiction than by enabling population growth addicts' addiction.

AMERICAN SENATORS AND REPRESENTATIVES

Have you recently heard a U.S. Representative or a U.S. Senator talk about wanting to grant *"amnesty"* to illegal aliens? Probably not. They might talk about "immigration normalization" or "earned legalization" or "guest worker programs" or "family reunification" or "compassion policies," but they are unlikely to use the word *"amnesty"* … except, of course, to say they don't believe in it. So, let me suggest a substitute word: *Reward*! Whenever you read or hear one of these Congressional euphemisms, just ask yourself, "What is the *reward* being offered for illegal behavior?"

For example: Among other things, the *reward* for entering America illegally and avoiding deportation for a certain number of years—no doubt by using illegally obtained identification documents and by illegally lying on any number of forms—will be … what?

- To have children receive in-state resident tuition to attend an American college?
- To cut in line for a green card ahead of tens of thousands of fellow applicants who are trying to enter America legally?
- To retain employment which was obtained illegally with an employer who hired illegally and who pays illegally "under the table" while a legal American worker—immigrant or native-born—is out of work?

Interestingly enough, a simple call to your elected representative's office may not be sufficient to determine his or her position on rewarding aliens for illegal behavior.

Representatives and their staffs know a majority of their constituents have enough common sense to not want to reward illegal behavior. Consequently, staffs often try to plead ignorance when people call and ask such questions as, "What is Representative So-And-So's position on House Resolution Such-And-Such?" Don't be fooled. Follow up and ask, "How did Representative So-And-So vote on House Resolution Such-And-Such? Oh! That's too bad." Or, "Please thank him/her for that vote."

AMERICAN STATE DEPARTMENT

There seems to be a tendency for this department to give more importance to serving the interests of citizens of other nations than to implementing American immigration laws which are serving the interests of American citizens. Here is an example of what I mean:

L-1 Visas

There is a visa category, *L-1*, which is designed to permit foreign companies to bring their citizens into America to work in those companies' American offices. That is a reasonable objective. For example, assume a foreign company establishes an office in America to implement a major engineering and construction project. It is reasonable to expect that company would want to send some key employees, e.g., accountants, engineers, managers, and others, to manage that project. *L-1* visas were designed for that very purpose, for those very people.

However, some clever immigration attorneys figured out a way to use *L-1* visas as they were never intended to be used. Some companies, particularly Indian information technology companies, use *L-1* visas to emigrate workers to their "offices" in America. Then, they turn around and hire out these workers to other American companies to do work at wage and benefit rates below the common rates for existing American workers.

According to an article by *San Francisco Chronicle* Staff Writer Carrie Kirby, an official at the Department of Homeland Security said this kind of use is fraudulent. The *L-1* visa was designated to let workers move from one office to another within a company. It was not designed to permit workers to move from a company to a client.

No brainer, right?

Not according to the State Department's Consular Affairs Bureau. They said this obvious misuse of *L-1* visas was not a misuse at all.

Looking at this example, what do you think? Is the Bureau serving other nations' citizens or protecting America's interests? You be the judge.

I cite this example of a State Department position simply to alert you to the problem. Whenever you hear of a dispute between the State Department and another federal department over the application of immigration laws or implementation of homeland security, decide for yourself how often our State Department seems to be more concerned about foreign nations and their citizens than it is about American citizens. That may explain why *L-1* visa holders, particularly from India, have increased at such a rapid pace, from approximately 120,000 for one year to approximately 315,000 the next.

Dual Citizenship

Here is another example of State Department failure to protect the meaning of American citizenship. When immigrants become American citizens, they take an oath of allegiance to America which says, "I absolutely and entirely renounce and abjure all allegiance and fidelity to any foreign prince, potentate, state, or sovereignty, to whom or which I have heretofore been a subject or citizen." Any question in your mind as to what that oath is saying?

There was no question in Teddy Roosevelt's mind as to what it meant when he called "dual citizenship," i.e., citizenship in two countries, a "rank absurdity." Since our State Department sees no problem with Mexico and certain other foreign governments encouraging such dual citizenship, perhaps Roosevelt would consider our State Department a "rank absurdity."

FANNIE MAE AND FREDDY MAC

I caught the tail end of a TV commercial by one of these two *gigantic* government-chartered, taxpayer "guaranteed" home mortgage finance entities—which one wasn't clear. What the commercial did make clear, however, was how proud this entity was that by 2010 there will be an additional 30 million people in America and that many of them will live in homes whose mortgages will have been financed by one of these two. The commercial didn't suggest how many of that 30 million will be in America illegally, nor did it suggest America might be a better place to live if less than 30 million were added to America's population or, indeed, if we had 30 million fewer residents. The thrust of the message quite simply was: "Keep 'em coming; we can keep financing mortgages for however many come!"

Now, I don't mean to pick on Fannie Mae or Freddy Mac, but it does rub this populationist the wrong way to hear a government-chartered entity bragging about the very thing that is *driving up home prices for Americans*—too many new homebuyers. Yep, when demand goes up, prices go up. More homebuyers means more demand which means higher prices.

So, are Fannie Mae and Freddy Mac proud of being enablers of America's population growth addiction which is driving up home prices? Do you think they will be as proud a generation or two from now when Americans wake up to the reason why it takes two workers in too many families to pay mortgages or why it takes two hours of commuting to live in houses younger Americans can afford?

POLICE CHIEFS AND POLICE COMMISSIONERS

It is a sad day indeed when the people we hire to enforce our laws instead take a stand to ignore laws they dislike—laws they consider to be politically incorrect. Laws such as immigration laws. Yes, too many police chiefs and police commissioners in major cities throughout America have taken a stand *against* enforcing America's immigration laws. Immigration laws are federal laws, they say, and they are too busy enforcing their own state and local laws to have time and resources to enforce federal laws. Besides, if they started arresting people who are in America illegally, soon they wouldn't be able to secure the cooperation of others of the same nationality—especially of those who are also here illegally.

Writing for *City Journal—Winter 2004*, in an article titled "The Illegal-Alien Crime Wave," Heather Mac Donald *[yes, the space between c and D is correct]* paints a devastating picture of the crime cost of such police "sanctuary policies." In page after page, Mac Donald details rapes, robberies, murders, and drug dealings and deaths which might have been avoided had police in California, Florida, or New York and federal authorities worked together to enforce immigration laws against known felons.

Mac Donald points out how major criminal organizations of the past were attacked by application of laws not necessarily tied directly to their primary criminal activities (think Mafia and tax laws). Then, logically summarizing a key point of her article, she writes: "However the nation ultimately decides to rationalize its chaotic and incoherent immigration system, surely all can agree that at a minimum, authorities should expel illegal-alien criminals swiftly. Even on the grounds of protecting non-criminal illegal immigrants, we should start by junking sanctuary policies. By stripping cops of what may be their only immediate tool to remove felons from the community, these policies leave law-abiding immigrants prey to crime." And the rest of us, as well.

Sanctuary Saints And Sinners

Many, but not all, sanctuary supporters are sectarian leaders and their followers. Sanctuary supporters, secular and sectarian, provide sanctuary from law enforcement for people who are in America illegally. In other words, they encourage illegal aliens to break America's immigration laws, thereby enabling America's addiction to population growth. This encouragement runs the gamut from providing food, clothing, and shelter, to providing referrals to lawyers who specialize in thwarting American immigration laws and to criminals who produce false documents for illegal aliens.

There are also cities which are sanctuary supporters. Such cities have instructed their law enforcement officers to *not* enforce laws with which the city officials disagree—laws such as immigration laws. City officials rationalize such instructions by saying such things as, "We don't want to frighten illegal aliens so they won't seek government protection from domestic violence," or "We want illegal aliens to be willing to provide police with information about, or act as witnesses to, serious crimes."

How easy do you think it is for sanctuary cities to educate their illegal alien populations as to which laws are OK to break and which laws must be obeyed?

STATE AND LOCAL OFFICIALS

Some legislators in some states have pushed to *reward* illegal aliens with driver's licenses, thereby providing them with legal standing—identification used to open bank accounts, purchase air travel tickets—for breaking our laws. This *legalization of an illegality,* of course, tells illegal aliens that those responsible for making state and local laws have no intention of enforcing federal laws. So, they tell compatriots back home, "Hey, if you can get in, by hook or by crook, Americans will eventually find a way to make your stay comfortable—and permanent." And so, rampant population growth is stimulated anew by these legislator-enablers.

Of course, these legislator-enablers argue, "We're simply facing reality. There are ten million illegal aliens (actually, they say 'undocumented workers') and they need to receive driver's licenses (a) so they can get to their jobs to support their families and/or (b) so they will be tested for competency to drive on our streets and highways."

Their argument reminds me of a group of teenagers who sneaked into a movie theater. Let me tell you why.

Welcome To Fantasy Theater

The latest movie rage at our fictional theater was a teenie-bopper-science-fiction-creepy-slasher-musical-comedy. Our fictional group of teenagers arrived at the theater in time to see a line of would-be ticket buyers extending down the street and around the corner. Instead of waiting to see how fast the line was moving or asking when the next showing would occur, one member of the group said, "I know how we can sneak inside through one of the 'Exit' doors."

"Let's do it," the others said—and they did.

Twenty minutes later they had occupied most of the front row in the center section of the theater and were enjoying popcorn and sodas a few of them had brought back from the lobby.

About that time the theater manager and some ushers started down the aisles asking people to show their tickets. Upon reaching the front row, they knew what to expect—no tickets. The manager and ushers were about to ask our imaginary group of teenagers to leave the same way they entered.

However, a spokesman for the group spoke up saying, "Hey, that's not fair. We've been here twenty minutes. We've purchased popcorn and sodas. We've watched all your screened commercials and listened to all your mediocre music. After all, we're sitting in seats other Americans won't sit in. Why don't you simply face reality … and give us tickets so we'll be like everybody else?"

The theater manager thought about it for a few seconds, then said, "You're right." Turning to one of the ushers he said, "Please go back to the lobby and get some tickets for these fine young people who haven't done anything wrong since they sat down here. And while you're at it, tell the fifteen people who bought tickets but haven't been able to find seats, we'll honor their tickets at the next showing."

I told you this was a fantasy. But ask yourself, "If our 'give-them-driver's-licenses' legislators owned this fictional theater, how long would they remain in business?"

Probably not very long once the public discovered that sneaking in paid off. That's right … they would stop illegal entry quickly or go out of business.

Too bad our legislators don't take a more proprietary interest in our country's welfare and demonstrate more concern about what illegal entry across our borders costs American taxpayers. Unfortunately, they like to be generous with other people's money.

Local Politicians

According to an article in my local newspaper, politicians in the tiny Texas border town of El Cenizo required "all business be conducted in Spanish." A reader responded to that article by suggesting how much money that requirement might save taxpayers, since "... all municipal employees, vendors, and subcontractors must be paid in *pesos* and not in dollars (which are written in English)..."

If I were in a charitable mood, I might suggest the politicians of El Cenizo were only thinking of the convenience of Mexican shoppers who cross the border in the morning to do their shopping in America and who return to Mexico in the evening. Unfortunately, I'm *not* in a charitable mood. So, telling it like it is, let's recognize what these particular politicians were doing—like too many fellow politicians around America are doing: *Enabling* Spanish-speaking, non-English-speaking illegal aliens to live in America without learning English, let alone obeying American immigration laws.

Policy Perverting Politicians

Most politicians have one goal in mind: To get reelected! If they can do that by representing their constituents, they will do so. However, if campaigning costs convince them they will be better served by serving big money-donating interests—such as industries which want to employ cheap labor—they will do that instead.

Now, don't get me wrong. I don't look down on all politicians—just most politicians. My own county is represented by four or five Congressmen—one of whom is a Congresswoman. Don't I know whether the correct number is four or five? Not really. Gerrymandering is a political science slightly more complex than astrophysics and I have trouble following the Congressional feet in their manipulative minuet.

Do you sometimes wonder how Congressmen (and Congresswomen) are able to follow the mathematical intricacies of gerrymandering Congressional districts, but can't manage to understand basic negative economic realities created by population growth?

A PECULIAR PRECEDENT

There is one enabler of America's addiction to population growth which I find as difficult to categorize as I find it difficult to understand. It is called "birthright citizenship" and it produces what are called "anchor babies." Let me explain. Perhaps you can decide where it belongs ...

A wealthy, pregnant Asian woman pays several thousand dollars to a specialized "travel agent" to arrange air transport to America and accommodations at a five-star American hotel until she can enter a first-class private hospital and give birth to a baby boy.

A poor, pregnant Latin American woman pays one thousand dollars to a "coyote" to smuggle her into America where she gives birth—without cost in a county hospital—to a baby girl.

A well-traveled, pregnant European woman accompanies her husband to America on a business trip and unexpectedly gives premature birth to fraternal twins—a boy and a girl.

If you ask, "So, what?" I understand. However, by a long-standing, strange tradition, each of those four babies would be American citizens with all the rights and privileges of other American citizens. So, America's population has just increased by four and those four may eventually petition to have some of their relatives join them in America, further increasing our population.

"OK, Ed, but how often do those kinds of things actually happen?"

Premature births in America by European—or other foreign—wives of businessmen? Not so often. Births by wealthy Asian women who pay big bucks to have their babies born in America? More often than you might think. Births by illegal alien mothers? Well, of course, hospitals located in border communities are well aware of the cost of serving "coyotes'" clients. However, consider additionally how many of the approximately 10 million illegal aliens scattered throughout America are women and, therefore, potential mothers. How many give birth in America? Your guess is as good as mine ... and, for that matter, as good as anyone else's.

How logical does it seem to you that babies should be declared American citizens simply on the basis of having been born in America? Such a strange tradition will not enable many wives of European businessmen to add to America's population. But such enabling does encourage and has encouraged tens of thousands of pregnant women, some wealthy, but most from third-world countries, to cross America's borders at least long enough to give birth and thereby establish an American citizen within their families.

If you wonder whether it is the norm around the world for countries to grant birthright citizenship to babies born on their shores, the answer is: *No,* it is not the norm. America's birthright citizenship tradition is abnormal. For example, Ireland had been the *only* member of the European Union to grant automatic citizenship for babies born in that country. And in the summer of 2004, Irish voters overwhelmingly approved a plan to end that practice.

If that wealthy, pregnant woman's "travel agent" accidentally transported her to any other Asian country to give birth, her son would not become a citizen of the Asian country in which he was born.

In the unlikely event that poor, pregnant Latin American woman asked to be smuggled into any other Central or South American country to give birth, her daughter would not become a citizen of the Central or South American country in which she was born.

And our well-traveled, pregnant European woman could give premature birth in virtually any other country in the world where her businessman husband traveled and there is virtually no chance their premature twins would be declared citizens of whatever country they happened to be visiting when the babies were born.

When will America end its birthright citizenship—a strange tradition which results in thousands of citizenship grants annually to thousands of "anchor babies?"

LOOKING BACK ... AND AHEAD

In this chapter, we have examined some of the governmental enablers of America's addiction to population growth. We discussed several branches of government and several levels of government playing the addiction enabling game—often to the consternation of their constituents—and making mockery of the term "public servants."

In the next chapter, we discuss non-governmental enablers of America's addiction to population growth. If you did not personally know any of the governmental enablers, you can almost bet you *will* personally know some of the non-governmental enablers.

As you read further, remind yourself: *Addictions can be broken! You* can join tens of thousands of others who are working to break America's addiction to population growth!

FOR REFLECTION AND DISCUSSION:

1. What was your reaction when you read that America's population had grown approximately 30% while five presidents studied the situation?
2. Who do you hold more responsible for America's failure to address its population growth addiction, American presidents or American senators and representatives?
3. How do you feel about police chiefs and police commissioners who instruct their personnel not to ask arrested criminals their residency status?
4. How do you feel about state legislators and local politicians who reward illegal aliens with identification documents and with "official" sanctuary?
5. What surprises did you encounter as you read about federal, state, and local governments' relationships to America's population growth?

QUICK FIX #10

Write a short letter to your Representative in the U.S. House of Representatives saying, "I saw your 'report card' at www.*NumbersUSA. com*" and explaining your reaction to what you saw. Appendix C, "Quick Fix References," contains three sample letters designed for three levels of NumbersUSA grades. Please feel free to borrow from the appropriate sample.

Chapter 11

THE ENABLERS

Non-Government

enabler *n.* A person or institution that allows or encourages destructive behavior patterns to continue.

"Man can always be blind to a thing as long as it is big enough."
— G. K. Chesterton

PSYCHOLOGICAL BLINDFOLDS

THE FOLLOWING IS REPRINTED BY permission from *Imprimis,* the national speech digest of Hillsdale College, *(www.hillsdale.edu).* Discussing "What's Wrong with the CIA?" Herbert E. Meyer said, "The analysts responded with the classic CIA reply: 'We have no evidence of that.' They wouldn't concede that it was the *logic* of the situation that comprised the evidence, rather than some purloined document from the safe of Leonid Brezhnev's office. One reason they wouldn't concede the point is that they simply didn't grasp it. Another reason—and I'm dragging my heels as I say this, because it's impressionistic rather than provable, but it simply must be said to understand the problem—that is, *they didn't want to see it."*

Some enablers of America's destructive population growth may not be able to grasp the connection between population growth and its deleterious effects. Others may be able to grasp the connection—but may not want to see it. They are wearing what my friend, Jack Weir, calls psychological blindfolds, obscuring that which is plainly before their eyes.

BLEEDING HEARTS

bleeding heart *n.* A person who is considered excessively sympathetic toward those who claim to be underprivileged or exploited.

Don't get me wrong—some of my best friends are bleeding hearts. When such a friend said the other day, "We can't get along without illegal aliens," I was reminded of that old joke about the little boy at the dinner table who refused to eat his vegetables.

His mother said, "Eat your vegetables, Tommy. In India there are half-a-billion people who would give anything to have your vegetables."

To which Tommy replied, "Name three."

Likewise I wanted to say to my friend, "Please name three illegal aliens America can't get along without."

In a nation of 300 million people, no one is indispensable—whether illegal alien, immigrant, or native-born. Perhaps you wonder if my friend is simply unfamiliar with the laws of economics and the fact that our economy would make adjustments—some of which might be "painful" to my friend and some of which might be "gainful" to her? Is that part of her problem—part of the problem of millions of Americans who have been bombarded with thousands of statements about American industries failing without illegal alien workers? *But America and its economy would survive!*

In her case, I believe the real problem is that she sees so many people standing on corners in our county waiting for offers of work or coming to the thrift store, where she volunteers, to buy secondhand clothing that she begins to believe that she and we—all Americans—have an obligation to make life better for all these people.

I have reminded my friend that there over six billion people in the world and that four or five billion of those people may have a poorer life than the people she is concerned about.

"Shall we invite those other four or five billion to America so we can make their lives better?" I ask her.

"No, we can't do that," she acknowledges.

But somehow, she can't quite get over the feeling that we—we Americans—should do something to help those who have come into our country, even when they have come here illegally. Which means, of course, we should do more to assist those who have *broken* our laws than to assist those who have *not broken* our laws. A strange reward system indeed.

where population is not increasing significantly, but housing prices are increasing dramatically.

Remember "Per Capita!" (There *Will* Be A Test!)

I may be wrong, but my impression is that economists, in general, tend not to think or to communicate in terms of "per capita." For example, they speak of *national* Gross Domestic Product (GDP) rising or falling. When was the last time you heard an economist writing or talking about *per capita* GDP rising or falling? Quite possibly, not in your lifetime. Consequently, when economists report, "GDP rose 2% between January 1 and ..." they don't tell you how much population rose during that same interval and, therefore, that GDP per capita (i.e., per person) may have actually declined.

Intentionally or unintentionally, many economists have become enablers of the population growth addiction. Too often they talk and write about growth—manufacturing and production growth, real estate and development growth, GDP growth—without noting the accompanying population growth which effectively reduces per capita growth. So, whether intentionally or unintentionally, many economists encourage us to enjoy growth for growth's sake without recognizing they may be hooking us on poisonous population growth.

ELITE OPINION MAKERS

The wealthy and the politically powerful—often the same people—are not like you and me. They have more money. They have more political power. They may walk like you and me, but they don't talk like you and me. They talk—among themselves—as if you and I aren't very bright. They talk—among themselves—as if we need the wealthy and the politically powerful to tell us how to live better lives.

Where are the elite opinion makers I refer to? Naturally, you find them in Washington, DC, in New York City, and in Hollywood, California—and, more accurately, throughout America in major metropolises. You find them in the executive suites of most major media and business organizations in America. You find them in the offices of American academia. You find them on the boards of most American charitable foundations.

How can you recognize an elite opinion maker in the unlikely event you should actually get to meet one in person? That's easy! They will tell you what you should do so you will live a better life. For example, complain to elite opinion makers about congested highways and you will be told:

- "You should pay higher taxes on gasoline.
- "You should move to a home close to your job.
- "You should ride a bike to work and to go shopping.
- "You should drive a smaller car that gets 100 mpg.
- "You should move your business to where your workers live.
- "You should … You should … You should …"

We are so fortunate to have such brilliant elite opinion makers who know so well what is best for us!

My local newspaper wrote a lengthy editorial titled, "Risky Population Trend." From the title you might think the editorial theme was, "Too many people." But, no. The actual theme was, "Too many people are ignoring our admonitions about how they should live their lives." (Those are my words, but here are their words; see if I missed their point):

"There are at least a couple of ways to counter this trend. One is to build attractive housing close to job centers and in older cities. The other is to bring more jobs to outlying areas …"

Just think about what they were suggesting:

- Real estate close to job centers is beyond the financial reach of most workers. Do these elite opinion makers propose to tax some workers to subsidize housing for other workers?
- Most workers do not choose to live in older cities. Do these elite opinion makers propose tax-paid subsidies to encourage workers to live where they do not choose to live?
- Employers establish places of employment where they think it is economically advantageous. Do these elite opinion makers propose tax-paid subsidies to make outlying areas more economically advantageous?

Rather than tinker with immutable economic and cultural realities, why don't America's elite opinion makers address the basic problem: Out-of-control population growth? Why? Because addressing America's population growth means, in the current decades, addressing net migration into America. That is not something about which elite opinion makers are comfortable offering opinions.

Journalists

During a TV interview about his book, Bernard Goldberg, author of *Arrogance: Rescuing America From the Media Elite,* said that diversity in journalism is only skin deep. According to Mr. Goldberg, most newsrooms make it a point to have a politically correct diversity of skin colors, genders, ethnic backgrounds, sexual preferences, etc., but have very little diversity in thinking or point of view.

Now, good journalists—and even some not-so-good journalists—can factor this into their reporting. That's nice, but what do journalists do when they don't even understand there are two sides to an issue? Take population growth, for example. What happens when they start from a position of: "America's population has always grown; America's population continues to grow; my bosses like to see America's population grow; America's population growth is good; America's population growth is inevitable!"

Well, if America's population growth is good and is inevitable—and if their bosses like it—there really isn't room for much thought, let alone many stories, about population decline or negative population growth or anything that might restrain population growth such as immigration reductions or efforts to discourage illegal aliens.

John Glennon, opinion page writer for my local newspaper, wrote a major piece titled, "Our Planet Is Overcrowded—Overpopulation of Earth Could Lead to Unprecedented Disaster." Now that sounds serious, doesn't it? In his article Glennon worried that 6.1 billion was double the global population of 1960, but he made no mention of the fact that California's population had more than doubled in that same period.

I couldn't help wondering if the reason Glennon's article talked about what we should do to save the world—but not what to do to save California or America—was because the media giant he worked for receives billions of dollars of advertising revenue from the people who sell the hordes of houses and crush of cars used to illustrate his article? Perhaps journalists will be able to improve their population education track record when "Mother Nature" buys multipage advertising supplements in newspapers.

ENVIRONMENTAL ORGANIZATIONS

Once upon a time, not so many years ago—say in the 1960s and '70s—U.S. environmental organizations considered stabilization of America's population a necessary prerequisite to protecting America's environment. By the late 1990s, environmental organizations and environmental journalists had lost their sense of the obvious: Human population growth inevitably depletes natural resources and diminishes the environment. Roy Beck and Leon Kolankiewicz in *Journal of Policy History* describe "The Environmental Movement's Retreat from Advocating U.S. Population Stabilization."

In 1969, the Sierra Club urged "the people of the United States to abandon population growth as a pattern and goal; to commit themselves to limit the total population of the United States in order to achieve a balance between population and resources; and to achieve a stable population no later than the year 1990."

However, as of this writing, the Sierra Club's website says its position is, "… to protect the global *[not the American]* environment and preserve natural resources for future generations by slowing *[not stopping]* population growth and reducing wasteful consumption."

Why the change? Sierra Club and like-minded environmental organizations like to say, "Overpopulation is a global problem and requires a global solution."

Whenever I read or hear that statement, it immediately suggests to me a gardener refusing to weed his garden until all of his neighbors have adequately weeded their gardens. Apparently, it provides a rationale for not getting dirt under one's fingernails.

Again, according to Beck and Kolankiewicz, "The nation's best-known population group, Zero Population Growth (ZPG)—founded by biologists concerned about the catastrophic impacts of ever more human beings on the biosphere—was outspokenly also an environmental group. However, in the late 1990s, ZPG changed its mission from stopping population growth to 'working to slow population growth.'" Eventually, they also changed their name to the noncommittal Population Connection.

If you would like a carefully documented and well-written explanation of why the environmental movement retreated from its position of advocating U.S. population stabilization to its present "If we save the world, America should be OK" position, the Beck/Kolankiewicz report is must reading. For now it is simply enough to note that instead of using their influence to reduce America's population growth and help preserve America's environment, most American environmental organizations have become enablers of America's population growth addiction.

FOUNDATIONS AND PHILANTHROPISTS

In an October 27, 2004 article in the *Los Angeles Times,* Staff Writer Kenneth R. Weiss wrote about a philanthropist who had apparently given more money to California conservation causes than anyone else—e.g., over $100 million to Sierra Club. One can't help but admire someone who uses his money for the benefit of others—particularly uses it to preserve wilderness and to teach young people about nature.

On the other hand, I had to raise an eyebrow when I read this philanthropist had told Carl Pope, Sierra Club's Executive Director, that he wouldn't give them another dollar, if the Club took an "anti-immigration" position. What do you suppose this gentleman considers an "anti-immigration" position? I can't help wondering if there is a philanthropist somewhere who is concerned about *America's* environment and who recognizes the detrimental effect rampant population growth is having on *America's* environment ... whether that rampant population growth is caused by births or by immigration?

Further, it is my impression that many foundations are managed by, largely staffed by, and often funded by people who are exceptionally sympathetic to other people who are less affluent than, say, middle-class Americans. Good! The world needs people who sympathize with almost everyone. Unfortunately, the "almost everyone" they sympathize with includes an awful lot of people—say *over five billion people*—most of whom do not live in America.

Because most of the foundations I am talking about are located in America and because most of their directors and staffs also live, primarily, in America, they are inclined to believe the world would be a better place if more of those *"over 5 billion people"* lived more like middle-class Americans ... in America! The result is that some organizations, supported by such foundations, feel constrained from addressing America's population growth *when it is caused by migration* of the very people upon whom their supporting foundations have bestowed their sympathy. Let me give you an example:

The goal of *In Growth We Trust,* the Edwin Stennett book mentioned previously, was "... to clearly and forcefully draw out the links between overpopulation and local, community-level problems." He focused on the Washington, DC metro area to illustrate "... how a community's quality of life steadily declines as its population continues to increase."

What's not to like about such a goal and such an understandable approach? The problem—at least from my perspective—is that Stennett noted America's current net inward migration is about one million per year and its total fertility rate is 2.05 children per woman. He suggested that if America were to lower its fertility rate to 1.8 children per woman and maintain it, America could continue to support net inward migration of 1 million per year *and* stabilize its population.

Stennett did point out the U.S. Census Bureau projects an *increasing, not decreasing,* birth rate in America to 2.2, due largely to the higher fertility rate of immigrant women. But, artfully dodging the U.S. Census Bureau's wet blanket, what he is really saying is: If Americans agree to have one million fewer babies per year—1.8 babies per woman per lifetime—America can continue to accept net inward migration of one million people per year and not have a population growth problem.

What Stennett wrote is correct: If Americans have one million fewer births than deaths, then we can have one million more immigrants than emigrants and still stabilize our population. That approach seemed to please Population Connection. As they wrote in their magazine, "We were thrilled to learn about Population Connection member Edwin Stennett's book …" But it doesn't thrill me. It simply provides one more example of how philanthropists and foundations—and the organizations they support—become enablers of America's addiction to population growth by advocating impractical, but politically correct, solutions to America's population growth problem.

IMMIGRATION ATTORNEYS

It seems to me most immigration attorneys earn their livings by helping aliens thwart American immigration laws. Perhaps that is not the way they would put it. They might say, "We help foreign-born people obtain the full benefit of American justice." That's sounds better. Of course, it does nothing to help America reduce its population growth. Please let me know, if you hear of an immigration attorney who, while in the process of helping a foreign-born person "obtain the full benefit of American justice," recommended his client leave America.

In an Associated Press article titled, "Visa cap leaves labor gap," Lisa Gentes writes about the "difficulties" some American businesses were having because they couldn't obtain enough *H-2B* visas entitling *seasonal* employees to work in America for nine months. The article was datelined "RI." Apparently, I'm not familiar with New England seasons. What is their *nine-month* season called?

The same article quotes an immigration attorney as saying it is beyond his imagination as to how to get workers in Florida to take temporary jobs in Colorado. Perhaps Gentes should have asked a businessperson rather than an immigration attorney trained and paid to bring more and more people into America. The response might have been, "Hit the college campuses early in the year, post attractive fliers with beautiful photos of your resorts. Talk about 'Free room and board. Free dances weekly. Free time for fishing, hiking, biking, and …'" Well, you get the idea. An immigration attorney might not have been the best person to ask.

There was one other aspect of this article I can't pass up commenting on. It ended with a paragraph about a seafood business in Alaska wanting to import 22 "temporary" workers from Japan because it was unable to find local workers with "the skills to properly grade" fish. Just think of that! Just think of the thousands of fishing families living in Alaska for centuries! Something smells fishy to me. I want to see my attorney—my immigration attorney!

LABOR UNION LEADERS

Sometimes power is measured in numbers of dollars, sometimes in numbers of constituents and, in the case of labor union leaders, in numbers of constituents and dollars. For decades American labor union leaders looked for additional constituents and dues dollars from the ranks of American workers. In return, American labor unions worked to protect American workers from the wage-reducing influence of low-wage-earning alien workers, particularly illegal alien workers.

Historically, labor union leaders had good reason to lobby for reduced immigration. Cornell economist Vernon M. Briggs, Jr., author of *Immigration and American Unionism,* wrote that, with only two exceptions, when immigration increased, labor union membership dropped. For example, after 1965 while immigrants increased from 8.5 million to 28.4 million (+231%), union membership dropped from 18.2 million to 16.3 million (-10%). Incidentally, the two exceptions to this negative correlation were 1897 to 1905 and 1922 to 1929, the former during a period of economic recovery and rapid industrialization and the latter during a period of assault on unions by business, government, and the courts.

Prior to 1980, labor union leaders supported every legislative action to reduce immigration and to enforce immigration laws. In the late 1980s, union leadership "began to waffle on the issue" and by the 1990s, its position was beginning to change. In February 2000, the Executive Council of AFL-CIO announced it would now support (1) expanded immigration, (2) lenient law enforcement, and (3) legislative agendas of immigrant organizations. AFL-CIO leaders said they were "championing immigrant rights as a strategic move to make immigrants more enthusiastic about joining unions."

At some point, some American labor union leaders appear to have concluded that since America is going to continue to import millions of additional workers from other countries they might just as well try to organize those workers, including illegal aliens, and begin collecting their membership dues. Consequently, those labor union leaders have switched from lobbying Congress for laws to restrict immigration of low-wage workers to lobbying Congress to increase immigration of low-wage workers and for laws to forgive illegal aliens for entering America illegally. What a rude awakening for millions of American workers.

ONE-WORLD WONDERS

I call them "One-World Wonders," because *one wonders* what world they are living in! These are the people who believe America should surrender its sovereignty to various worldwide bureaucracies such as United Nations, World Court, International War Crimes Tribunal, Law of the Sea Treaty, International Conference on Population and Development in Cairo, and so on.

In case you wonder, yes, these are the same people who complain when the result of America surrendering its sovereignty to *some* worldwide bureaucracy produces a different result than the One-World Wonders want. (Think International Monetary Fund, World Bank, and World Trade Organization.)

How do the One-World Wonders become enablers of America's addiction to population growth? Well, basically, they don't really believe in nations and national borders. They have watched too many *Star Trek*® movies and think we have evolved to a point where a universal government should be able to take over the world, if not the universe, and make all the "right" decisions for everybody.

The important point is this: Since One-World Wonders don't believe in nations, they don't believe the residents of one geopolitical entity should be restricted from moving to any other geopolitical entity that they choose to move to, i.e., people all over the world should be free to migrate at will between geopolitical entities.

Since One-World Wonders don't believe in nations or borders, they don't believe in immigration laws and they don't believe there should be limits to the populations of geopolitical entities. Consequently, they don't believe there should be any limit to the population of America. Therefore, they support virtually any and every plan that will enable America's addiction to population growth whether by politicians who vote to subsidize families with more than three children or by organizations lobbying for increasing immigration.

Incidentally, aside from being caring, many religious leaders are susceptible to becoming "One-World Wonders." In the back of many of their minds there is always the belief that "God is *really* in charge of everything everywhere, so what is there for humans to worry about?" Religious leaders who otherwise favor family planning see nothing wrong, let alone irresponsible, about those who encourage more and more aliens—legal and illegal—to migrate to America. Perhaps it is time for all one-world wonders to ask themselves, "Just how many people can America sustain comfortably?"

SMART GROWTH PROMOTERS

Imagine an unimaginably enormous building containing a hospital, schools, stores, and apartments for 1,000 people all of whom work and study in that building. Now, imagine business in the building's stores becomes so good the building's owners add additional floors for residences for an additional 1,000 employees imported from another county or country. With this "smart growth" approach, they have just solved sprawl and environmental degradation problems, haven't they?

Would that it were so! Unfortunately, additional acres would be required somewhere to grow food for the additional residents. Additional water would be required from somewhere. Additional energy would need to be generated somewhere. And, sad to say, additional traffic would be created to transport additional food and supplies for the hospital, schools, and stores for the additional 1,000 residents.

There is another basic problem with smart growth: Most Americans do not want to live the way smart growth promoters propose! Countless surveys demonstrate this, but let me give you a more anecdotal illustration.

Population Connection's magazine, *the reporter,* printed an excerpt from a *New Yorker* article by David Owen. Titled, "Green Manhattan: The Environment Needs More Big Cities," it is Owen's two-page paean to that "smartest" of all smart growth American cities. However, in this piece he writes that when he and his wife had their first child, they moved to a small town in northwestern Connecticut, because they didn't want to raise "... our tiny daughter in a huge city." Welcome to reality, Mr. Owen! *Most* Americans do not want to raise their tiny daughters—or tiny sons—in huge cities.

Once again: *To solve a problem we must first accurately define the problem!* America's problem is not too many cars or too many quarter-acre lots or too many vacant lots. America's problem is too many people. Population growth is the problem. Population growth—smart or not-so-smart—will simply exacerbate that problem! As a letter published in my local newspaper put it:

"There is an 800 pound gorilla on the mountain rolling boulders into our valley, destroying our schools, homes, highways, and quality of life. Instead of organizing villagers to shackle the gorilla, village elders are encouraging villagers to roll the boulders into pretty patterns they call 'smart growth.'

"The 800 pound gorilla is Congress and the boulders are unrestrained population growth.

"Congress can stop subjecting us to one million legal immigrants and one-half million illegal aliens—40% of whom live in California—anytime it wants. In the meantime, Congress and our village elders must accept responsibility for what can only be called 'dumb growth.'"

WHITE FLAG FLYERS

You are likely to hear white flag flyers say, "America's population growth is inevitable! It can't be stopped because we can't stop the poor and oppressed of the world from sneaking into America in search of better lives."

As someone once wrote, "When you hear someone say something is inevitable, you know you are dealing with ideology, not reason."

To take one example: "No matter how many border patrol agents we put on our borders, we can never keep out people who want to get into America."

Well, yes and no. There may always be ways for some aliens to get into America if they really want to, but that doesn't mean border enforcement is a failure. Just as important as border patrolling is interior enforcement, e.g., *prosecuting employers of illegal aliens.* Common sense tells us fewer illegal aliens will want to enter America, if they find they have no paying jobs when they arrive.

Border enforcement and interior enforcement are equally important— and America has not exercised *both simultaneously* for many years.

Speaking of exercise: Border enforcement without interior enforcement is similar to a person trying to improve his physique by dieting, but without exercising, or by exercising but continuing to eat excessive amounts of food. We know neither approach is likely to work. Nevertheless, all the white flag flyers tell us we can't enforce border security, but neglect to tell us that *some of the most important "border enforcement" work is not done at the borders.*

The white flag flyers want us to believe we should eliminate logical immigration laws, because *enforcing* them is impossible. As Heather Mac Donald wrote:

"Advocates for amnesty argue that it *[amnesty]* is the only solution to the illegal alien crisis, because enforcement clearly has not worked. They are wrong in their key assumption: Enforcement has never been tried. Amnesty, however, *has* been tried—in both an industrial-strength version in 1986, and in more limited doses ever since—and it was a clear failure. Before we proceed again to the ultimate suspension of the nation's self-definition, it is long past time to make immigration law a reality, not a charade."

LOOKING BACK ... AND AHEAD

In this chapter, we have examined some of the non-governmental enablers of America's addiction to population growth. We considered how some of these individuals and organizations may be handicapped by psychological blindfolds as well as other reasons why some may have become enablers.

In the next chapter, we will discuss what needs to be done to help America recover from its addiction to population growth and what *you* can do to support that recovery. You will have an opportunity to practice *thinking like a populationist.*

As you read the next two chapters I hope you will conclude: *"Addictions can be broken! I* will join tens of thousands of others who are working to break America's addiction to population growth!"

FOR REFLECTION AND DISCUSSION:

1. What experience have you had with people wearing psychological blindfolds regarding population growth?
2. Under what circumstances do you think you might qualify for the dictionary's definition of bleeding heart, i.e., "A person who is considered excessively sympathetic toward those who claim to be underprivileged or exploited?"

3. What is your reaction to environmental organizations which express concern for America's dwindling wild lands and wildlife, but refuse to express concern for America's population growth?
4. How many societal and environmental problems exacerbated by population growth can you think of which are not mitigated by smart growth?
5. Why do you think so many politicians and elite opinion makers insist on saying nothing can be done to stop America's population growth?

QUICK FIX #11

Visit or ask a friend to visit *www.NumbersUSA.com* and click on "Report Cards" to look for one of your U.S. Senator's population growth "grade." Then record the date and the "grade" in Appendix C, "Quick Fix References."

Chapter 12

TREATMENT AND WITHDRAWAL

Contribute Your Thinking

treatment *n.* Administration or application of remedies to a patient.

withdrawal *n.* 1. Discontinuation of the use of an addictive substance. 2. The physiological and mental readjustment that accompanies such discontinuation.

"Destiny is not a matter of chance; it is a matter of choice. It is not a thing to be waited for; it is a thing to be achieved." —William Jennings Bryan

A POPULATION GROWTH REFRESHER COURSE

HOPEFULLY, AS YOU HAVE READ *The Population Fix* you have thought about what you have read and, perhaps, you have thought about how many people *you* would like to see in America seven generations from now. If you haven't done so already, perhaps you now can begin training to *think like a populationist.* It takes little time and only a little practice. I'll give you a practice exercise below. But first, let's review the causes of population growth discussed in Chapter 2, "An Overview" and Chapter 3, "The Addiction" to ensure we are all singing off the same sheet of music.

Worldwide, two factors determine population change—births and deaths. If births exceed deaths, population increases. Therefore, world population can only be reduced (a) by reducing births (i.e., reducing fertility rates) or (b) by increasing deaths (i.e., reducing life spans).

In a geographic entity such as America, three factors determine population change—births, deaths, and net migration (immigration minus emigration). If births exceed deaths and immigration exceeds emigration, America's population will increase. Therefore, America's population can only be reduced by (a) reducing births, (b) reducing immigration, (c) increasing deaths, or (d) increasing emigration.

Today, the primary cause of America's population growth is the amount by which immigration exceeds emigration. Once we have an Administration and a Congress which have kicked the population growth habit, they can address both relatively easily by reducing immigration levels through changes in immigration laws and by encouraging aliens illegally in America to emigrate back to their homelands through workplace law enforcement.

However, the secondary cause of America's population growth is the higher-than-replacement fertility rates of certain categories of residents. Some can be categorized by religion, some by ethnicity, and some by culture. One example:

According to Lee Green writing in *Los Angeles Times Magazine*, excluding Latinos, the birthrate for other Californians, both American citizens and legal immigrants, is essentially 2.0. However, the birthrate for women from Mexico and Central America is "more than three children per mother."

"More than three children per mother!" Do you remember from Chapter 7, "Rehabilitation," how a couple with two children and an Adjusted Gross Income (AGI) of $44,000 paid federal income tax of $574 while a couple with the same AGI and four children paid no federal income tax and instead *received a $2,356 check* from Uncle Sam?

Congress can certainly revise tax law to eliminate tax subsidization of families with four or more children by taxpayers with three or fewer children. Meanwhile, nonprofit family planning organizations can continue their education and resource efforts to enable all who want to, to be able to plan family size.

THREE POSSIBILITIES, FOUR POSITIONS

Before proceeding let's consider the only three possibilities for America's population: (1) It can increase, (2) it can stabilize, or (3) it can decrease. Therefore, it seems to me there are only four positions an American can have regarding America's population: (1) To want it to increase, (2) to want it to stabilize, (3) to want it to decrease, or (4) to have no position.

In America, of course, the last position—no position—is actually one of condemning future generations of Americans to population increase. Remember, 99 of the past 100 years have seen America's popu-

lation increase. Therefore, unless you want to condemn future generations of Americans to a population of *one billion,* you have a duty to take
a position and express your position to those who are in a position to do
something about changing the direction of America's population.

"WHAT SHOULD I DO?"

I'll return to that question shortly, but first I want to acknowledge you
have done something useful already simply by reading *The Population
Fix.* If you have read this book and if you have reflected on what you
have read, you are well on your way to being part of an influential group
of Americans who *think like populationists!*

Like all thinking Americans you have many other commitments
in your life—commitments to others and commitments to yourself.
Consequently, I want to answer the "What should I do?" question in a
way that will permit you to also consider your other commitments. To do
so, my answers are arranged from the least time-consuming to the most
time-consuming. For that purpose answers are organized according to
potential contributions (1) of thinking, (2) of time, (3) of money, and
(4) of additional energy. The first, contribute thought, will be discussed
in the remainder of this chapter. The remaining three, contribute time,
money, and additional energy, will be discussed in the next chapter.

CONTRIBUTE YOUR THINKING

*If you do no more than read this book and continue to think carefully
about what you have read, you will have taken a first step toward breaking America's addiction to population growth.* Think about what you have
learned. Think about unanswered questions. Think about points with
which you disagree. Visit *www.ThinkPopulation.org,* if you have time,
and let me know your thoughts. Even if you don't have time for that, I
trust you will look at America's—and the world's—problems differently
and listen to politicians' and other leaders' "solutions" differently than
you did before.

Decide "How Many Are Enough?"

The first—and in my opinion, *the most important thing you can do*—is
to answer for yourself the question asked at the beginning of this book:
"How many people are enough?" How many people would *you* like to
see in America two, three, four—or as some American Indians might
say—seven generations from now? If your answer is, "About one billion,
more or less," then the answer to the "What should I do?" question is,

"Do nothing." If you do nothing, in a few generations America's addiction to population growth will almost certainly take its population to one billion—more or less.

"Ed, do you *really* think America's population could reach one billion in seven generations?"

Yes, I really do. Let me show you why I do.

Let's assume a generation is 30 years, i.e., a newborn baby becomes a parent in approximately 30 years. We learned in Chapter 3, "The Addiction," that America adds 3.3 million to its population each year. Seven generations equals 210 years (30 years x 7 generations). Two hundred-ten years times 3.3 million added per year equals 693 million Americans added in seven generations. Add 693 million to today's 300 million and you get 993 million Americans seven generations from now. Not quite one billion, but close enough for our purposes, wouldn't you say?

"But seven generations … that's a l-o-n-g time, isn't it?"

Perhaps. But consider a person's parents, grandparents, and great-grandparents and that person's children, grandchildren, and great-grandchildren. Three generations of ancestors, three generations of descendants, plus that person equals seven generations. Perhaps that is why some American Indian tribes think in terms of seven generations.

So, please think about it. How many Americans would *you* like to have living in America? One-quarter billion? One-half billion? One billion? More? As I said before, there is no right answer. Every reader—every politician—every American—is entitled to his or her own answer. In my view, *the only wrong answer is to have no answer!* I believe it is an incomplete and unsatisfactory answer to say, "I support tax and welfare subsidies for families of four or more children" and/or "I support increasing immigration," but not be willing to complete the sentence, "*because I believe an America of one billion or more residents is a worthy goal!*"

There Is No Right Answer

Let me tell you a couple of stories which I believe will illustrate my point about there being no right answer to the "How many are enough?" question. When I reported to my detachment in Inchon, South Korea, I replaced a Special Agent named Logan. He was what I called "a New Yorker's New Yorker." I liked to say he was born in a high-rise hospital, raised in high-rise apartments, educated in high-rise schools, married in a high-rise chapel, employed in high-rise offices, resided in a high-rise

condominium, and someday would be inurned in a high-rise colum-
barium. I don't know how much of it was true, but I liked to say it.

Now, let me tell you about a trout fishing trip my wife and I took
with my wife's cousin, "Bud." He wanted us to see his favorite trout fishing stream before we had to return to California from Colorado. We
left his cabin at about 8,500′ and *climbed from there!* First we drove to
the end of the pavement, then to the end of the gravel, then to the end
of the dirt, then to the end of two ruts. Then, we parked … and started
hiking.

We hiked through a forest unlike any I had ever seen with half the
trees downed and lying in our path. I don't know how long we climbed
and clambered over fallen trees but I do know that by the time we finished climbing and clambering, the parts of our legs that weren't black
and blue … were bloody!

Suddenly, we broke out of the forest into the most spectacular high
mountain meadow I had *ever* seen! It was many miles across with beautiful peaks on all sides and an *amazing* trout stream meandering from
one end to the other.

Across the meadow, *far* in the distance, we could see a couple of
specks. We city folks couldn't make out what they were, but with his
outdoorsman's eyes "Bud" studied the specks for awhile then declared,
"They're fishermen." He studied the specks a half-minute longer then
turned to us and said apologetically, "It's usually not this crowded."

My point in telling you about Logan and "Bud" is so you can sense
how different people might have different perspectives about how many
residents America should have. I suspect "Bud's" number would be much
smaller than Logan's, while your number may fall somewhere between
the two. I also suspect numbers provided by people who immigrated
into America from Bombay, Calcutta, Hong Kong, Mexico City, and
Singapore would be larger than the numbers provided by people who
immigrated into America from Mongolia or Patagonia. But I could be
wrong …

The important thing is that *you* think about how many people—
and people-exacerbated problems—you think future generations of
Americans should have to deal with.

"What Is Ed's Answer?"

Perhaps you are wondering, "What is Ed's answer? He must have given
it a lot of thought. How many does he think is enough?"

Since you asked, I will give you my answer, not expecting it to be your answer or anybody else's answer, for that matter. But first, let me say a few words about some experts' answers to that question.

I would say people who approach the question from an environmental perspective (e.g., saving wilderness and wildlife) and those who approach the question from an economic perspective (e.g., depleting natural resources, water, farmland) tend to arrive at numbers between 100 million and 200 million. Writing in 2004, Lindsey Grant guessed fellow writers concerned with optimum population would support an American population of approximately 150 million, i.e., America's 1950 population. I am sympathetic to such numbers, but ...

Frankly, I would be satisfied—indeed, I would be delighted—if our politicians and the power-elite would establish an American population goal of 250 million—one-quarter billion. How did I arrive at that number? To begin with, I think it may be doable. It would still take many decades to achieve and the population situation would continue to get worse before it began to get better no matter what we did. But I believe one-quarter billion is an achievable long-term goal.

Second, it was the approximate population of America in 1990, the end of the last decade before we drifted, rudderless, into decades of *more than 30 million residents added every ten years.*

Finally, as you know by now, I like to keep numbers simple, if practicable. One-quarter billion is a nice, simple number to remember and, in case anyone cares, at 250 million, America would likely be the fourth most populous nation in the world.

What Is *Your* Answer?

I don't believe I can emphasize this too much: *It is critically important that you come up with your own number!* Why? Because unless you can say to others, "I think an America of *(insert your number)* million people is a reasonable population goal," it seems to me it is difficult, if not impossible, for you to criticize actions of others who are contributing to America's population growth addiction. If you have no number *you* have determined to be your environmental and cultural carrying capacity for America, then you cannot logically criticize any number, including undefined, unspoken, and unknown numbers.

Garrett Hardin, bioethicist and Professor of Human Ecology wrote, "Carrying capacity is inversely related to quality of life. When dealing with human beings, there is no unique figure for carrying capacity. So when a pronatalist asserts (Revelle, 1974) that the world can easily support 40 to 50 billion people—some many times the present population—he need not be contradicted. If everyone lived on the energy budget of the Ethiopians, the earth might support 60 times the present population, or about 300 billion people." Only by having a self-drawn bulls-eye to aim for, will you know whether America is moving toward your target or moving toward an Ethiopian standard of living.

Remember, you need not make a research project out of deciding how many you think are enough nor need you cast your first answer in stone never to be revised. You know now that America's population is approximately 300 million, that America is the third most populous nation in the world, and that, as it adds approximately 3.3 million people per year, it has the fastest growing population of any developed nation in the world.

If you do not already know the population of your state, simply by keeping your eyes and ears open, you will soon learn what it is. As you increasingly *think like a populationist,* you will begin to recognize dozens of problems—nationally and in your state—which have been exacerbated by America's addiction to population growth and you will begin to draw your own conclusions about America's environmental and cultural carrying capacity by calibrating from today's population of approximately 300 million.

Think Like A Populationist

"OK, Ed," you might say, "now that I understand the causes of population growth and now that I know something about the producers, pushers, enablers, and especially about the addicts and victims of America's addiction to population growth, how do I *think like a populationist?*"

It's easy. *Think population!* That's it. That's all there is to it. Every time you hear about, read about, or think about a world, national, regional, state, or local problem, *think population!* Think, *"Will this problem be easier to mitigate or more difficult to mitigate if population continues to grow?"*

Sounds easy? You can do it, right? Then, let's try a little practice session.

Let's Try A Particularly Peculiar Problem

Not so long ago, there was a fellow who wanted permission to float blimp-like rubber containers filled with Northern California water down the California coast to alleviate Southern California's water shortage. Really, I'm not making this up!

Wow, that sounds costly and complicated, doesn't it? This fellow would have to get permission to take water from a couple of Northern California rivers—permission that would require many months, if not years, of court battles and financial negotiations with Northern Californians who really don't want to give up their water.

This fellow would have to design and construct these enormous containers to hold enormous amounts of water.

This fellow would have to obtain coastal authority permission to build loading and unloading facilities in Northern and Southern California to take on and to off-load these enormous amounts of water.

This fellow would have to build and/or hire oceangoing tugboats capable of moving these enormous containers of water along the coast.

This fellow would have to find water authorities in Southern California willing to pay enormous amounts for his Northern California water.

Is this an impractical idea or what?

How might a populationist look at this story? Rather than getting tangled up in the legal and logistic complications, a populationist might say, "More impractical than this idea are the politicians who allowed tens of millions of people to *inhabit* a semiarid part of Western America."

Without being distracted by all the ins and outs and controversies of this fantastic scheme and its endless court battles, a populationist would ask, "Will this water shortage problem be easier to mitigate or more difficult to mitigate if population continues to grow in Southern California?"

Obviously, it will be more difficult to mitigate.

Would this fellow be dreaming his dream and scheming his scheme, if population had stopped growing in Southern California?

Probably not.

So, perhaps the solution resides in considering what we might do to discontinue the continuing population increase in Southern California rather than worrying about or debating this fellow's idea.

Does that make sense?

Perhaps you say, "It makes sense, Ed, but we can't stop population growth in Southern California, can we?"

Actually, yes, we can. As a matter of fact, without immigration and births to immigrants, California's current population would be decreasing, not increasing! *More native-born Americans are moving out of California to other states than are moving into California from other states*—and Congress, not chance, determines how many immigrants come into America and California.

The Test I Warned You About

Do you remember in Chapter 11, "The Enablers," I wrote, "I may be wrong, but my impression is that economists, in general, tend not to think or to communicate in terms of 'per capita?'" Here is your chance to "remember 'per capita'" and to *think like a populationist*.

Here is an example taken from a speech given by an economist: "Controlling for inflation, household assets rose from $6 trillion to $41 trillion between 1945 and 1998."

I am sure we could easily find dozens of similar statements about scores of different economic measurements from hundreds of different economists—and they would all be overlooking a basic populationist concern. Now that you are *thinking like a populationist,* what is that overlooked concern?

Right! This economist controlled for inflation, but not for *population growth!*

So, how does our legitimate concern affect this economist's statement? Well, if we take his statement at face value, we might say, "Hmm. Household assets grew nearly seven times between 1945 and 1998." ($41 trillion divided by $6 trillion = 6.83.)

However, *thinking like populationists* we might ask, "How much did population grow between 1945 and 1998? Oh, it grew from 140 million to 270 million. That means *per capita* household assets were worth $43,000 in 1945 ($6 trillion divided by 140 million people) and *per capita* household assets were worth $152,000 in 1998 ($41 trillion divided by 270 million people). Hmm. *Per capita* household assets grew from $43,000 to $152,000 or only 3.5 times ($152,000 divided by $43,000). That's good, but not as good as the good professor might have led us to believe."

And good for you, if you have learned to remember *"per capita"* and to think about the effect of population growth when you hear or read economists, politicians, and news pundits speaking or writing about "growth" of one kind or another.

In the next chapter, I'll tell you more about action you can take to ensure Congress understands your concern with the problems created by America's addiction to population growth. But, for the moment, the issue isn't how to solve America's problems. The issue is how to identify the overriding and omnipresent problem of population growth—how to *think like a populationist.*

Just as doctors may not be able to cure certain kinds of cancers, they still want to know when their patients have cancer and what kinds of cancer they have so they can do as much as is medically practicable to help their patients. In other words, even if we might not do anything to reduce population or population growth in a particular situation, we still want to know whether or not population growth is exacerbating a problem.

Watch And Listen For Media Bias Favoring Population Growth

Here are examples of the kind of bias you will undoubtedly find:

Remember in Chapter 2, "The Overview," we talked about the fallacious argument that population growth is getting smaller in percentage terms and I used the analogy of trying to pour eleven gallons of gasoline into a ten gallon container? Another example: A newspaper wrote that according to census figures, the population growth rate (percentage increase) for the 1990s was the slowest of any single decade.

To illustrate just how meaningless that kind of statement is, let me give you some facts and figures about America's population growth: Between 1900 and 1910, America's population grew 21%, whereas between 1990 and 2000, America's population grew only 13%.

"Well, Ed, doesn't that demonstrate that America's population growth has slowed down considerably between the beginning and the end of the 20th century?"

Unfortunately, no it doesn't. Because between 1900 and 1910, America's population grew by 16 million whereas between 1990 and 2000, it grew 33 million, i.e., more than twice as much! As you now understand, it is *the number of people for each square mile or for each acre in America* that determines how few acres are available to support each American. Thirty-three million more people on the same number of acres may very well mean each acre will be asked to do more than it is capable of doing.

Here is another example: In a 2004 *USA TODAY* report by Barbara Hagenbaugh headlined, "Slower population growth could have dual impact," she reported, "… population will rise 49% by 2050." She then went on to write that number was "… down from an 87% gain" for the 50 years prior.

Unfortunately, when it comes to providing acres to support people, the "87%" represents a growth of just under 130 million people, while the "slower 49%" represents almost 140 million people! The moral: When somebody talks about population growth in terms of percentages, try to determine (a) whether or not they understand the issue, (b) whether or not they have a population growth bias, or (c) both. If you have time, drop them notes, write letters to editors, or make telephone calls and ask which it is!

Encourage Friends And Acquaintances To Think Like Populationists

You might begin by giving or loaning a thinking friend or acquaintance a copy of *The Population Fix*. Whether you buy your friend or acquaintance another copy of *The Population Fix* or simply let them borrow this copy, the result will be the same from my standpoint. The more people you and I can encourage to read this book and to begin *thinking like populationists,* the more likely it is future generations of Americans will live in an America which has not been destroyed by population growth.

Here is another action you can take which will take only a little time and money: Invite potential populationists to lunch—or to breakfast or to dinner. What do potential populationists look like? Probably about the same as people who have little potential for becoming populationists. What sets them apart is their ability to think logically, to ask themselves challenging questions, and to arrive at answers which may not be politically correct nor personally convenient.

Do you know some such people? Probably. If so, get together— one-on-one or one-on-two—in an informal setting and let them know what you have been reading about and thinking about. Judge their reactions and see if they might be candidates for reading a copy—used or new—of *The Population Fix.*

Even in less planned settings, let others know what you have been reading about and what you have been thinking about. In such settings you will discover—as I have—many others who share your concerns about America's addiction to population growth, but who have been persuaded by addicts, producers, pushers, and enablers that there is nothing to be done about it. Let them know you believe that message is self-serving, defeatist propaganda delivered by addicts, producers, pushers, and enablers for their own economic and political power benefit. Perhaps they should read a copy of … Well, you know.

When you encounter people who appear hostile to your populationist perspective, offer them Professor Bartlett's challenge. You remember it was posed in Chapter 1, "The Populationists":

"Can you think of any problem on any scale, from microscopic to global, whose long-term solution is in any way aided, assisted, or advanced by having larger populations at the local level, state level, nationally, or globally? Can you think of anything that will get better, if we crowd more people into our towns, cities, states, nations, or world?"

Encourage people, whether hostile or supportive of your populationist perspective, to accept Professor Bartlett's challenge and try to answer his questions. It should lead to some interesting conversations!

The point is, you understand the births-minus-deaths and immigration-minus-emigration equations. You understand birthrates and fertility rates are just fancy ways of talking about births, that life spans and mortality rates are not-so-fancy ways of talking about deaths, and that net migration to America is simply the number of immigrants minus the number of emigrants. Share your understanding with others. It takes little time and you may be surprised at how surprised others are that you understand and that you have made it so easy for them to understand as well.

Ask Others: "How Many Are Enough?"

At the beginning of this book I asked you, "How many are enough?" Now, each time a friend or acquaintance—or perhaps someone you have just met—advocates an action which, as a thinking populationist, you know *encourages population growth* in America, ask that person, "How many people do you think America should have?"

They will probably answer, "I don't know," or "I haven't really thought about it," or "That's not the issue."

Go right after them: "Yes, that is the issue! You are proposing to increase America's population. You are proposing to push America's addiction to population growth. Therefore, I would like to know at what point in America's population growth you will concede enough is enough—for you and for future generations. In other words, how many people do you think America should have? Unless you have an answer to that question, I challenge your right to condemn future Americans to crowded lives of diminished quality!"

By getting *just one more person*—a friend or an acquaintance—to begin thinking about America's addiction to population growth, you will have made a significant contribution toward America's withdrawal and recovery.

LOOKING BACK ... AND AHEAD

In this chapter, we have examined how *you* begin the addiction treatment and withdrawal process simply by *thinking like a populationist* at every opportunity and then by encouraging friends and acquaintances to *think like populationists*. Begin by training yourself to always ask the basic populationist question: *"Will this problem be easier to mitigate or more difficult to mitigate if population continues to grow?"* and you will soon be asking others the same question. They in turn will begin asking themselves and then others. And the treatment and withdrawal process will have begun.

In the next chapter, I will outline additional steps you can take, besides *thinking like a populationist*, to treat and cure America's addiction to population growth.

As you read further, remind yourself: *Addictions can be broken! You* can join tens of thousands of others who are working to break America's addiction to population growth!

FOR REFLECTION AND DISCUSSION:

1. How comfortable are you with the idea of explaining to others the two factors which determine whether or not world population grows and the three factors which determine whether or not a nation's population grows?
2. How will you go about selecting your own number for America's long-term population target?
3. What local or state problems can you think of which you believe should be addressed from a populationist's perspective, but seldom are?
4. What national problems can you think of which should be addressed from a populationist's perspective, but seldom are?
5. How might younger people, who may not have seen the effects of many years of population growth, nevertheless be encouraged to consider its long-term ramifications?

QUICK FIX #12

Write a short letter to your first U.S. Senator saying, "I saw your 'report card' at www.*NumbersUSA.com*" and explaining your reaction to what you saw. Appendix C, "Quick Fix References," contains three sample letters designed for three levels of NumbersUSA grades. Please feel free to borrow from the appropriate sample.

Chapter 13

TREATMENT AND WITHDRAWAL

Contribute Time, Money, And/Or Energy

"The only thing necessary for the triumph of evil is for good men to do nothing." —Edmund Burke

NOW THAT YOU HAVE HAD time to think about thinking like a populationist, *let's consider how you can translate your populationist thinking into action.*

CONTRIBUTE YOUR TIME

When politicians, federal, state, or local, advocate actions which you know will result in population increases, call or write and ask them to tell you how many *they* think are enough—enough people in America, in your state, or in your local political entity. They will twist and turn like Harry Houdini to avoid giving you an answer, but keep after them. For example, you might write:

"I see by your voting record you believe America and *(insert the name of your own state, county, city, or town)* should have more people. Personally, I believe *(insert your number)* million people would be a sustainable population for America and *(insert your number)* people would be a rational population for *(insert the name of your own state, county, city, or town)*. But since you obviously believe that America should have more than its present 300 million people and that *(insert the name of your own state, county, city, or town)* should have more than its present population, you must have some objective targets in mind. So, please, tell me, what are *your* targets for America's and *(insert the name of your own state, county, city, or town)* populations?"

What are the chances that you will get firm numbers in reply? What are the chances you could fly, if you just flapped your arms fast enough? That's OK! The politician you wrote to now knows there is *another* populationist out there watching and recording. At some point that politician will realize there are more of you than previously recognized.

Also, your local newspaper may be happy to print a letter from you saying, "Here is a letter I sent to … *(Then, insert your letter to the politician.)* Unfortunately, *(name of politician)* was unable to provide me with an answer regarding an ultimate population for America and for *(insert the name of your own state, county, city, or town)*."

Remember this, even letters to editors which do not get printed or calls to radio and television stations which do not get read over the air have an effect! Print editors and program producers are made aware that people are reading, listening, and watching carefully. They understand that for every reader, listener, and viewer who takes time to write or call, there are many more who observed the same non-journalistic bias, but didn't take time to write or to call. Since most media outlets want the public to trust their objectivity, your letters and calls *will* affect future reporting.

Cancel Subscriptions And Tell Why

Remember, media owners and executives are population growth addicts. Columnists and journalists are, for the most part, population growth pushers and enablers. How much moral and financial support do you want to commit to people and corporations who are motivated to increase their numbers of readers at the expense of overcrowding America?

I'm not saying you shouldn't read newspapers and magazines. I'm just saying, don't make it easy for them to lock you into *their* population growth fix by getting you hooked with subscriptions. Pick up occasional magazines and newspapers. You may find you can live without having every issue of the magazines and newspapers you cancel. Also, you may want to try some different publications, possibly finding some less inclined to disparage your populationist viewpoint.

Have I practiced what I'm preaching? Yes. My wife and I canceled our subscription to our local newspaper and now pick it up three days a week at a newsstand. Perhaps a better example:

Some years ago I canceled my subscription to a major newspaper. I had begun reading that newspaper when I was an undergraduate student in college oh-so-many years ago. I became hooked. Or as a friend once said—when he traveled to places where that newspaper was not available, he wondered if the world still existed, because he couldn't read about it in that prestigious newspaper. I understood his feeling. Nevertheless, I broke my habit and went straight—"cold turkey."

What finally induced me to break the habit? Quite simply, I came to believe this widely acclaimed newspaper allowed its open borders policy to influence its reporters, columnists, and editors. For example, it published an editorial which, it seemed to me, misrepresented a particular Congressman's position on an immigration issue.

When I read it I assumed editors wouldn't have printed it, if they didn't know it to be correct. But, because their editorial didn't match what I *thought* I knew about the Congressman's position, I called his office and asked if I had misunderstood the Congressman's position. His office staffer said, "No. The editorial was wrong," but also said it took a lot of editorial misrepresentation to get their boss's dander up. A few days later another misrepresenting editorial was published which apparently *did* get his dander up and the next thing I saw was a letter from the Congressman correcting them!

Later, another reader's letter was printed in which he decried the fact that the newspaper had described him as an anti-immigration activist even though he wrote that he had never said a word about immigration. He expressed hope that this newspaper's support for open borders was founded upon more research than its reference to him.

Lastly, after many years of periodically responding to editorials, opinion pieces, and reports which supported this newspaper's open borders policy, one of my letters was finally published—but with a key phrase deleted and my address shown as New York, even though my letter was submitted on my California letterhead!

Anyway, goodbye lifetime subscription. And when they called to ask why, I gave them the examples you have just read. Do they care? I suspect they do, even though it is only one lost subscription out of millions. As every marketing professional will tell you, it costs many times more to obtain a new customer than it does to retain an old customer. And word-of-mouth from satisfied customers is still a marketer's best friend.

Thus, when you cancel your subscription to addict, pusher, and enabler publications, *you should let them know* you are tired of their consistent beating of drums in support of America's addiction to population growth. With some publications, you will receive a telephone call asking why you canceled your subscription. Tell the caller. But don't stop there! Write a short letter or email to the editor or publisher explaining your reason. You can cite an example, if you choose. But it isn't necessary. Publishers know about their addiction. You are simply reminding them you also know!

CONTRIBUTE YOUR MONEY

Contribute Money To Populationist Organizations

As you read in Chapter 3, "The Addiction," America's present population growth is caused by two factors: (1) a high rate of net migration (immigration exceeding emigration) into America and (2) higher-than-replacement fertility rates among certain groups, e.g., adherents of some religions as well as some groups of legal immigrants and illegal aliens. There are several national organizations which address the first cause and one major national organization which addresses the second cause.

In Appendix B you will find my descriptions of some of these organizations. Ultimately, I recommend you contact those organizations whose interests appear to match your own and decide for yourself which are the "best fit." Each of the organizations described in Appendix B can be reached via *www.ThinkPopulation.org*. There you will also see what rating, if any, each organization has been given by Better Business Bureau's Wise Giving Alliance. Each organization's Internet website will tell you how you can provide financial, volunteer, and/or moral support.

Contribute Money To Populationist Environmental Organizations

There are four major national environmental organizations which exhibit an interest in population issues and which I believe may merit support from populationists: Izaak Walton League of *America* (IWLA), *National* Audubon Society (NAS), *National* Wildlife Federation (NWF), and *Sierra* Club (SC). These are the four organizations which have separate staffs to address the issue of environmental degradation caused by rampant human population growth. Each manifests its particular concern for the environmental impact of population growth in its own particular way. For a more detailed look at each organization's approach, visit *www.ThinkPopulation.org*, click on "Think Environment," and then click on "Think Population-Environment Scorecard."

In the previous paragraph, in the names of these four organizations, I italicized words which suggest why I think they should share my position as stated at our website: "We are not concerned about population growth in America *only*, but we are concerned about population growth in America *especially*." Izaak Walton League of *America* clearly should be concerned about *America*. I'm sure the nation referred to by the *National* in *National* Audubon Society and *National* Wildlife Federation is America. And, in case there is any confusion, the mountain range referred to in *Sierra* Club is Sierra Nevada, not Sierra Madre.

Unfortunately, of these four organizations, only IWLA has distributed information about that part of America's addiction to population growth which is fed by net migration from other nations. Fortunately, members of all four organizations are not so restricted and it is not unusual to see letters from members printed in those organizations' publications expressing concern about net migration into America and occasionally chastising an organization's hierarchy for not including this subject within policy considerations.

If you have not contributed to one of these four organizations in the past, you might consider doing so in the future. At the same time, as you become familiar with limitations to an environmental organization's policies and activities regarding America's population growth, write to their publication's editor and/or to their Executive Director and say that you are disappointed the organization does not take a stand on America's addiction to population growth, which includes net migration as well as fertility rates.

In addition, should you decide to reconsider the size of future support of environmental organizations which make little or no effort to address the effect of human population growth on the environment, drop a note to the Executive Director or other executive briefly explaining why you are doing so.

I do want to mention two worthy organizations which do not score well on the "Think Population-Environment Scorecard" because their missions are somewhat different than those of the organizations which do score well on the Scorecard. One is The Nature Conservancy (TNC) which is primarily focused on engaging in real estate transactions to protect land—often land in the path of human population growth. The second is World Wildlife Fund (WWF) which is primarily driven by international environmental concerns rather than domestic concerns. While the work of these two organizations is not well reflected in the criteria of the Scorecard, their publications occasionally remind readers of the environmental cost of rampant human population growth wherever it occurs, whether in America or internationally.

CONTRIBUTE YOUR ENERGY

Contribute Your Energy To Populationist Organizations

If you simply *think like a populationist* and encourage others to *think like populationists,* you will have done a good deal to break America's addiction to population growth. If you are able to contribute money to some of the organizations listed in Appendix B, you will have done still more in that endeavor. If you are also able to contribute time to that mission, you will begin to see immediate feedback and payoff for your efforts.

Several populationist organizations make it quite easy for you to communicate with politicians and media editors regarding your concern about America's addiction to population growth. In addition, several of these organizations provide opportunities for you to meet other populationists and participate in grassroots political activities. You will generally find meeting other populationists and participating in group activities will "recharge your batteries" and provide you with fresh inspiration to work even harder on behalf of Americans yet unborn. Read about these organization in Appendix B. Then, visit *www. ThinkPopulation.org* to learn more about each organization. Finally, link from there to visit the home pages of those populationist organizations which particularly interest you.

Hire Legal Workers—And Their Employers

If you interview potential baby-sitters and gardeners, you can hopefully make enough conversation to extract a sound basis for deciding the legality or illegality of someone you propose to hire. If the candidate for work doesn't speak English well enough for you to make such a judgment, he or she probably doesn't speak English well enough to do the job you have in mind.

What do you do when you hire a contractor? How do you know whether the contractor's employees are American citizens, legal immigrants, or illegal aliens? You probably don't. However, at the time you are negotiating or describing your job to the contractor or the contractor's English-speaking representative, make it clear: You do not want illegal aliens on your property and you want to be able to converse with workers in English. If either of those requirements presents a problem for the contractor, you should probably look for another contractor.

What do you say if your contractor says, "I can meet your requirements for an all-legal crew that speaks English, but frankly, it will cost another $1,000 since I can't pay them in cash and will have to pay payroll withholding taxes?"

You say what your conscience tells you to say. But remember, if you want to cure America's addiction to population growth, you don't want to become an addict yourself.

Fire Illegal Workers—And Their Employers

Let businesses know your decision to do business with them may be affected if they hire illegal aliens rather than American citizens and legal immigrants. The business may be no larger than a local restaurant hiring busboys and dishwashers, or as large as Wal-Mart or Tyson Foods. There is no need to threaten to take business away nor to disparage products or services. Simply advise them with a telephone call that you are concerned about America's present unsustainable population growth and that you cannot support any activities designed to further that population growth.

If you learn—legally—that someone you have hired—legally—has broken immigration law and is in America illegally, fire them—legally. Did I emphasize "legally" too much? Probably not. Congress has gone out of its way to make it difficult for employers to know what questions they may and may not ask of people they hire and justifications they may and may not use regarding the firing of people they hire. For larger employers, Congress talks about creating a system using Social Security Numbers and a central data base to verify the legality of present and prospective employees. In fact, some in Congress talk as if they have already accomplished this. Talk, especially in Congress, is cheap—except for taxpayers. Forgive me for not cheering just yet.

Telephone, Fax, Mail, Or Email Politicians And Editors

Did you happen to notice that politicians are discussed in three chapters of this book as addicts, as pushers, and as enablers? That is not coincidence. As Lindsey Grant wrote:

"The people who suffer most from population growth are poor and unskilled. Money talks. The political calculus may change if unemployment [*and underemployment*] continues to rise and begins to hurt the more prosperous (as it already hurts engineers and computer programmers). The complaints may become more insistent, and Congress may begin to hear them.

"But we don't need to wait for a depression to address the problem. The crowding that afflicts suburban and exurban America is a problem of the prosperous, but most of them do not see its source. The message to those people is: You are hacking at the branches, not the roots. Your problem starts, not with the shopping mall or rising local taxes or water shortages, but with the population growth that drives those symptoms.

"America's population growth is a function of migration. Immigration policy is made by Congress. State and local governments could do much more than they do now to encourage and help the federal government to enforce the immigration laws we now have, but the fundamental decisions rest with Washington. Take your problem to your Senators and Congressman. You cannot solve it locally."

You *can* take problems exacerbated by population growth directly to your Senators and Representative by calling their Washington, DC and/or local offices. You may be surprised to hear how responsive and attentive their staffs are to your calls. You can also send emails, letters, and/or faxes to their Washington, DC and local offices. Some of the organizations listed in Appendix B make it quite easy to make telephone calls and to send faxes to your Senators and Representative.

You can also communicate with your Senators and Representative indirectly by writing letters to the editor of your local newspaper. Such letters will give other readers as well as your elected representatives occasion to think about the connection between population growth and resulting societal and environmental problems!

Thank Populationist Politicians And Media People

Most important of all, tell your Senators, your Representative, and media people "Thank you" in emails, faxes, letters, and telephone calls to their offices, and in letters to the editor of your local newspaper, when they take stands, register votes, and write editorials or columns designed to help break America's addiction to population growth!

There is a minority of politicians, program producers, editors, columnists, and journalists who are more concerned about America's future quality of life than they are about the quantity of constituents, readers, viewers, and listeners they attract. When you find them, they deserve your support and your "Thanks." A brief "Thank you" note will help to counteract some of the beatings about the neck and shoulders such populationist politicians and media people take every day for trying to protect America's future.

Complain To Population Growth Addicts, Pushers, And Enablers

There are so many population growth addicts, pushers, and enablers in America, you can't possibly react every time you read, hear, or see something that suggests someone is advocating an action which will further increase America's population growth. So, pick your spots carefully … or sleeplessly. If something you've read, heard, or seen angers you so much you have difficulty putting it out of your mind when you should be sleeping, that is probably a good candidate for action!

Make a telephone call or write a letter or fax and ask, *"How many people do you want in America? And if you don't know, how dare you support America's addiction to population growth which is pointing us toward a population of one billion!"* Enough angry calls, letters, and faxes and some of the addicts, pushers, and enablers will begin rethinking their positions and their public images.

Incidentally, you may have noticed I didn't suggest you contact *producers* of America's addiction to population growth. That is because the producers live on, and therefore live for, America's population growth addiction. There is nothing you can say to any of them which will in any way sway their dedication to thwarting, knowingly or unknowingly, America's quest for a sustainable population.

DON'T BLAME GOD

Remember, population growth in America is not an act of God—it is an act of Congress. As fellow populationist David M. Bell wrote, "The demographic consequences of decades of reckless mass immigration policy have already placed us on a disastrous population trajectory running well ahead of even the highest estimate of the U.S. Census Bureau, an estimate that portends a billion people within this century. If this future is not averted through immediate and significant reductions in current immigration levels, such population momentum will result in America squandering its natural legacy and the country mortgaging its future with overpopulation, environmental degradation, wage and living standard depression, balkanization, and terrorism."

Future generations of Americans are counting on you to contribute your thinking, your money, your time and/or your energy to prevent this dismal prediction from becoming reality. Please don't let them down! Decide for yourself how many are enough. Decide what *you* want the population of America to be.

Then, do what *you* can do to help America break its addiction to population growth … and move America toward *your* population target.

LOOKING BACK ... AND AHEAD

In this and the previous chapter, we have examined things *you* can do to help America withdraw from its addiction to population growth. Because I know you have other commitments in your life besides populationist commitments, I have tried to give you a variety of choices which you can relate to the time and/or money available to you.

In the next chapter, I will tell you (1) why I am optimistic that we *will* cure America's addiction to population growth, (2) how you can monitor the recovery process, and (3) how you can often respond to seemingly complex questions with a simple populationist answer.

As you read the next chapter you will surely conclude: "*Addictions can be broken!* I *will* join tens of thousands of others who are working to break America's addiction to population growth!"

FOR REFLECTION AND DISCUSSION:

1. Who do you know who might be candidates to read *The Population Fix*?
2. Who do you know who might be candidates to learn to think like populationists?
3. How do you feel about allocating your donations to American environmental organizations according to the degree to which they make the population-environment connection?
4. How would you respond to contractors or other employers who told you hiring legal residents as employees would increase prices you pay?
5. How do you feel about making "Thank you" calls or writing "Thank you" notes to politicians, media people, and others who show concern about America's population growth?

QUICK FIX #13

Visit or ask a friend to visit *www.NumbersUSA.com* and click on "Report Cards" to look for your other U.S. Senator's population growth "grade." Then record the date and the "grade" in Appendix C, "Quick Fix References."

Chapter 14

PROGNOSIS AND CURE

prognosis *n.* 1. A prediction of the probable course and outcome of a disease. 2. The likelihood of recovery from a disease.

cure *n.* 1. Restoration of health. 2. Recovery from disease.

"There are no 'good' people or 'bad' people. Some are a little better or a little worse, but all are activated more by misunderstanding than malice."
—Tennessee Williams

IN THIS BOOK I HAVE repeatedly written that America's addiction to population growth *can* be broken! Nevertheless, I realize reading a catalog of the addicts, the victims, the producers, the pushers, and the enablers could leave one asking, *"Can one person—me—really have an effect on the outcome of this battle?"* I have good reason to believe the answer is ... *Yes!* Let me illustrate why I feel that way.

REASONS FOR OPTIMISM

I belong to a professional organization for writers and independent publishers. At the beginning of each meeting, attendees stand up, introduce themselves, and say a few words about the status of books they are working on. The first time I stood up and said, "I'm writing a book about America's addiction to population growth ..." I was interrupted by applause (not the norm!) and by people saying such things as, *"It's about time!"* A month or two later, I was a guest at a similar meeting for writers and *the same thing happened!*

Another example: In casual conversations in all kinds of situations with all kinds of people, talk may turn to someone asking me what I am working on. When I mention *The Population Fix,* without any cues on my part, questioners often launch into tirades about problems created in their lives *because of rampant population growth!*

And another: During the late 1980s and the 1990s, Congress passed half-a-dozen bills rewarding illegal aliens for breaking America's immigration laws. After 1999, several Representatives and Senators introduced many additional bills to reward illegal aliens. *Virtually all were stopped,* some before they made their way to committee. For example, in the spring of 2004, the hotel and tourism industry pressured Congress to introduce a "Save Our Summer Act" which would have increased special hospitality industry visas from 66,000 to 106,000. The bill *never even came up for a vote.* One wonders how many additional young Americans obtained summer jobs as a result?

And another: Early in his bid for reelection in 2004, President Bush announced a plan to reward, with work visas and fast track legal residency, millions of illegal aliens already in America and to invite millions of additional foreigners to legally immigrate to America "to do work Americans won't do." Within 48 hours, Mr. Bush and his advisors surely knew they had made a miscalculation—whether they were willing to admit it or not. At a time when America was concerned about Americans losing jobs and about America being attacked from within its borders, rewarding lawbreakers and offering American jobs to foreigners was not a winning idea and *the White House switchboard had the statistics to demonstrate the public's opposition!*

And another: When I first became concerned about America's addiction to population growth—though I didn't realize it was an addiction at that time—there were *few* letters to editors about the havoc population growth was causing in America and even less coverage of the issue on radio and television, or in newspapers and magazines. Today, *hardly a week goes by* that a letter to the editor isn't published in my local newspaper or in one of the many environmental magazines I read decrying the havoc created by rampant population growth in America or in a particular state, county, city, or town. *Every week* there is radio and television coverage of the issue. (Think *Lou Dobbs Tonight.*) Magazines such as *Business Week, The Economist, Free Inquiry, Forbes, Newsweek,* and *Time* have felt compelled to devote major articles to the subject of population growth ... or feel they were missing *a changing tide of public opinion.*

Recent example: Congressman Tom Tancredo (R-CO) has been a longtime, and sometimes lonely, exponent of reforming immigration laws. Several times in the past few years he has offered an amendment in Congress which would prohibit any city with a sanctuary policy for illegal aliens from receiving federal funds to reimburse them for costs of providing medical care and other services to illegal aliens. Leadership of both parties and the White House opposed his amendment.

A couple of years ago, Tancredo's amendment received a respectable protest showing of 122 votes. In 2004, his amendment received 148 votes. In May 2005, his amendment received about 160 votes. In June 2005, his amendment received 204 votes with only 222 votes against it. Without taking sides on this issue, I wonder what the vote might have been if the leadership of both parties and the White House had not been opposed to his amendment? Also, again without taking sides, I don't have to wonder about the position of the voters—and taxpayers—in the districts of those Representatives who have changed their votes over time.

The point is: There are many more Americans upset by the damage done by rampant population growth than I had, and perhaps you have, realized. There are many more unhappy Americans—citizens and legal residents—than there are producers, pushers, and enablers. If you add *your* voice to those tens of thousands saying, *"It's about time ...,"* I have no doubt we can turn our societal and environmental problems into financial and political problems for the producers, pushers, and enablers.

COMMON SENSE AND MATHEMATICS

Common sense as well as mathematics tell us America will *eventually* break its addiction to population growth. We just don't know when. We do know America cannot continue to double its population every two or three generations and remain the America we know and love. China let their 300 million become 600 million *before* they began to address their population problem. Yet their population is now *1.3 billion* and is projected to reach *1.5 billion* before it begins to decline.

Can you visualize what would happen in America if its population grew to 600 million *before it began* to address its population growth addiction? I can imagine dramatic—and drastic—events occurring, but I'm not enough of a futurist to predict what they would be. Obviously, there would be severe political and economic ramifications and lifestyle adjustments would be major. Would America survive? Probably. Would America be the place you envision for future generations? Probably not. A cure will come; the question is: When and how?

ARE WE CURED YET?

How will we know when America is no longer addicted to population growth? That's a little like asking, "How will I know when I no longer have the flu?" How did you know you had the flu in the first place? Did your radio alarm come on in the morning with an announcer announcing, "Traffic is a bit heavier than usual for this hour. And, by the way, you have the flu!" I don't think so.

Maybe you had a headache, felt a little dizzy, and your digestive system might not have been up to snuff, and you had soreness in muscles not usually susceptible to soreness, a constricted throat, tender glands, etc. Not all at once, perhaps, but nevertheless, you correctly said, "Darn, I've got the flu!" Likewise, diagnosing overpopulation is a bit like self-diagnosing the flu. There is no single symptom that says, "This is definitely overpopulation!"

Likewise, there is no single criterion by which we can definitely say, "America's addiction to population growth is ended." When radio traffic reports go from every thirty minutes, with little to report, to every ten minutes, with lots to report, we may be addicted to population growth. When radio traffic reports return to every thirty minutes or when they have little to report, we may be breaking the addiction.

When news reporters write and talk incessantly about America being short of teachers and short of nurses and short of open space and short of water and so on, they may actually be talking about being "long" on people. When they stop talking about such matters, we may be breaking the addiction.

When your friends complain about congested and failing highways, about exorbitant prices for houses and apartments, about crowded parks and recreation areas, they may actually be complaining about population growth. When they stop complaining about those things, we may be breaking the addiction.

CLUES TO LOOK FOR

Your mission, as the old TV spy show used to say, should you choose to accept it, is to keep your eyes and ears open for the kinds of clues which will indicate to you whether or not more people are thinking about population and whether or not more people are becoming populationists. When enough Americans begin thinking about population growth and about the damage it is doing to America and about the difficulties it adds to the mitigation of America's problems, America will begin to kick its population growth habit.

What are some additional clues you might look for?

- Do you see an increase in the number of letters to the editor of your favorite newspaper relating population growth to some local, state, national, or international problem?
- Do you see increasing Op-Ed pieces in your favorite newspaper presenting the populationists' viewpoint that population growth makes problem mitigation more difficult?
- Do you hear radio and TV newscasters talking more about what the rate of population growth is in your community or state?
- Do you find your Congressional Representative is being careful not to say anything which could be construed to suggest that he or she wants to encourage population growth?
- Do you find your friends and acquaintances listening more carefully when you explain to them how America's addiction to population growth is going to degrade the quality of life for future Americans?
- Do you see the number of Representatives in the Congressional Immigration Reform Caucus growing?
- Do you see Congressional votes on population issues moving in the direction of reversing population growth? Some organizations listed in Appendix B will help you track these clues.
- Do you see environmental organizations doing more about the connection between America's population growth and America's environmental degradation? You can track this clue at The Population-Environment Connection Scorecard reached via *www.ThinkPopulation.org.*
- Do you see more environmental organizations joining Alliance for Stabilizing America's Population (ASAP)? You can track this clue at the Population-Environment Balance Scorecard reached via *www.ThinkPopulation.org.*
- Do you see the populationist organizations you support increasing their membership and their receipts? You can track these clues by asking for annual reports or by simply asking organizations for that information.

These are just a few of the clues you may observe, if and when, America begins to kick its addiction to population growth. It won't happen "cold turkey," unfortunately, and you will probably observe occasional backsliding. Kicking a habit is a difficult task. Just as if you were helping a drug addict recover, you will have to be understanding but firm, patient but persistent. You will have to keep after the addicts, the pushers, and the enablers until America's future generations are safe from the ravages of America's addiction to population growth.

ARE YOU AN ALTRUIST? ARE YOU—OR COULD YOU BECOME—A POPULATIONIST?

You may remember Chapter 1 "The Populationists," began with those two questions. Perhaps, those are also appropriate questions with which to begin the ending of this book.

If you are an altruist—in fact, *only* if you are an altruist—will this book provide value to you. Your generation and my generation are unlikely to see much improvement in America's population growth during our lifetimes. We will hopefully live to see some changes in political leaders' perspectives and changes in policies. But because it takes so long for policy changes to slow, stop, and ultimately reverse population growth (remember China), we are unlikely to see a population decline in America during our lifetimes. Our reward must be the satisfaction of trying to make America better for future generations.

If you are—or if you become—a populationist, I believe you *will have* the satisfaction (1) of communicating with others who share your concerns, (2) of recognizing logical mitigation to problems confounding others, (3) of observing gradual shifts in perceptions of the general public to the costs of population growth, and (4) of seeing a growing awareness by politicians that their constituents are restless for a cure to the addiction.

I have felt the satisfaction of each of these during my time as a populationist and I believe you will too, especially as changes continue to come at a faster pace!

A SIMPLE ANSWER FOR COMPLEX QUESTIONS

One final thing you may want to remember: You can answer many questions and resolve many arguments simply by saying or writing, "I believe in an America with a population of (insert your number) million. If you want an America with many more people or if you don't know how many people you want America to have in the future, then you and I have quite different attitudes about our responsibilities to future generations of Americans. I am concerned about America seven generations from today. I am an altruist and I am a populationist."

Thank you for reading this book, for thinking about "How many are enough?" and for sharing my concern about America's addiction to population growth.

FOR REFLECTION AND DISCUSSION:

1. What do you think will happen to American society, if America continues to double its population every two or three generations?
2. What have you read, heard, or experienced which gives you reason to be optimistic that America will break its addiction to population growth before it is too late?
3. What additional clues can you think of which might suggest America is breaking its addiction to population growth?
4. How has your view of yourself as an altruist and/or as a populationist changed since you began reading this book?
5. How would you complete the sentence, "I believe in an America with a population of … because …?"

QUICK FIX #14

Write a short letter to your other U.S. Senator saying, "I saw your 'report card' at *www.NumbersUSA.com*" and explaining your reaction to what you saw. Appendix C, "Quick Fix References," contains three sample letters designed for three levels of NumbersUSA grades. Please feel free to borrow from the appropriate sample.

"I'm all in favour of free expression provided it's kept rigidly under control."
—Alan Bennett

EPILOGUE—"THE MAVEN"

(With Apologies To Edgar Allan Poe)

Once upon a morning dreary, while I pondered bleak and bleary
Over many a quaint and curious lot of demographic lore—
While I nodded, nearly napping, suddenly there came a snapping
As of someone gently wrapping, wrapping at my hallway door.
"'The *Journal* carrier," I muttered, "wrapping at my hallway door—
Only that and nothing more."

Open here I flung the portal, saw departing some staunch mortal
On my step a *Wall Street Journal* wrapped for rainy days and more;
Not a drop of water on it, sheltered by its plastic bonnet;
So unwrapped with rapt attention perched it on that
ski invention Model Number 4;
Perched upon a paper holder on my skiing exerciser Model No. 4
For reading, as I have before.

Turning to the editors' writing, quickly felt my flame a-lighting,
"Doubtless," said I, "what they write is their only stock and store
Bought from some unhappy Pope, with little logic, lots of hope."
Skiing fast and reading faster but one message all the writings bore.
'Till the burden of the reading had become a melancholy bore.
Only that and nothing more.

Water and our air polluted, roads for land are substituted
And each morn reporters tell us that our roads can take no more.
Still the *Journal* says solutions are at hand for these pollutions,
Faith in science and the Pope will sail us to some wondrous shore,
Simple faith in Pope and science sail us to some wondrous shore,
Only this and nothing more.

Immigration problems mounting, crime statistics up—and counting,
Every page another issue to be solved by less, not more.
While the *Journal* in its preaching, common sense it seems is leaching;
Like some maddened maven's senseless spoutings
for the senseless to adore,
Repeating endless words of faith in growth, the senseless to adore.
Repeating this for ever more.

"Don't be concerned about pollution. Concentrate on absolution!
This great nation is much greater as we open up our door.
Every immigrant we love, each conception's from above.
Each city should become an American Singapore.
Pile house on house on house on house as they do in Singapore."
Quoth the maven, "Pile on more."

"Don't curse the rivers rapid drying nor the wildlife lands a-dying.
Our scientists will find a way to help us find some more.
Curse the doubled border guards, the 'biometrics' ID cards,
Curse reformers and the rest whose 'closed-door' policies we abhor.
How much longer must we fight those closed-door policies we abhor?"
Quoth the maven, "Ever more!"

And the maven, never flitting, still is sitting, still is sitting
On the pallid dust of skiing exerciser Model Number 4;
And its "Ayes" have all the seeming of a demon's that is dreaming,
While I, the reader o're it screaming throws the *Journal* to the floor;
And my soul from out that prattle that lies gloating on the floor
Shall be lifted … nevermore!

ECH—1996

PS: I am considerably more optimistic now, than when I wrote this.

HOW TO ORDER THIS BOOK

IF YOU ENJOYED THIS BOOK and would like another copy to pass on to someone, please visit our website *www.ThePopulationFix.com.*

- Or to place a telephone order, call **800-852-4890.**
- Or to place fax order, copy this page and fax it with your credit card information to **707-838-2220.**
- Or to place a mail order, copy this page and mail it with your check or credit card information to **Rayve Productions, P.O. Box 726, Windsor, CA 95492-0726.**

Please send me:

_____ copies of *The Population Fix* (hard cover) at $24.50 $ _____

_____ copies of *The Population Fix* (soft cover) at $18.50 $ _____

Subtotal $ _____

Discounts: If subtotal is over $100 deduct 20%,
    over $200 deduct 30%, over $400 deduct 40% $ _____

California residents please add 7.75% sales tax $ _____

Shipping: $5.50 for the first copy and $2.00
    for each additional copy $ _____

Total $ _____

Please *print* information as shown on your credit card account:

Name_____

Address _____

City _____ State_____ Zip _____

Telephone_____ email _____

Credit Card Number _____/_____/_____/ _____

Expiration date: _____/_____

Or check with your local bookstore or favorite online bookseller.

APPENDIX A
Contact Information

How to Contact Ed Hartman:

- Regarding a speaking engagement

- Regarding a textbook version of *The Population Fix*

- Regarding an audio version of *The Population Fix*

- Regarding a documentary film about America's addiction to population growth

- Regarding a short story contest about one billion Americans

- Regarding a demographic board game about population growth

- Regarding an educational interactive video game about population growth

Please email: *info@ThePopulationFix.com*

APPENDIX B

Populationist Organizations

IN CHAPTER 13, "TREATMENT AND Withdrawal," I suggested you consider contributing money and, if possible, energy to populationist organizations. The following are descriptions of some populationist organizations you may want to consider for your financial and/or volunteer support.

You can reach the home pages of each of these organizations via *www.ThinkPopulation.org*:

ORGANIZATIONS CONCERNED WITH FERTILITY AND NET MIGRATION

Californians for Population Stabilization (CAPS) is committed to stabilizing the population of California and America and dedicated to preserving the natural environment from its greatest threat—a continuing increase in human population. CAPS is unique in that it addresses both causes of population growth in America—high birthrates and high immigration levels. Consequently, CAPS works with national and regional organizations concerned with high birthrates and/or high immigration levels and/or environmental degradation.

CAPS is determined to fill the gap created by the failure of conventional environmental organizations to oppose continued American population growth. Fortunately, it has a special niche in the population-environment movement. Several of its board members hold, or have held, leadership positions in national environmental organizations.

CAPS is known for its major media television and radio ads, its public events featuring nationally recognized speakers, its contributions to opinion pages of print and online newspapers, its testimony before public bodies, its speaking engagements before civic and educational groups, and its demographic studies. CAPS staff and board members—several of whom are senior university professors or *emeriti* in physics, biology, and history—are regularly quoted in news articles and are interviewed on radio and television programs in many parts of the country.

Izaak Walton League of America (IWLA) has a reputation for conciliation rather than conflict, consistently looking for points of agreement with business, with government, and with other environmental organizations. It has been concerned with the issue of human population growth since 1970 when its members first enacted a policy on carrying capacity. It launched its advocacy and education campaign on population and sustainability in 1993, and has consistently framed its message in terms of environmental concern and commonsense solutions.

In early 2005, IWLA launched a campaign to encourage outdoor journalists to take on the issue of population. To begin this campaign, it issued a pair of publications intended to inspire, engage, and assist outdoor journalists to reacquaint themselves with the potentially explosive consequences for natural resources of human population growth.

One of its two publications provides outdoor journalists with basic information about population growth in the world and in America—how populations are changed by births, deaths, and human migration. The second publication contains essays by five prominent journalists on the effects of population growth on outdoor recreation. This campaign, carried to its ultimate potential, makes IWLA a clear leader among environmental organizations on *www.ThinkPopulation.org's* Population-Environment Connection Scorecard.

ORGANIZATIONS CONCERNED WITH FERTILITY

Planned Parenthood Federation of America (PPFA) establishes medical standards and protocols and provides educational information, technical support, and financial assistance for its approximately 130 affiliates, which include approximately 875 health centers in most states and the District of Columbia. PPFA's national office disseminates teaching materials and assists with affiliate education program fact sheets. Background information on issues are also provided to affiliates.

The national office also monitors reproductive technology, conducts research, educates the public about health care services available at the affiliate clinics, and advises government agencies and the pharmaceutical industry on reproductive issues. In addition, through advocacy, education, and litigation, PPFA defends and campaigns for expansion of reproductive rights including ensuring health insurance coverage for contraception. PPFA publishes a bimonthly newsletter, *Marketing Exchange*, which provides a forum for outreach into the community and details strategies for improving customer satisfaction.

PPFA's Family Planning International Assistance program provides technical assistance and direct support to family planning and reproductive health projects in developing countries throughout the world. Through advocacy efforts, PPFA promotes legislation increasing funds for foreign reproductive rights and policies concerning the status of women worldwide.

Population Connection (PC), formerly Zero Population Growth, believes the well-being and even the survival of humanity depends on the attainment of an equilibrium between population and the environment. Continued population growth is foremost among the factors aggravating deforestation, wildlife extinction, climate change and other critical environmental and social problems. It also erodes democratic government, multiplies urban problems, consumes agricultural land, increases volumes of waste, heightens competition for scarce resources and threatens the aspirations of the poor for a better life.

PC participates in coalitions; influences governmental policies on the international, national, state, and local levels; works extensively with the media; engages in teacher training and public education programs; and produces educational materials. PC conducts research, interprets and applies the research of others, and provides a population perspective on social and environmental problems.

Because the United States is the chief consumer of the world's resources, PC believes slowing its population growth is disproportionately important for protecting the global environment. It is PC's view that immigration pressures on the U.S. population are best relieved by addressing factors which compel people to leave their homes and families and emigrate to the United States. PC also supports the removal of all taxation incentives and subsidies for procreation and larger families.

ORGANIZATIONS CONCERNED WITH NET MIGRATION

Center for Immigration Studies (CIS) is an independent, nonprofit organization founded in 1985. It is the nation's only think tank devoted exclusively to research and policy analysis of the economic, social, demographic, and environmental impact of immigration on America. It is the Center's mission to expand the base of public knowledge and understanding of the need for an immigration policy that gives first concern to the broad national interest. The Center provides a variety of services for academics, policymakers, journalists, and other interested parties.

CIS studies are thorough and academically rigorous and its publications are lucid and compelling. It often invites journalists and Congressional staffers to attend releases of new studies. This provides opportunities to ask questions of study authors as well as other experts in the fields under study. Consequently, CIS studies and the CIS staff are particularly well regarded and their counsel is often sought by journalists and Congressional staffers. The CIS staff is also sought by and seen and/ or heard on prominent national and regional TV and radio programs.

Federation for American Immigration Reform (FAIR) is a national, nonprofit, public interest membership organization of citizens united by their belief in the need for immigration reform. Founded in 1979, FAIR believes America can and must have an immigration policy that is nondiscriminatory and designed to serve the environmental, economic, and social needs of our country. FAIR advocates immigration rates consistent with American population stabilization, e.g., annual levels of approximately 200,000.

FAIR is a nonpartisan group whose membership runs the gamut from liberal to conservative. FAIR's grassroots networks help concerned citizens use their voices to speak up for effective, sensible immigration policies that work for America's best interests. FAIR's publications and research are used by academics and government officials in preparing new legislation. National and international media regularly turn to FAIR to understand the latest immigration developments and to shed light on this complex subject.

FAIR's publications to its supporters are succinct and easy to understand. Its Executive Director appears frequently on national and regional TV and radio programs presenting FAIR's perspective on existing and proposed immigration policies.

NumbersUSA (NUSA) believes the most important public policy issue concerning immigration is the numbers. This is true in terms of the way immigration affects housing, schools, streets and roads, public transportation, bridges, and other infrastructure, wages, social services, taxes, urban sprawl, traffic, natural habitat, air and water quality.

NUSA is an efficient and effective population stabilization organization. NUSA's website provides visitors (a) with understandable information about net migration and (b) with simple means of communicating with legislators. Active volunteers strive to help journalists maintain equilibrium in the often slanted world of immigration reporting.

NUSA's staff on Capitol Hill motivates Congress to move immigration legislation in the direction many constituents would prefer, i.e., a reduction in net migration. NUSA is particularly good at keeping supporters advised (a) about what grassroots supporters are doing and (b) about legislative victories and defeats.

OTHER POPULATIONIST ORGANIZATIONS

There are some additional national organizations as well as several regional organizations and groups that are concerned about America's addiction to population growth. Space limitation does not permit a complete list. The following are a few which can be reached via *www. ThinkPopulation.org* and, if you become an active populationist, you will soon be introduced to other populationists and populationist organizations with a variety of causes and interests, such as:

Carrying Capacity Network (CCN), as its name suggests, is concerned that America not exceed its capacity to support its existing population, let alone its rampantly increasing population. What is carrying capacity? Well, if you remember the discussion in Chapter 3 "The Addiction," about the number of acres of land supporting each American dwindling from 105 acres in 1800 to approximately 8 acres in 2000, then you have a basic appreciation for carrying capacity. CCN's publications provide thorough, but easily understood surveys of what is happening to America's carrying capacity. If you would like to learn more, visit CCN's website.

Diversity Alliance for a Sustainable America (DASA) is a nonprofit organization dedicated to educating the media, politicians, policymakers, and residents across America about the impact of population growth which is driven mainly by record levels of legal and illegal immigration, plus American-born children of immigrants. DASA advocates replacement-level fertility (two children per family) and replacement-level immigration (reducing the current number from over one million to around 200,000 annually) so that America can achieve population stability in the long run.

DASA's leaders and supporters are racially, ethnically, and politically diverse. Its Executive Director is an immigrant with extensive prior experience helping people emigrate to America. The diversity of DASA's leaders and supporters permits entree into counsels and channels which might be closed to other groups with less obvious diversity. DASA's tenacious and tireless Executive Director appears frequently on regional radio and TV programs and her letters and Op-Ed pieces appear in newspapers throughout America. If you want to learn more, visit DASA's website.

Negative Population Growth (NPG) takes the position that America has already exceeded its carrying capacity, if Americans wish to have the quality of life enjoyed by past generations. In other words, NPG believes 300 million and growing is too many and it is time to reverse population growth and return to a more manageable population. If that is a position you would like to understand better and might want to support, visit NPG's website.

Population-Environment Balance (BALANCE), as its name suggests, is concerned about the damage America's addiction to population growth is doing to America's environment. The environmental community is well represented on its Board of Directors and its National Advisory Board. BALANCE is sponsor of Alliance for Stabilizing America's Population (ASAP), an alliance primarily of regional environmental groups with a common desire to see America kick the population growth addiction. If you are particularly concerned about environmental degradation caused by America's addiction to population growth, you may want to visit BALANCE's website.

APPENDIX C

"Quick Fix References"

Editor's Name _____

Publication name: _____

Address: _____

_____

Telephone No.: _____

Sample letter for editor of your newspaper or newsmagazine

(date)

Mr./Ms. _____, Editor
(publication name)
(address)
(address)

Dear Mr./Ms. _____ :

I have been reading a book explaining why America has become addicted to population growth and telling readers what they can do to help break that addiction before America's population reaches <u>one billion!</u> It is called *"The Population Fix—Breaking America's Addiction To Population Growth."*

I hope your reporters, columnists, and editors will keep this addiction in mind and ask themselves, "How many of the problems we write about would be easier to solve, if America's population was stabilized?"

Thank you.

(your name, address, and telephone number)

Contact information and "grade" for your U.S. Representative

U.S. Representative's Name: _____

Local Address: _____

_____

Local Telephone No.: _____

Wash. DC Address: _____

_____

Wash. DC Telephone No.: _____

NumbersUSA.com grade as of ____/____/____: _____

NumbersUSA.com grade as of ____/____/____: _____

NumbersUSA.com grade as of ____/____/____: _____

NumbersUSA.com grade as of ____/____/____: _____

NumbersUSA.com grade as of ____/____/____: _____

NumbersUSA.com grade as of ____/____/____: _____

NumbersUSA.com grade as of ____/____/____: _____

NumbersUSA.com grade as of ____/____/____: _____

NumbersUSA.com grade as of ____/____/____: _____

NumbersUSA.com grade as of ____/____/____: _____

NumbersUSA.com grade as of ____/____/____: _____

NumbersUSA.com grade as of ____/____/____: _____

Contact information and "grade" for one U.S. Senator

Senator's Name: _____

Local Address: _____

_____

Local Telephone No.: _____

Wash. DC Address: _____

_____

Wash. DC Telephone No.: _____

NumbersUSA.com grade as of ____/____/____: _____

NumbersUSA.com grade as of ____/____/____: _____

NumbersUSA.com grade as of ____/____/____: _____

NumbersUSA.com grade as of ____/____/____: _____

NumbersUSA.com grade as of ____/____/____: _____

NumbersUSA.com grade as of ____/____/____: _____

NumbersUSA.com grade as of ____/____/____: _____

NumbersUSA.com grade as of ____/____/____: _____

NumbersUSA.com grade as of ____/____/____: _____

NumbersUSA.com grade as of ____/____/____: _____

NumbersUSA.com grade as of ____/____/____: _____

NumbersUSA.com grade as of ____/____/____: _____

Contact information and "grade" for other U.S. Senator

Senator's Name: _____

Local Address: _____

_____

Local Telephone No.: _____

Wash. DC Address: _____

_____

Wash. DC Telephone No.: _____

NumbersUSA.com grade as of _____/_____/_____: _____

NumbersUSA.com grade as of _____/_____/_____: _____

NumbersUSA.com grade as of _____/_____/_____: _____

NumbersUSA.com grade as of _____/_____/_____: _____

NumbersUSA.com grade as of _____/_____/_____: _____

NumbersUSA.com grade as of _____/_____/_____: _____

NumbersUSA.com grade as of _____/_____/_____: _____

NumbersUSA.com grade as of _____/_____/_____: _____

NumbersUSA.com grade as of _____/_____/_____: _____

NumbersUSA.com grade as of _____/_____/_____: _____

NumbersUSA.com grade as of _____/_____/_____: _____

NumbersUSA.com grade as of _____/_____/_____: _____

Sample letter for U.S. Senators or Representative asking him or her to keep population growth in mind

(date)

The Honorable (full name of Senator or Representative)
United States Senate (or) U.S. House of Representatives
(address)

Dear Senator (or) Dear Representative (last name:)

I have been reading a book explaining why America has become addicted to population growth and telling readers what they can do to help break that addiction before America's population reaches <u>one billion</u>! It is called *"The Population Fix—Breaking America's Addiction To Population Growth."*

I would appreciate it if you will keep this addiction in mind and ask yourself, "(1) How many of the problems we address with legislation would be easier to solve, if America's population stabilized?" and "(2) Will legislation I am drafting or I am voting on tend to increase or decrease America's population?"

Thank you.

(your name, address, and telephone number)

Sample letter for U.S. Senators and Representatives with scores of "A" through "B"

(date)

The Honorable (full name of Senator or Representative)
United States Senate (or) U.S. House of Representatives
(address)

Dear Senator (or) Dear Representative (last name:)

Recently I saw your "report card" at www.NumbersUSA.com and was pleased to see you have a grade of (enter grade of "A" through "B"). As you clearly recognize, it is difficult to think of a problem faced by our nation or our state that is not made more difficult to solve because of our rampant population growth. Your continued recognition of that fact as you draft and vote on legislation will increase our chances of finding satisfactory solutions to many of those problems.

Incidentally, I have been reading a book explaining why America has become addicted to population growth and telling readers what they can do to help break that addiction before America's population reaches <u>one billion!</u> It is called *"The Population Fix—Breaking America's Addiction To Population Growth."* If you or your staff would like to learn more about that book, you may visit www.ThePopulationFix.com.

Thank you.

(your name, address, and telephone number)

Sample letter for U.S. Senators and Representatives with scores of "B-" through "C-"

(date)

The Honorable (full name of Senator or Representative)
United States Senate (or) U.S. House of Representatives
(address)

Dear Senator (or) Dear Representative (last name:)

Recently I saw your "report card" at www.NumbersUSA.com and saw you have a grade of (enter grade of "B-" through "C-"). When I viewed that grade I wondered if you have considered how hard it is to think of a problem faced by our nation or our state that is not made more difficult to solve because of our rampant population growth. I would appreciate it if you will consider that as you draft and vote on legislation which will result in still more population growth.

Incidentally, I have been reading a book explaining why America has become addicted to population growth and telling readers what they can do to help break that addiction before America's population reaches <u>one billion!</u> It is called *"The Population Fix—Breaking America's Addiction To Population Growth."* If you or your staff would like to learn more about that book, you may visit www.ThePopulationFix.com.

Thank you.

(your name, address, and telephone number)

Sample letter for U.S. Senators and Representatives with scores of "D+" through "F"

(date)

The Honorable (full name of Senator or Representative)
United States Senate (or) U.S. House of Representatives
(address)

Dear Senator (or) Dear Representative (last name:)

Recently I saw your "report card" at www.NumbersUSA.com and saw you have a grade of (enter grade of "D+" through "F"). When I saw that grade I wondered if you have considered how hard it is to think of a problem faced by our nation or our state that is not made more difficult to solve by our rampant population growth. If you will begin to consider that as you draft and vote on legislation I believe you will both improve your "report card" and improve America's chances of finding satisfactory solutions to many of those problems.

Incidentally, I have been reading a book explaining why America has become addicted to population growth and telling readers what they can do to help break that addiction before America's population reaches <u>one billion!</u> It is called *"The Population Fix—Breaking America's Addiction To Population Growth."* If you or your staff would like to learn more about that book, you may visit www.ThePopulationFix.com.

Thank you.

(your name, address, and telephone number)

REFERENCES

Abernethy, Virginia, *Population Politics: The Choices that Shape Our Future,* Plenum Press, NY, NY, 1993; Chair, **Carrying Capacity Network,** Board Member, **Population-Environment Balance.**

AFL-CIO, Executive Council, www.aflcio.org (May 2000). See also www.ourfuture. org/projects/next_agenda/ch13_1.cfm-47k (Aug 30, 2005). **[178]**

Alliance for Stablilizing America's Population; see **Population-Environment Balance.**

American Farmland Trust, 1200 18th St., NW, Ste. 800, Washington, DC 20036, info@ farmland.org, 202-331-7300. **[98]**

American Heritage Dictionary of the English Language, Fourth Edition, Houghton-Mifflin, Boston, New York, 2000. **[29, 33, 34, 39, 51, 63, 75, 93, 111, 127, 141, 153, 167, 168, 169, 183, 207]**

Associated Press, www.ap.org. **[82, 100, 105, 176]**

Austin, Mary, *Land of Little Rain,* Modern Library, Random House, Inc., NY, 2003. **[76]**

Barnett, Don, October 2003. See **Center for Immigration Studies (CIS). [136]**

Bartlett, Albert A., Univ. of CO. "The World's Worst Population Problem (Is There a Population Problem?)" in *Wild Earth: A journal for creatures who care about their habitat,* Richmond, VT, Vol. 7, No. 3, Fall 1997, 88–90; see also other writings. **[32, 194]**

Beck, Roy and **Leon Kolankiewicz,** "The Environmental Movement's Retreat from Advocating U.S. Population Stabilization," *Journal of Policy History,* Pennsylvania State University Press. **[174]**; also **Presidential Policy. [154]**

Bell, David M., population activist, **www.ThinkPopulation.org. [205]**

Borjas, George, immigration economist, Harvard University, Cambridge, MA, ksgfaculty.harvard.edu/george_borjas, gborjas@harvard.edu. **[146]**

Boulding, Kenneth, www.colorado.edu/econ/kenneth.boulding. **[170]**

Briggs, Vernon M., Jr., *Immigration and American Unionism,* Cornell University, Ithaca, NY: ILR Press, 2001. **[177]**

Burnett, John, National Public Radio (NPR), from transcript of Sat., Feb. 21, 2004, reporting on the hospitality industry in Vail, Colorado, www.npr.org. **[67]**

Brooks, David, columnist, *The New York Times.* **[121]**

California Energy Commission, Media and Public Communications Office, 1516 Ninth Street, MS-29, Sacramento, CA 95814-5512, www.energy.ca.gov. **[79]**

Californians Against Waste Foundation, 921 Eleventh St., Ste. 301, Sacramento, CA 95814, 916-443-5422, www.cawrecycles.org. **[105]**

Californians for Population Stabilizaftion (CAPS), 1129 State St., Ste. 3D, Santa Barbara, CA 93101, 805-564-6626, info@capsweb.org. **[147]**

Camarota, Steven A., "Back Where We Started: 1996 Law Failed to Cut Overall Immigrant Welfare Use," **CIS** report, March 2003. **[86]**

Carrying Capacity Network (CCN), 2000 P St., NW, Ste. 310, Washington, DC 20036, 202-296-4548, www.carryingcapacity.org; carryingcapacity@covad.net **[32]**; see also **CCN** publications, *Action Alert,* Nov. 2004 **[57]**, *Focus* **[154]**

Center for Immigration Studies (CIS), 1522 K St. NW, Ste. 820, Washington, DC 20005-1202, 202-466-8185, www.cis.org. [66, 86, 101, 120, 128, 136, 145]

Chang, Jack, article, *Contra Costa Times.* [69]

Chute, Tanya, volunteer in La Ceiba, El Salvador, *a Common Place* magazine, Mennonite Central Committee, Akron, PA, www.mcc.org. [96]

Consumer Reports, Consumers Union, Yonkers, NY, www.consumereports.org. [80]

Contra Costa Times, Contra Costa Newspapers, Walnut Creek, CA, www.contracosta times.com. [35, 60, 69, 86, 113, 132, 135, 149, 162, 172, 173, 180]

Cristie, Les, *"Money,"* Cable News Network (CNN), www.cnn.com. [78]

Daleiden, Joseph L. *The American Dream: Can It Survive the 21ˢᵗ Century?,* 1999, www.amazon.com.

de Soto, Hernando, *The Other Path: The Economic Answer to Terriorism,* 1989, and *The Mystery of Capital: Why Capitalism Triumphs in the West and Fails Everywhere Else,* 2000, Basic Books, Lima, Peru. Acceptance speech for "Milton Friedman Prize for Advancing Liberty" from Cato, Institute, May 6, 2004; founder of the Institute for Liberty and Democracy in Peru, ILD Las Begonias 441 Of. 901 - Lima 27, Perú, t.(51-1)222-6800, www.cato.org/special/friedman/desoto/books.html. [135]

Dirty Pretty Things, film, (BBC Productions, with Celadon Productions, JonesCompany Productions; director, **Stephen Frears**; writer, **Steven Knight**), distributed by Miramax Films, Corp., USA, 2003. [81]

Diversity Alliance for a Sustainable America (DASA), 1904 Franklin St., Ste. 517, Oakland, CA 94612, 510-835-5017, www.diversityalliance.org. [69, 84, 131]

Duluth Trading Company Catalog, Item no. 91006, *Spanish on the Job: How to Get the Work Done.* Belleville, WI, www.duluthtradingcompany.com. [80]

Economist Newspaper Limited (The), 25 St. James's St., London SW1A 1HG, United Kingdom, 44 (0) 20 7839 2968/9, www.economist.com. [143]

Elko Shopper, Affordable Advertising, Elko, NV, compconn@inreach.com. [107]

Erhlich, Paul and John Holdren, "The Ehrlich/Holdren Formula"; see also Ehrlich, P., A. Ehrlich and J. Holdren, "Availability, Entropy and the Laws of Thermodynamics," in *Valuing the Earth: Economics, Ecology, Ethics,* eds. Herman E. Daly and Kenneth Townsend, MIT Press, 1993. [47, 78]

Farmingville, film, **Carlos Sandoval & Catherine Tambini,** producers, Public Broadcasting System (PBS), June 22, 2004, www.pbs.org.pov; www.farmingvillethemovie.com. [82]

Federation for American Immigration Reform (FAIR), 1666 Connecticut Ave., NW, Ste. 400, Washington, DC 20009, 202-328-7004, www.fairus.org. [87, 102, 114]

Frears, Stephen, director; see *Dirty Pretty Things.*

Friedman, Milton, Senior Research Fellow, Hoover Inst., www.hooverpress.org. [143]

Gentes, Lisa, "Visa cap leaves labor gap," *Associated Press.* [176]

Glennon, John, "Our Planet Is Overcrowded—Overpopulation of Earth Could Lead to Unprecedented Disaster," opinion page, *Contra Costa Times.* [173]

Goldberg, Bernard, *Arrogance: Rescuing America from the Media Elite,* Warner Books, Inc., NY, 2003; TV interview about his book. [173]

Grant, Lindsey, *The Collapsing Bubble: Growth and Fossil Energy,* Seven Locks Press, Santa Ana, CA, 2005; *Too Many People: The Case for Reversing Growth,* Seven Locks Press, 2001; *How Many Americans? Population, Immigration, and the Environment,* co-author, Leon F. Bouvier, Sierra Club Books, San Francisco, 1994; editor, *Elephants in the Volkswagen: Facing the Tough Questions about Our Overcrowded Country,* W. H. Freeman, NY, 1992; *Foresight and National Decisions: the Horseman and the Bureaucrat,* University Press of America, Lanham, MD, 1988 [188, 203]; see *Negative*

Population Growth, Alexandria, VA, www.npg.org. [**53, 154**]; **Presidential Policy.** [**154**]

Green, Lee, "Infinite Ingress: A human wave is breaking over California, flooding free-ways and schools, bloating house costs, disrupting power and water supplies. Ignoring it hasn't worked," Jan. 25, 2004, *Los Angeles Times Magazine.* [**184**]

Hagenbaugh, Barbara, "Slower population growth could have dual impact," report 3/18/2004, *USA Today.* [**192**]

Hanson, Victor Davis, *Mexifornia: A State of Becoming.* Encounter Books, San Francisco, CA, 2004, www.encounterbooks.com. [**81**]

Hardin, Garrett, "Cultural Carrying Capacity," 1986, www.garretthardinsociety.org. [**188**]

Healy, Melissa, *Los Angeles Times.* [**104**]

Heavens, Alan J., article, March 28, 2004, *Knight Ridder Newspapers,* referring to **Professor James Johnson Jr.** [**57**]

Heminger, Steve, exec. dir., (California) Metropolitan Transportation Commission, 101 8th Street, Oakland, CA 94607, 510-817-5700, www.mtc.ca.gov. [**99**]

Hinrichsen, Don, Karin Krchnak, and Katie Mogelgaard, "Population, Water, and Wildlife: Finding a Balance," **National Wildlife Federation.** [**87**]

Holdren, John; see **Ehrlich.** [**78**]

Izaak Walton League of America, 707 Conservation Lane, Gaithersburg, MD 20878, 800-453-5463, www.iwla.org. [**88, 200**]

Islam in Africa, www.IslamInAfrica.org. [**138**]

Iyer, Pico, "The Magic of Flight," *Via,* magazine, California State Automobile Assoc., San Francisco, CA , Nov./Dec. 2003, 59. [**137**]

Johnson, James, Jr.; see **Heavens, Alan J.**

Jordan, Mary; see **Sullivan, Kevin.**

Kenney, George, former U.S. diplomat, in *Contra Costa Times.* [**113**]

Kirby, Carrie, staff writer, "Visa's use provokes opposition by techies, L-1 regarded as threat to workers," *San Francisco Chronicle,* Sun., May 25, 2003. [**157**]

Knight, Steven, writer; see *Dirty Pretty Things.*

Kolankiewicz, Leon; see **Beck, Roy.**

Krchnak, Karin; see **Hinrichsen, Don.**

Krikorian, Mark, exec. dir., CIS. "Flawed Assumptions Underlying Guest Worker Programs," Feb. 2004. [**66**]; "Dried-on-the-Vine" production, from "Statement on H.R. 4548, *Guestworker Programs . . .*" June 15, 2000, www.cis.org/articles. [**101**]

Kuper, Alan, president, Comprehensive U.S. Sustainable Population (CUSP), Cleveland Heights, OH, cuspscore@earthlink.net, www.uscongressenviro-score.org, in *The New York Times.* [**122**]

Los Angeles Times, www.latimes.com. [**100, 104, 175**]

Mac Donald, Heather, "The Illegal-Alien Crime Wave," Winter 2004, *City Journal,* published by The Manhattan Institute, NY. [**159, 181**]

Malkin, Michelle, *Invasion: How America Welcomes Terrorists, Criminals, and Other Foreign Menaces to Our Shores,* Regnery Publishing, Inc., A Division of Eagle Pub-lishing, Washington, DC, 2002. "Home loans for illegal aliens?" Aug. 29, 2003, World Net Daily.com, Inc., Grants Pass, OR, www.worldnetdaily.com. [**106**]

Marston, Ed, "The Son of Immigrants Has a Change of Heart," February 3, 2003, *High Country News,* Paonia, CO, www.hcn.org. [**133**]

Martin, Philip L., "Promise Unfulfilled: Why Didn't Collective Bargaining Transform California's Farm Labor Market?" January 2004, CIS, article adapted from his book, *Promise Unfulfilled: Unions, Immigrants, and Farm Workers,* Cornell University Press, Ithaca, NY, 2003. [**120**]

Meyer, Herbert E., "What's Wrong with the CIA?" *Imprimis*, Hillsdale College, Hillsdale, MI, www.hillsdale. edu, October 2003. [167]

Mogelgaard, Katie; see Hinrichsen, Don.

Mooney, Alan, "Shoddy home construction," in *Consumer Reports*. [80]

Moore, Charles, pres., Criterium Engineers, "Trashed: Across the Pacific Ocean, plastics, plastics, everywhere," *Natural History*, www.naturalhistorymag.com, November 2003. [42]

Mumford, Stephen, *Focus*, from Carrying Capacity Network, Presidential Policy. [154]

Munroe, Tappan, chief economist, Capital Corp. of the West, pres., Munroe Consulting, Moraga, CA, "NAFTA is still a work in progresss," *Contra Costa Times*. [132]

Naik, Gautam, "Tunisia Wins Population Battle," Aug. 8, 2003, *Wall Street Journal*, Chicopee, MA, www.wjs.com, gautam.naik@wsj.com. [138]

National Association of Home Builders (The), NAHB Research Center, 400 Prince George's Blvd. Upper Marlboro, MD 20774, 800-638-8556, www.nahbrc.org. [79]

National Association of Realtors (The), 430 N. Michigan Ave., Chicago, IL. 60611-4087, 800-874-6500, www.realtor.org. [79]

National Audubon Society, 700 Broadway, NY, 10003, 212-979-3000, www.audubon. org. [88, 200]

National Wildlife Federation, 11100 Wildlife Center Dr., Reston, VA 20190, 800-822-9919, www.nwf.org. [87, 88, 200]

Nature Conservancy (The), 4245 N. Fairfax Dr., Ste. 100, Arlington, VA 22203-1606, 703-841-5300, www.nature.org. [42, 88, 115, 201]

Navarrette, Ruben, Jr., *A Darker Shade of Crimson: Odyssey of a Harvard Chicano*, Bantam Dell Publishing, Random House, Inc., NY, 1994; syndicated columnist. [77]

Negative Population Growth (NPG), 2861 Duke St., Ste. 36, Alexandria, VA 22314, 703-370-9510, www.npg.org. [53, 154]

New York Times (The), www.nytimes.com [121, 122]

9/11 Commission Report: Final Report of the National Commission on Terrorist Attacks Upon the United States, by National Commission on Terrorist Attacks, NY: W. W. Norton & Company, Inc., 2004. www.9-11commission.gov/. [116]

Numbers USA (NUSA), 1601 N. Kent St., Ste. 1100, Arlington, VA 22209, 703-816-8820, www.NumbersUSA.com.

Owen, David, "Green Manhattan: The Environment Needs More Big Cities," excerpted from a *New Yorker* magazine article in *the reporter,* the magazine of Population Connection, Winter 2005. [180]

Pfeiffer, Dale Allen, "Eating Fossil Fuels," Carrying Capacity Network, www. copvcia.com., *From the Wilderness* Publications, 2004. [32]

Poe, Edgar Allan, poem "The Raven" by Edgar Allan Poe (1809–1849), inspiration for "The Maven" by Edward C. Hartman, www.ThinkPopulation.org. [215]

Population Coalition, P.O. Box 7918, Redlands, CA 92375, www.popco.org. [97, 108]

Population Connection, 1400 16th St. NW, Suite 320, Washington, DC 20036, 202-332-2200, 800-POP-1956, www.populationconnection.org. [122, 169, 174, 176, 180]

Population-Environment Balance, 2000 P St. NW, Ste. 600, Washington, DC 20036, 202-955-5700, www.balance.org. [55]; Alliance for Stabilizing America's Population.

Population Press, publication of Population Coalition, www.popco.org/press. [97, 108]

Presidential policy on population growth, 40 years of data: see Mumford, Stephen; Grant, Lindsey; Beck, Roy and Kolankiewicz, Leon. [154]

Pritchard, Justin, "Showdown at the Border: Critical Issues in Covering U.S. Immigration and Border Policy," Polk Award, 2004, L. A. Bureau, *Associated Press*. [82]

reporter (the), magazine of the **Population Connection.** [169, 180]

Revelle, R., "Food and Population," *Scientific American,* 1974, 231:161–170, cited by Garrett Hardin, "Cultural Carrying Capacity," 1986. [188]

San Francisco Chronicle, 901 Mission St., S.F., CA 94103, 415-777-1111, www.sfchron.com. [84, 157]

Sandoval, Carlos, producer; see *Farmingville.*

Schwartz, James, "How Much Is Enough?" Desert Valley Financial Planning, LLC, 20 W Juniper Ave., Ste. 101, Gilbert, AZ 85233, 480 855-4209. [31]

Scientific American, "Sex for Pleasure," April 2004, www.scientificamerican.com. [40]

Sierra Club, 85 2nd St., 2nd Flr., S.F., CA 94105, 415-977-5500, www.sierraclub.org. [88, 174, 200]

Sperling, Bert, *Best Places* guides, Portland, OR, www.bestplaces.net. [60]

Sprawl City, "Defining Sprawl & Other Terms/What Is Sprawl?" www.SprawlCity.org. [98]

Stennett, Edwin, "What about Metrorail?" *In Growth We Trust: Sprawl, Smart Growth, and Rapid Population Growth,* Growth Education Movement, Gaithersburg, MD, 2002. [101, 175, 176]; see also **Population Connection.**

Stolzenburg, William, "Just the Facts: Isn't There Always Another Fish in the Sea?" *Nature Conservancy,* Winter, 2003. Arlington, VA, www.nature.org/magazine. [42]; see also **Nature Conservancy.**

Strauss, Valerie, "A Case for Smaller Schools," 8/8/2000, *Washington Post.* [85]

Strom, Ken, Field Director, Population and Habitat Campaign, Global Stewardship Initiative, "Population and Habitat in the New Millennium," published by **National Audubon Society,** NY, www.audubon.org. [88]

Sullivan, Kevin, with **Mary Jordan,** *Washington Post.* [133]

Takada, Hideshige, environmental geochemist, and colleagues, Tokyo University; referred to in **Moore, Charles,** "Trashed . . ." [42]

Tambini, Catherine, producer; see *Farmingville.*

Think Population, www.ThinkPopulation.org.

Uhl, John, *Life on a Crowded Planet: How You Can Help Create a Sustainable Future,* download free at www.lifeonacrowdedplanet.com.

United States Bureau of Labor Statistics, www.bls.gov. [78]

United States Census Bureau, www.census.gov. [48, 52, 53, 57, 77, 85, 99, 176]

United States Centers for Disease Control, www.cdc.gov. [104]

United States Immigration and Naturalization Service. [114, 132, 148]

USA Today, a division of Gannett Co. Inc., McLean, VA, citing U.S. Census Bureau statistics, Jan. 1, 2004, www.usatoday.com. [53, 192]

Van Ry, W. J., "Why Get Involved: The U.S. Population and the Health Care Challenge," Spring/Summer 2004, *Population Press.* [97]

Vaughan, Jessica, "Be Our Guest: Trade Agreements and Visas," *Backgrounder,* December 2003, **CIS.** [128]

Verzosa, Bernadette, "Second Chance Cafe," *Gourmet* magazine, publisher, Epicurious, www.epicurious.com. [84]

Vote Smart, www.votesmart.org. [49, 62, 73]

Washington Post, 1150 15th St. NW, Washington, DC 20071, 800-627-1150, www.washingtonpost.com. [85, 98, 133]

Wasserman, Jim, *Associated Press.* [105]

Weikel, Dan, "The Road More Heavily Traveled," July 5, 2004, *Los Angeles Times.* [100]

Weir, Jack, letters to the editor, *Contra Costa Times.* [35]

Weiss, Kenneth R., staff writer, *Los Angeles Times.* [175]

World Health Organization, www.un.pk/who. [104]

World Wildlife Fund, 1250 24th St., NW, Washington, DC 20037, 202-293-4800, www. worldwildlife.org. [201]

Yeh, Ling-Ling, exec. dir., **Diversity Alliance for a Sustainable America, (DASA),** *Contra Costa Times* [69]; "Advice for Arnold, Part II: Advice on immigration to the immigrant governor-elect," *San Francisco Chronicle,* Nov. 16, 2003, [84]; "Mexican Immigration and the Political Future of the United States," *The Journal of Social, Political and Economic Studies,* Vol. 29, No. 4, Winter 2004. [131]